FROM
AIRSHIPS
TO AIRBUS

Proceedings of the International Conference on the History of Civil and Commercial Aviation
W. David Lewis, General Editor

The International Conference on the History of Civil and Commercial Aviation was held in August 1992 at the Swiss Transport Museum in Lucerne. Organized cooperatively by aviation historians at Auburn University, the National Air and Space Museum of the Smithsonian Institution, and the Swiss Transport Museum, the conference focused attention on the political, economic, social, and cultural aspects of commercial flight, and on the influence of such contextual forces throughout civil aviation history.

FROM
AIRSHIPS
TO AIRBUS

THE HISTORY OF CIVIL
AND COMMERCIAL AVIATION

Volume 1 ☆ Infrastructure and Environment

EDITED BY

WILLIAM M. LEARY

SMITHSONIAN INSTITUTION PRESS
WASHINGTON AND LONDON

Copy Editor: D. Teddy Diggs
Production Editor: Duke Johns
Designer: Kathleen Sims

Library of Congress Cataloging-in-Publication Data
International Conference on the History of Civil and Commercial Aviation (1992 : Lucerne,
　　Switzerland)
　　　From airships to airbus : the history of civil and commercial aviation.
　　　　p.　cm.—(Proceedings of the International Conference on the History of Civil and
　　Commercial Aviation ; v. 1–2)
　　Includes bibliographical references.
　　　Contents: v. 1. Infrastructure and environment / edited by William M. Leary—v. 2. Pioneers
　　and operations / edited by William F. Trimble.
　　　ISBN 1-56098-467-8 (v. 1 : alk. paper).—ISBN 1-56098-468-6 (v. 2 : alk. paper)
　　　1. Aeronautics, Commercial—History—Congresses.　2. Private flying—History—
　　Congresses.　I. Leary, William M. (William Matthew), 1934–　.　II. Trimble, William F.,
　　1947–　.　III. Title.　IV. Series: International Conference on the History of Civil and
　　Commercial Aviation (1992 : Lucerne, Switzerland). Proceedings of the International Conference
　　on the History of Civil and Commercial Aviation ; v. 1–2.
　　TL515.I53　1992
　　387.7′09—dc20　　　　　　　　　　　　　　　　　　　　　　　　　　　　　94-26006

British Library Cataloguing-in-Publication Data is available

Manufactured in the United States of America
02　01　00　99　98　97　96　95　　5　4　3　2　1

Contents

██
██
██ W. David Lewis

Prologue

An Idea Takes Flight

The idea of organizing an international conference on the history of civil and commercial aviation occurred to me during an unforgettable visit to Central and Eastern Europe in July 1989. Spending two days in Lucerne, Switzerland, I was deeply impressed by the Swiss Transport Museum, a superb institution featuring a remarkable range of exhibits and artifacts devoted to the history of transportation in all of its many phases and manifestations. My imagination was stimulated by the sheer majesty of the setting in which the museum is located, with cloud-capped Mount Pilatus looking down on the city's unique octagonal stone tower, its famed wooden bridge, and the picturesque paddle steamers navigating the Vierwaldstätter See. I was also overwhelmed by the hospitality extended to me by Museum Director Fredy Rey and Head Curator Henry Wydler, now vice-director of the institution. It was a magical experience.

Everything about the Swiss Transport Museum, including its heavy reliance on private funding from a group of about 20,000 devoted patrons, marked it as an exceptional institution, fully justifying its claim as Europe's most comprehensive museum of its type. Opened to the public in 1959, its sprawling facilities cover an area of about 40,000 square meters and attract between 500,000 and 600,000 visitors per year. It maintains one of the most important railway collections in Europe, with more than 60 locomotives and coaches; a cable rail-way exhibition, including the cabin of the Wetterhorn Lift, the second licensed passenger cable railway in the world; a road transport hall, containing more than 30 historic automobiles and a large assortment of bicycles, sleighs, coaches, and other vehicles; a navigation hall, with functioning machinery of the 1895 steamship *Pilatus* and 200 model ships; two halls devoted to various means of communication ranging from Morse telegraphs to a television studio in which visitors can indulge themselves in role-playing as announcers or pro-ducers; the Hans Erni Planetarium, the only facility of its type in Switzerland, capable of accommodating 300 persons in a domed auditorium equipped with 150 projectors that offer spectacular views of solar eclipses and other phenome-na; an astronautics section with a Mercury capsule, a moon suit, and rock frag-ments from the lunar surface; and a giant cosmorama with 36 projectors and 18 individual screens on which viewers can see significant milestones in American and Russian space travel.

As an important component of Switzerland's national effort to promote tour-ism, the museum has a Swissorama that provides stunning 360-degree views of Alpine scenery. But the institution also has a scholarly mission. Its archives contain approximately 150,000 documents, 15,000 glass disks and negative plates, 70,000 photographs, 3,500 technical plans, 50,000 postcards, and 12,000 placards and posters. Its founder, Dr. Alfred Waldis, now retired but still active in his role as honorary president, is a world-renowned expert in the history of transportation, with a phenomenal publication record.

As a historian of aviation, I was particularly impressed by the aeronautics exhibition. Its crown jewel is a 1931 Lockheed Orion 9-C, resplendent in red-and-white Swissair livery. But the museum also owns more than 30 other air-craft, ranging from the earliest Swiss biplane, piloted by Armand Dufaux in 1910 in the first flight over Lake Geneva, to a 1945 Douglas DC-3 and a 1962 Convair CV-990 Coronado that stand in a large central plaza where visitors can ascend boarding ramps and explore the cabins and cockpits. Other exhibits in-clude a Chanute hang glider; a 1913 Blériot XI monoplane; a Stierlin helicopter; 100 models of historic airplanes; imaginative dioramas depicting various modes of flight; a control tower, complete with an exact reproduction of a traffic controller's radar console; and a video projection system that simulates a trans-atlantic flight on one of Swissair's modern passenger jets.

During my visit Rey mentioned that the museum also had excellent confer-ence facilities and said that he was highly receptive to having them used for public events. In 1987 a projected conference on significant milestones and an-niversaries in the history of aviation had failed to materialize at my home institution, Auburn University, for lack of extramural funding. Now, suddenly, it occurred to me that something even broader in scope might somehow take place in the heart of Central Europe: the world's first international conference devoted to the history of civil and commercial aviation, a once-neglected area of research that in recent years has begun to attract increasing scholarly attention. I was particularly interested in holding a conference at which contextual questions involving political, economic, social, and cultural aspects of commercial flight could be fruitfully addressed. Experts in military aviation had been holding such conclaves for many years; why not hold a meeting focusing on peacetime operations? Switzerland's long tradition of neutrality made holding such an event on Swiss soil all the more logical.

After returning to Auburn, I shared my thoughts with Gordon C. Bond, head of the history department, who had given me unstinting support in my efforts to build a graduate program in the history of technology, a program that strongly emphasizes aerospace history. With Bond's encouragement, I discussed my ideas with David R. Hiley, then associate dean of liberal arts, and Paul F. Parks, who, as vice president for research, had funded many of my previous projects. Bond later became dean of liberal arts at Auburn, and Parks became provost and vice president for academic affairs. With their support, which I deeply appreciate, I wrote an exploratory letter to Fredy Rey, outlining the type of conference I wanted to hold and the range of subjects that it would cover.

Rey's enthusiastic response led to further preliminary planning and a second trip to Switzerland in 1990. During this visit, the structure and details of the conference took much firmer shape, and we discussed potential sources of funding. On my way back to Auburn, I stopped at the National Air and Space Museum (NASM) and shared my idea with the head of its aeronautics department, Tom D. Crouch. After consulting with Museum Director Martin Harwit and other officials, Crouch informed me that NASM was willing to join Auburn University and the Swiss Transport Museum in sponsoring the projected conference. Soon after I returned to Auburn, Crouch appointed R. E. G. Davies, curator of air transport at NASM and a distinguished author of many books on the history of commercial aviation, to represent the museum in planning the conference. Along with Crouch and Davies, Wendy Stephens, Dominick Pisano, Robert van der Linden, and other staff members at NASM gave generous help and advice in the process that lay ahead. I am most grateful to them.

I also received valuable encouragement from Felix C. Lowe, director of the Smithsonian Institution Press, who has published a large number of books on all aspects of the history of aviation. Lowe expressed a strong interest in having the proceedings of the conference appear under his colophon, ensuring them widespread attention from scholars and aviation enthusiasts who might not be able to attend the event. I greatly appreciate the help given me by Lowe and his staff in all phases of the project.

During the months and years of planning that followed, I corresponded frequently with Rey and Wydler. The rapidly accumulating number of fax transmissions between us made me thankful that I had embarked on such a venture at a time when advances in the instantaneous transmission of data made it easy to keep in touch with these two extremely congenial associates. At one point, as our preparations intensified, I found a greeting card with an evocative picture of a 19th-century clipper ship, the *Three Brothers*. Impressed by the congruence between the fastest transportation that a bygone era could offer and the speed with which jet aircraft now carry passengers from one part of the planet to another, I sent the card to my Swiss friends as a symbol of our relationship. They were quick to reciprocate my friendly gesture, and we henceforth became the "Three Brothers," united in a mutual quest that became more and more fulfilling with the passage of time.

Trusting that our project would be successful, even though I was still unsure of sources for sufficient funding, I invited a number of scholars to prepare papers and chair sessions if such aid became available. Because their contributions form the contents of the proceedings that follow, it would be superfluous to mention them by name. Most belong to the Albatrosses, a group of aerospace historians who are members of the Society for the History of Technology (SHOT). As secretary of the Albatrosses and an editor of the group's newsletter, I maintain frequent contact with more than 100 scholars all over the world and encourage networking among them. I was greatly heartened by the responses I received from the people I contacted. Slowly, but with ever-increasing momentum, a project that had started as a mere idea began to gain form and substance.

Since 1919, when the first regularly scheduled international air routes connected London and Paris, civil and commercial air transport has been a force for globalization. A conference on the history of civil and commercial aviation would therefore have to include scholars from many nations. Inevitably the United States, with its large number of professional aerospace historians, would be heavily represented, but I was determined that American scholars would constitute no more than half of the participants. As it turned out, this was the exact proportion that resulted from the long planning process. I was also eager for young scholars to take part and for a wide variety of viewpoints to be represented. Colleagues from the sponsoring institutions fully supported these aims, providing much valuable advice about potential invitees and the topics that they would discuss.

Even with optimal financial support, it was clear that only a few of the many potential subjects appropriate to the history of commercial aviation could be covered. From a list of possible topics, we ultimately decided on the history of airports; the evolution of the technical infrastructure that had undergirded progress in civil and commercial aviation; economic and social constraints affecting the development of commercial aircraft; early problems involving operations, logistics, and routes; connections between flight and society; links between military and commercial aviation; and fresh insights on great pioneers in the growth of the airline industry.

For a time, it was not clear that even this severely limited range of topics could be examined. If the conference was to take place at all, we needed funds well in excess of the amounts that Auburn, NASM, and the Swiss Transport Museum could commit to the venture. From the outset, Swissair strongly supported our efforts. In addition, the following parties came to our aid: the Association of Aviation Writers in Zurich; the City of Lucerne; the Swiss Federal Railway; Hallwag Publishers in Bern; the Hotel Montana and Hotel Union AG in Lucerne; the Lake of Lucerne Navigation Committee; the Nidwaldner Museen in Stans; the Public Bus VBL in Lucerne; the Lucerne Tourist Office; the Swissair Fokker Team, dedicated to the preservation of aircraft that had figured importantly in Swissair's history; and officials at several outstanding Swiss facilities who later cooperated in arranging field trips for the conferees. It is a pleasure to thank all of these parties for their generous support.

Ultimately, prospects appeared good that several airlines and airframe manufacturers, including Airbus Industrie, Boeing International Corporation, Fokker Aircraft B.V., McDonnell Douglas, and SNECMA/cfm international, would join Swissair in providing financial aid. It is a pleasure to acknowledge this assistance, which materialized late in 1991 and without which our conference could not have been held. Encouraged by our progress, Rey came to Washington, D.C., in November 1991 for a meeting at NASM, bringing Waldis and Wydler with him. Parks joined me in representing Auburn University, and Lowe attended on behalf of the Smithsonian Institution Press. Crouch, Davies, Pisano, and van der Linden represented NASM. A detailed list of sessions, topics, and speakers was agreed on, and a budget was adopted. At the time, the possibility of having a session on the connections between military and commercial aviation was undetermined, but a deeply appreciated contribution from General Electric Company early in 1992 enabled us to add this subject to those already approved. By that time, the final outlines of the conference were firmly in place.

Preparations for the conference moved rapidly ahead as scholars who had previously indicated their willingness to take part now accepted the formal invitations. In a most welcome development, Roger Béteille, who had played a key role in the emergence of Airbus Industrie, agreed to give the keynote address. We were also able to add several distinguished people, including Genrikh Novozhilov, head of Russia's Ilyushin Design Bureau, to our roster of speakers as a result of the gift from General Electric. At Auburn University, the appointment of Martha Graham Viator as a part-time administrative assistant aided me in making final preparations. Patricia Manos gave me unstinting secretarial help; Barbara Connell advised me in budgetary procedures; and Sandra Rose rendered valuable assistance in word processing. Meanwhile, across the Atlantic, Christine Boesiger, Renate Bueche, Tonia Annen, Corinna Braun, and other members of the Swiss Transport Museum staff attended to a multitude of local arrangements under the direction of Rey and Wydler. Swissair granted special rates to participants and their spouses, and the Swiss Transport Museum agreed to provide meals and lodging.

Although our budget could cover only our speakers, their spouses, and a relatively few officials from the sponsoring institutions, we wanted others to attend the conference and take part in the discussions if they could obtain funding to do so. We therefore sent invitations to members of several scholarly and professional organizations, including the Society for the History of Technology, which would hold its annual meeting at Uppsala, Sweden, during the week immediately preceding our own event. We were pleased that several people accepted this offer, among them Antoin Dalton, of Aer Lingus; Michele A. Fistek, of Plymouth State College, United States; John Edward King, of the Croydon Airport Society, England; Kurt Offenloch, of J. W. Goethe University, Frankfurt, Germany; Leonard Reich, of Colby College, United States; Edward Walters, of the University of Texas at Dallas, United States; and Hans Wittenberg, of Delft University of Technology, Netherlands. Their enthusiasm and their comments following the papers contributed much to the success of the conference.

Others who took part in our meetings included Peter Bachmann, of the Zurich Airport Authority; Armin Baltensweiler, former president of Swissair; Lewis Bateman, of Airbus Industrie; Vladimir Belyakov, of the Ilyushin Design Bureau; Walter M. Borner, manager of special assignments for Swissair; Michel Déchelotte, director of internal relations of Airbus Industrie; Hansjochen Ehmer, representing the German Aerospace Research Establishment; Michel Julliand, general manager of engines sales, SNECMA/cfm international; Werner Latscha, retired chief executive, Swiss Federal Railway; Otto Loepfe, president of Swissair; Erich Meier, of the Association of Aviation Writers,

Zurich; Paul Maximilian Müller, a member of Swissair's executive management team; Jean Roeder, senior vice president of Airbus Industrie; Ernest Schlecht, of the Zurich Airport Authority; and Richard Schilliger, head of Swissair's Fokker Team and a retired airline captain.

Everyone who participated in the event received a handsome preliminary brochure and a large ring-bound volume containing the official program of the conference. Both of these impressive productions, beautifully designed by the Swiss Transport Museum, featured a dramatic logo with the outline of a modern jetliner superimposed on a rotorcraft sketched by Leonardo da Vinci, with boldly stylized letters and numbers heralding "ICCA 92," as our International Conference on the History of Civil and Commercial Aviation was now designated. In a further gesture of hospitality, the Swiss Transport Museum commissioned special commemorative watches to be given to conferees and other people whose help had been instrumental in making ICCA 92 possible. One of my most pleasant tasks as president and director of the conference was to distribute these timepieces with appropriate expressions of thanks. I did this so many times during the course of the proceedings that I became known as "Mr. Rolex."

The conference took place during the week of August 23–29, 1992. Participants gathered on the first evening of the event for a plenary session, followed by an elegant banquet hosted by the City of Lucerne. Welcoming addresses were given by Fredy Rey and Franz Kurzmeyer, lord mayor of Lucerne, followed by responses from representatives of the American cosponsors. Adolf Ogi, Swiss federal minister of transport and energy, extended an official greeting, paying tribute to the cumulative achievements of pioneering fliers and recalling the role that Switzerland had played in the conquest of the air.

In an opening presentation, I tried to capture the spirit that had brought us together in the first international meeting specifically devoted to the history of civil and commercial, as opposed to military, aviation. Shortly before the conference opened, my wife, Pat, and I stood on the balcony of our hotel at daybreak and watched three balloons rising slowly above Lake Lucerne as the rising sun broke through the haze with an unearthly splendor. As I would tell the conferees, it seemed like a good omen for the meeting that was about to begin.

Later that same day, Pat and I ascended Mount Pilatus, starting on foot and then continuing on an aerial lift and a cable car that took us across yawning chasms to the lofty peak. After admiring the view, we descended the steep mountainside on a cogwheel railway and returned to Lucerne on a lake steamer. The various modes of transportation provided an appropriate prelude to a conference on a significant aspect of the human urge to move people and goods from one place to another. The large complex of buildings atop the mountain, every component of which had been brought to the summit in a striking display of human ingenuity, reminded me of the zest for achievement that drives people onward in an endless creative process, of which technology, like any other cultural activity, is a part.

In my opening presentation, I reminded those present that historians, as the great American scholar Carl Becker once said, are the memory keepers of the human race and that what had brought us together was our responsibility to preserve and interpret as much remaining evidence as possible about the rich heritage of civil and commercial aviation. The epic of flight, I stated, is full of mixed meanings and consequences. In its most fearful and malevolent aspects, it is a story of the pitiless mass destruction of such places as Guernica, Dresden, and Hiroshima. At its best, however, it is a record of the peaceful accomplishments that have brought the human community closer together in increasingly interdependent relationships, making us more of a planetary family than ever before and yielding opportunities for the mutually beneficial interchange of goods and ideas.

The rest of the conference presentations are contained in the proceedings that follow. I will allow them to speak for themselves, but I want to thank all of the scholars who prepared them and chaired the sessions in which they were delivered. I am under particular obligation to William M. Leary and William F. Trimble, both of whom participated in the conference, for meeting with me in Atlanta shortly after the conference and agreeing to edit the proceedings. I deeply appreciate the time and effort that they put into this challenging project, requiring them to deal with papers written in a number of languages and reflecting diverse styles of scholarly presentation and documentation. Rather than force the papers into one common mold, they have wisely retained the methods of citation and source identification used by the various authors.

The nature and content of the seven working sessions of the conference will become clear in the pages that Leary and Trimble have edited. Instead of focusing on these meetings, I will complete this brief introduction with an account of the general setting within which the papers were presented and the field trips that took place throughout the conference. All of the sessions were held in a large, well-equipped hall that was decorated with travel posters colorfully evoking various stages in the history of passenger flight. Virtually every seat was occupied at all of the sessions, despite the lure of nearby tourist attractions in one of the world's most beautiful cities. Animated discussions occurred after each presentation and carried over into luncheons at the museum's "Cockpit" restaurant. Because of the difficulty of transcribing and editing these dialogues, only the papers themselves have been published. English was the official language of the conference, but participants were free to speak in their native tongues, and headphones were available for simultaneous translation. The outstanding manner in which this highly demanding task was performed by skilled interpreters typified the excellent logistical arrangements provided by the Swiss Transport Museum.

Along with having the pleasure of lodging at fine hotels in Lucerne, conferees had several evenings free to wander about the city for shopping, dining, and sightseeing. Free bus service was provided to and from the museum, and a well-staffed conference office rendered a variety of helpful services. Just before the conference began, a furious storm drenched the area with rain and blew down a few large trees along the Lido, yet the weather throughout the event was all that could have been hoped for.

The field trips were among the most memorable aspects of the conference, epitomizing the hospitality for which Switzerland is justly renowned. On the second day of the meeting, participants and their spouses were taken to Zurich for a tour of the airport and an inspection of Swissair's maintenance operations. The Zurich Airport Authority and Swissair's Technical Department made this event a rewarding experience, highlighted by a demonstration of fire-fighting equipment. The Swissair Fokker Team and its leader, Richard Schilliger, arranged a display of historic aircraft. Daniel Sporri, deputy managing director of the airport authority, gave an informative talk on the history of the huge international facility, including a discussion of political, economic, and environmental issues that the traditionally cautious Swiss voters have had to face throughout the development and expansion of the installation. Afterward, Swissair provided a much-appreciated banquet, graciously hosted by Otto Loepfe in his capacity as chief executive officer of the airline.

The next day the conferees visited the Pilatus Aircraft Factory at Stans, which makes trainers, and a maintenance base of the Swiss Aircraft Logistics Command at Buochs. Walter Gubler, president of Pilatus Aircraft Ltd., and Hansreudi Rüetschi, a colonel in the Swiss Air Force and director of the Buochs Branch of the Logistics Command, hosted these visits. The Pilatus facility is currently the only aircraft-manufacturing plant in Switzerland. The performance capabilities of the aircraft were dramatically demonstrated by a test pilot, Hans Galli, who performed a spectacular aerobatics demonstration against the backdrop of breathtaking Alpine scenery. Although conferees were not able, because of security reasons at the maintenance base, to tour the maze of subterranean hangars extending deep under the mountainous terrain, they got a good sense of the rigorous procedures followed in keeping Switzerland's Mirage III jet interceptors in constant readiness to meet any external threat to the nation's security. Conferees wanting to continue the tour after seeing the aircraft facility and maintenance base visited Fürigen, a historic mountain fortress of World War II vintage, before returning to Lucerne.

After the morning session on the fourth day, participants took a field trip to the Swiss Air Force Museum at Dübendorf, hosted by Walter Dürig, former general and commander of the Swiss Air Force and manager of the museum. Hugo Muser, a former air force colonel and retired Swissair captain, also addressed the group, relating information about Swiss military aviation going back to its origins as a balloon corps for artillery observation in 1899 and its first maneuvers with heavier-than-air craft in 1911. The Dübendorf facility, begun in 1972 and opened to the public six years later, houses a large number of historic aircraft including a Haefeli DH-1 biplane dating from 1916, a Dewoitine D-27, a Bücker Jungmeister, a Messerschmitt Me-109 E, a Junkers Ju-52, a P-51 Mustang, and a Mirage III-C. Like the Swiss Transport Museum, the installation exemplifies a heavy reliance on private support, provided by such organizations as the Friends of the Swiss Air Force Museum Association, founded in 1979. An extension that was begun in 1985 and opened in 1988 was funded through creation of the Swiss Air Force Museum Trust.

The final field trip, on Friday, August 28, took conference participants to the Swiss Federal Aircraft Factory and Wind Tunnel at Emmen and was hosted by the managing director of that facility, Hansjürg Kobelt. One of six federal armament factories maintained by Switzerland's Defence Technology and Procurement Agency, the Emmen plant and its sister installations have built and modified many aircraft under license for use in Swiss military service, as well as coordinating other projects carried out by subcontractors scattered throughout the country. Covering 35 acres and employing 800 persons, the ultramodern Emmen plant not only provides research, development, and production capability for various facets of the Swiss aviation program but also maintains final assembly and testing facilities for space and guided missile systems including the Dragon and TOW antitank missiles and the Rapier antiaircraft missile. The installation also performs contract work for foreign manufacturers.

The conference concluded with a plenary meeting later that same day. It featured a provocative address by Davies, "Facing the Transportation Gridlock of the 21st Century," and a French film on the beginnings of aviation and highlights of the "Golden Age" preceding World War II. The next morning, the participants enjoyed a guided tour of the Swiss Transport Museum after Fredy Rey had presented an informative history of the institution. The tour was followed by a farewell shipboard luncheon in an unforgettable trip down Lake Lucerne.

The sky was clear, the sun shone brightly, and the water sparkled as we sailed past Alpine forests and charming villages flanked by such storied peaks as Rigi and Burgenstock. Conversing with one another as they reveled in the scenery, the conferees were plainly enthusiastic about their week-long experience. Perhaps the greatest reward of the time we had spent together, over and above the information and insight that we had gained from the papers and discussions, was an enhanced sense of belonging to an international community of scholars for whom the history of civil and commercial aviation had become an endlessly exciting frontier for research, writing, and teaching. Fostering and promoting this sense of community is one of my most cherished professional goals, deriving from my conviction that a shared passion for reliving and reinterpreting the past is fundamental to the fulfillment of our scholarly goals.

For this reason I will never forget what happened shortly before our excursion boat returned to its mooring place in Lucerne. Before reaching the dock, it stopped by the Lido near the Swiss Transport Museum to discharge some of our party while the rest, including Pat and myself, stayed aboard for the final minutes of the trip. As we waved farewell to the group on the shore, and they waved back, the joy and enthusiasm uniting both groups was overwhelming. That was all I needed: I knew that everything that had happened since my first visit to Switzerland three years earlier had been well worth the effort. I was delighted that the idea I had conceived in response to Rey's remark about his conference facilities had taken flight in such a wonderfully rewarding way. The two volumes that follow will provide a lasting record of the extremely memorable event held amid Alpine grandeur in the summer of 1992.

Roger Béteille

Introduction

Airbus; or, the Reconstruction of European Civil Aeronautics

With a work force of around 450,000,[1] the aerospace industry in Western Europe (airframes, engines, equipment) is of the utmost economic importance, annually exporting approximately 25 billion ecus of products and services. A major part of this activity is dedicated to commercial aircraft,[2] thanks to the success of the Airbus family of aircraft, enabling a situation that was in jeopardy at the beginning of the 1970s to be put back on an even keel.

During World War I the European aeronautical industry produced 166,000 aircraft, more than four times the output of the United States. The technical and industrial capabilities available after 1919 were exploited in part to develop transport aircraft and to open air routes, first of all almost exclusively for postal and then for passenger service.

The industries and markets were purely national, and in spite of sometimes far-fetched ideas, it was only in the years preceding 1940 that efficient and fairly safe aircraft allowed commercial exploitation on a somewhat regular basis. Some of these aircraft pursued a commercial career just after the war, such as the Junkers 52 and the Bloch 161. But apart from the Ju-52, which benefited from extensive wartime production, none of these aircraft were produced in truly industrial quantities.

In 1945, apart from the English industry, Europe needed to be rebuilt. Germany, which had built 119,000 aircraft in six years, was "out of the running" for many years, and Italy was only slightly active. Only France and later the Netherlands recovered and made an attempt to return to the civil aviation market as England was doing, taking advantage of its intact industry. During the 10 years that preceded the advent of jet transport, England and France produced, with virtually prewar technologies, "national" aircraft such as the Avro Tudor, the Vickers Viking and Ambassador, the SE-2010 Armagnac, and the Bréguet Deux Ponts. Their distribution was generally limited to the airlines in the manufacturer's country. But beginning in 1952 England opened the way for turboprop aircraft with the Bristol Britannia and especially the Vickers Viscount, whose commercial success (438 aircraft) was considerable for that time. During this period the U.S. industry, on the basis of the aircraft produced in high quantities for the war effort, was placing its best-sellers, the Douglas DC-3 and DC-4, and was developing the Douglas DC-6 and DC-7 long-haul and the Lockheed Constellation and Super Constellation aircraft worldwide. The quantities and especially the reliability of the engines and equipment ensured the success of these aircraft.

Commercial jet aviation was born first in England with the De Havilland Comet, then in France with the SE-210 Caravelle. Although the Comet suffered at the outset from "mysterious" accidents that considerably undermined its sales,[3] the same cannot be said of the Caravelle, and we must ask ourselves why, after such a promising start and in spite of the British perseverance (the VC-10, BAC One-Eleven, Trident), Europe found itself, at the end of the 1960s, nearly eliminated from the civil aircraft market.

At the end of the 1960s and the start of the 1970s, even though a fairly high number of European civil transport aircraft were still in service, none of the offered models were selling except in almost negligible quantities and under very marginal economical conditions. The aircraft offered by the American manufacturers (Boeing 727/737/747, Douglas DC-9/DC-10, Lockheed 1011) were monopolizing the market, even in Europe and even with airlines still operating previously acquired European aircraft.

In my opinion the reasons for this situation are located on a European scale and not in a coordinated attempt by the American industry to eliminate the competition. The American manufacturers were only doing "their job" by industrially developing and producing reliable high-performance aircraft geared to suit the airlines' needs, by actively selling the aircraft at a competitive price, and by providing a good after-sales service.

Unlike in the United States, geography, politics, and history do not combine

⊘Historical domination of US suppliers

Jetliners delivered through end 1969

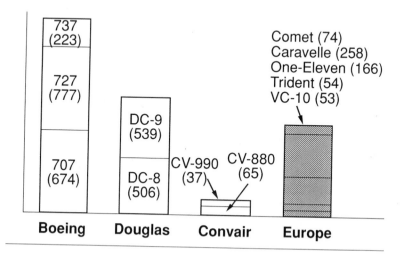

1.1. Historical domination of U.S. suppliers. (Courtesy Airbus Industrie)

in Europe to make a "large aeronautical market"[4] in which local manufacturers can sell substantial fleets of aircraft with short time-scale deliveries, ensuring production rates compatible with cost-effectiveness and rapid acquisition of extensive operational experience. But customers do give preference to local manufacturers, particularly when new models are launched—justified by communication, intervention, and relational considerations, especially important at the outset. And when a model has been retained to initially build up a fleet, the economical advantage of conserving this model is very high (investments, training of personnel, etc.), giving manufacturers an edge over any possible competitors.

The intrinsic insufficiency of the European market was aggravated by national compartmentalization and the dispersion of efforts. Although the U.S. market could reasonably support competition between the DC-9 and the Boeing 727/737, Europe could not economically support the trio composed of the BAC One-Eleven, the Caravelle, and the Trident. More important, an excessive "national preference" in the choice of the avionics equipment did not always encourage the suppliers to make the necessary efforts to obtain reliability and de-

🌀 European mainline turbine-powered airliners

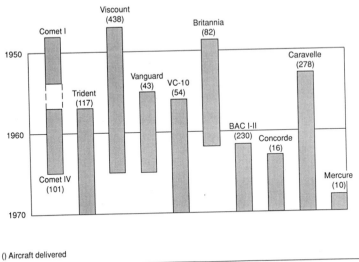

() Aircraft delivered

1.2. European mainline turbine-powered airliners. (Courtesy Airbus Industrie)

velop a competitive after-sales service. As a result, the reputation of European manufacturers seriously suffered.

The initial accidents that plagued the Comet and remained unexplained for far too long, and the delay that this caused in producing reliable aircraft (Comet 4), left the field open for competitors, who were able to corner the long-haul market with the Boeing 707 and the Douglas DC-8, both particularly successful. The later models of the Comet and the DC-10 were not sufficiently competitive to overcome the handicap.

At the beginning, the Caravelle benefited from an important asset: It was the first "medium-haul jet." The Caravelle succeeded in spite of the fact that certain important airlines, "hooked" on the turboprop (Lockheed Electra), were having some difficulties in accepting this revolutionary formula. Yet this advantage was fairly quickly lost as Caravelle failed to make the industrial effort required to optimize the commercial characteristics of the aircraft (in particular the fuselage cross section to provide sufficient baggage storage).[5] Cooperation with Douglas, initiated on request from the American airlines, who were extremely interested, stumbled essentially on this point; this encouraged Douglas to satisfy its customers with the DC-9, which was, at the outset, essentially a Caravelle tailored to suit the requirements requested by the American airlines.

Two reasons explain the behavior of the people in charge of Caravelle at that time. The first was the hope to sell the aircraft "as such" to TWA[6] (which seemed to go against Douglas's judgment on market requirements), a hope that was thwarted following difficulties within TWA, in particular the relations with Howard Hughes. The second was the excessive priority accorded at that time to supersonic transport, the first French definitions of which were "medium-haul" and were given the evocative name of Super Caravelle.

The Trident mainly suffered from too closely following the requests of the launch airline (British European Airways, BEA), requests tailored to national requirements too specific for the rest of the market. The result was an aircraft that was too small and too difficult to enlarge to follow growth in traffic and was therefore not really competitive when up against the Boeing 727 model series (727-100, 727-200).

Although the European companies (and governments) were counting to a large extent on the lead taken at that time in the supersonic field with the French-English Concorde project, they were aware that even if the Concorde turned out to be a resounding success, sufficient and profitable activity could not be maintained if they were eliminated from the subsonic market, especially since Boeing, Douglas, and Lockheed were almost simultaneously heralding the "widebody" age with the 747, DC-10, and L-1011.

Three main European airlines—Air France, British European Airways, and Deutsche Lufthansa—predicted that their medium-haul traffic would increase enough during the next decade for 200- to 250-seat aircraft to be required on their trunk routes. Coordinating their points of view during 1966, they published their desiderata during the last quarter, indicating that they would be ready to acquire aircraft of this type in the near future, and suggested that the manufacturers carry out studies and make proposals along these lines.

On the basis of preliminary individual studies, the main manufacturers in England and France, aware of the extensive facilities needed to develop large-size aircraft, joined their efforts and formed two groups. The first one united Sud-Aviation and the British Aircraft Corporation (BAC), also cooperating on the Concorde, and the other joined De Havilland and Bréguet. On their side, the five German manufacturers set up a joint office (Arbeitgemeinschaft Airbus) to examine the possibilities of a return to the civil market.

The governments, whose backing was sought, designated (for national industrial political reasons) Sud-Aviation in France and De Havilland in England as the main actors in this field. Joined by the German office, these manufacturers agreed to jointly produce a 250-seat medium-haul twin-engine with characteristics similar to the requests made by the European airlines. During the summer of 1967, the three governments agreed to provide financial help to the associates—a small sum in the first preliminary definition and market approach phase, possibly followed by substantial help for the manufacturing phase if the results of the first step were sufficiently promising.

One of the main reasons behind the decisions concerning both the number of engines and the size of the aircraft was that the American manufacturers (Douglas and Lockheed), aiming for a greater operating range (transcontinental) and higher performance (Denver airport), had both opted for the trijet formula, which led quite naturally to a larger aircraft (over 300 seats). With Boeing devoting its efforts to the 747, the Europeans hoped to avoid, at least initially, direct competition, allowing them to more easily penetrate the market.

The program defined in mid-1967 combined, in principle, an airframe produced by Sud-Aviation and De Havilland (having equal shares, 37.5 percent) and the German manufacturers (Deutsche Airbus, 25 percent) with Rolls-Royce engines. Rolls-Royce said that, with the help of the government, it could develop a suitable (high bypass ratio) engine, the RB 207. Very partial and limited subcontracting was possibly envisaged in the production phase for the French (SNECMA) and German (MTU) engine manufacturers. The progress in the technical definition of the aircraft and the analysis of its suitability to the widest possible market (which implied taking into account the opinion of many airlines and, in particular, the American airlines) highlighted a fundamental contradiction in the first months of 1968. On the one hand, the cost of the RB 207 engines and the technological possibilities available for the airframe implied increasing the aircraft capacity to above 300 seats to obtain an acceptable operating cost per seat,[7] but on the other hand, the market requirements were for 200 to 300 seats.

Two events would lead to a solution of this contradiction. First, without openly admitting it,[8] Rolls-Royce transferred the essential part of its manpower from the RB 207 program to the 211 program after the choice of the latter by Lockheed for the L-1011. The possibility of having a 207 engine operational in good time became, therefore, extremely doubtful. In parallel, the price of the 211 was fixed by Rolls-Royce at a level so low, when compared with the 207, that the twin jet lost a good part of its economic competitiveness with the trijet. Second, the launching by Douglas of the long-haul version DC-10-30 led to the development by General Electric and Pratt & Whitney of engines sufficiently powerful to equip a 250-seat medium-haul twin.

The project in progress was then completely revised and led, in the autumn of 1968, to the proposal of the Airbus as we know it today, that is, a 250-seat aircraft, equipped with two jet engines also developed for long-haul trijets. The result was a significant reduction in the development costs, better reliability guarantees, and, by initiating competition between the engine suppliers, acquisition conditions that were clearly more favorable. The potential customer airlines and the French and German governments reacted very favorably, but the revision led to the withdrawal of the British government.

Since the agreement of summer 1967 among the three governments to financially back the first exploratory stage of the associate industrial companies, the situation had changed significantly in the eyes of the British administration. On the one hand, Rolls-Royce (the flagship of the country's industry and therefore a "sacred cow" in the eyes of the government) had practically thrown in its lot with the Lockheed 1011 and had no good reason to encourage competition from the Airbus twin.[9] On the other hand, the British Aircraft Corporation[10] was proposing fully British solutions (airframe and engines)—the BAC Two-Eleven (180 to 200 seats, comparable to the Boeing 757) and the BAC Three-Eleven (220 to 240 seats, comparable to the Airbus)—for which this manufacturer could quite rightly take advantage of the technical and commercial experience gained on the BAC One-Eleven.

Not very optimistic about the success of a program that it could not direct at will and that, in case of success, would compete with the L-1011, the British administration advised the government to withdraw from the envisaged three-party cooperation. It also thought that this decision would ipso facto lead to the termination of the Airbus program. The government, which was looking for ways to save money and was not very politically motivated toward European industrial cooperation, took the administration's advice.

France and Germany, however, encouraged by the strength of their cooperation and convinced that the program in progress could succeed, decided to continue together. An attempt by BAC to obtain continental cooperation and, in particular, aid from the Germans for the British BAC Three-Eleven program, an attempt conducted more by the administration than by BAC itself, failed. Indeed, the BAC Three-Eleven project, associated with the Rolls-Royce engines, did not appear to be technically and economically competitive with the A300B project, and such a change in strategy was therefore not justified.

The British manufacturer HSA,[11] convinced of the benefits of the program abandoned by its government, then proposed to risk a substantial part of its own funds to stay with the project as subcontractor with participation in risks. This proposal was doubly attractive because it allowed continued benefits to be drawn from HSA's experience, work force, and industrial possibilities and also showed that a large industrial group judged the project sufficiently well directed and promising to invest heavily in it. Under these conditions, the French and German governments reached an agreement in June 1969 to financially back the program of their manufacturers on an equal-shares collaboration basis. The Airbus program could then continue and contribute, if successful, to the renaissance of European civil aeronautics.

In mid-1969 the European civil aeronautics industry consisted of three areas: national programs in progress; collaborative ventures; and national projects. The various national programs in progress included the following: (1) small aircraft, business and regional aircraft (Falcon, HS 125, Fokker 27,[12] HS 735), which could hope for a reasonably active career but represented only a small part of the turnover when compared with the overall possibilities of the industry; (2) 80- to 125-seat short- to medium-haul transport aircraft (Caravelle, BAC One-Eleven, Trident), which were being forced out of the market by the success of the 727/737 and the DC-9; and (3) the Fokker 28, which was smaller than the American competitors and would later have some success.

Two future collaborative ventures were the Concorde (Franco-British), the first civil supersonic transport aircraft, the initial prototypes of which were being completed even though the program was well behind initial schedule, and the Airbus (Franco-German with private participation from HSA), a 250-seat medium-haul twin-engine whose introduction into service was planned for 1974.

Among the various national projects were the Dassault Mercure, which was a potential competitor for the 737 and the DC-9 and which would have a very limited success (10 aircraft produced for Air Inter), and the BAC Two-Eleven/Three-Eleven, an Airbus competitor that was not developed because financial backing requested from the British government was not granted.

The start of the 1970s was marked by the first "oil shock," which, through its impact on fuel prices and the world economy, considerably slowed down the growth in air transport. The Concorde program came to a virtual standstill; only Air-France and British Overseas Airways Corporation (BOAC), which benefited from exceptional acquisition conditions, were able to introduce aircraft into service (12 aircraft). In addition, the airlines' rush to acquire new aircraft, particularly large-capacity aircraft, experienced a distinct slowdown, and the interest in fuel-saving aircraft, such as the Airbus twin promised to be, increased.

Overall, this situation turned out to be favorable to the Airbus program. During the few years spent demonstrating that an aircraft produced in cooperation could be ready within the specified deadlines and could satisfy its first customers both from an operational performance and from an after-sales service standpoint, the aircraft's market was not, as it could have been, saturated by the trijets.

From 1969 to 1975 the Airbus program accomplished the following: (1) definition and setting up of a technical, industrial, and commercial cooperative organization on an unusual but efficient basis in which a specialized legal entity (Airbus Industrie G.I.E.)[13] coordinated the partners' activities and all customer relations (promotion, sales, support); (2) enlargement of the group, with full participation from Spain and partial participation from the Netherlands; (3) development and certification of the aircraft within scheduled times; (4) setting up of the industrial and production tooling for the first series-production aircraft; and (5) satisfactory introduction into service with the first customers.

By the middle of the decade, the European industry had a good "horse" at its disposal with the Airbus A300 (that cooperation had not transformed into a "camel," as the saying goes) and an efficient tool for cooperative work under competitive conditions. Nevertheless, commercial success was far from certain. The market had stagnated, and competitors, although they did not have directly comparable aircraft, used the overcapacity argument to push the excellent 727-200.

It was soon confirmed, during the certification tests, that the initial technical definition of the Airbus included, as hoped, large development possibilities, in particular in takeoff and operating range performance. This opened medium- to long-haul markets for the twin[14] and allowed it to use airports that demanded optimum performance (South Africa, Iran, Denver). Commercial success, both in the Far East, where the regional routes seemed to be made for the Airbus performance and capacity characteristics, and in the United States, where Eastern Airlines selected the Airbus to replace the L-1011s, followed in spite of several difficult periods.

Nevertheless, toward the end of the decade, it was clear that substantial technical progress had been made in the world and, in particular, in Europe and that the aircraft designed 10 years previously could be greatly improved by incorporating this progress. Airbus profited from this technical improvement to reduce the capacity of the aircraft slightly to comply with the falloff in growth caused by the oil shocks. This led to the A310, ordered simultaneously by Swissair and Lufthansa in 1979, and then to the A300-600, the modernized A300 without reduction in capacity.

This European reaction was especially necessary since Boeing, which for a long time had publicly criticized the wide-body twin formula supported by Airbus, had just become a convert and launched the 767. When the A310 was launched the British government, faced with the continental success, changed its mind and reentered the program, which finally allowed HSA[15] to become a full member in the Airbus Industrie G.I.E.

✍ The Airbus product line

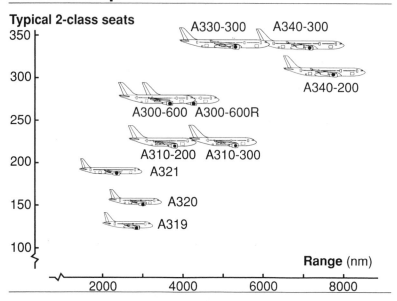

1.3. The Airbus product line. (Courtesy Airbus Industrie)

At the start of the 1980s, the A310 and the A300-600 put Europe in a choice position in the 200- to 300-seat, medium- to long-haul aircraft category, in which these two aircraft had conquered half of the world market. Throughout the 1970s, the European manufacturers had also tried to fill civil slots other than that of the wide-body twin. In general, the engine industry and the equipment industry had accepted transatlantic cooperation by associating with American firms and allowing them to obtain satisfaction on the world market from both a quality and a quantity standpoint. The equal-shares association between General Electric and SNECMA for the 10-ton engine (CFM 56) is a particularly good example. Also, participation in engines of 20 tons and more of the General Electric range, cooperation between Pratt & Whitney, Rolls-Royce, MTU, and the Japanese in the IAE group, and of course the recovery by Rolls-Royce of its reputation after the initial setbacks with the RB 211 have largely contributed to the excellent health of the European civil engine industry, which is now no longer exclusively British.

For the aircraft manufacturers, a distinction must be made between two classes. The first consists of aircraft of less than 100 seats. National programs—

HS 146 in England, F 50 and F 100 in the Netherlands (in line with the F 27 and F 28)—were successfully undertaken in a field relatively neglected by the American competitors. In addition, a Franco-Italian collaborative venture (ATR42/71), organized more or less along the Airbus lines, has succeeded in obtaining an enviable place in the world market for regional twin-turboprop aircraft.

The second class consists of medium-capacity aircraft (130–150 seats). Europe's exclusion from this market by lack of successors to the Caravelle, the BAC One-Eleven, or the Trident, all eliminated by the American competitors, could not of course be accepted without some reaction, especially since it clearly appeared that the wide-body aircraft of the Airbus type could not alone make the civil industry viable. This is why various attempts were made, on the one hand, on a national level in France by Dassault to develop the Mercure with CFM engines and, on the other hand, in cooperation with two groups, CAST and Europlane, the latter being essentially composed of Airbus participants. None of these attempts, in spite of the opening of exploratory negotiations to form cooperations with the American industry, reached a credibility level that justified continuation.

After the efficiency of the cooperation in the Airbus Industrie system had been demonstrated, associated with a growing reputation among customers, it became possible to seriously propose to the partners an extension in the Airbus range so that a true "family" could be proposed, eliminating the need for customer airlines to contact competitors for other aircraft for their fleets.

Two fields needed to be covered: the 150-seat and the long-haul. A careful study of a predictable change in the market led to the priority given to a technically highly developed 150-seat aircraft, the A320, which from the outset met with unprecedented success for a European aircraft. In parallel with the natural developments of this formula (A321/A319), Airbus then entered the long-haul range by launching the A340/A330 pair, which also enjoyed an enormous success thanks to the excellent requirement adaptation provided by the choice offered between the four-engine and the two-engine versions and a very high technological level. Thus, today's "Airbus family" symbolizes, to a great extent, the completion of the European civil aircraft industry's renaissance.

Many in the past qualified Airbus as the "improbable if not impossible European dream." Its success proves, however, that with a competent and qualified work force and a solid industrial base, this type of dream can come true. The Airbus industry group has shown that it can draw an inheritance from a long history by establishing a true in-house "culture," surpassing national obstacles without depriving itself of the input that a multinational structure inherently

🌀 Family tree

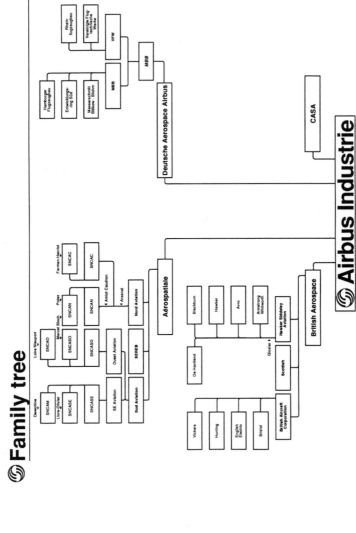

1.4. Airbus Industrie family tree. (Courtesy Airbus Industrie)

provides. This culture has enabled Airbus to develop efficient industrial cooperation throughout the world, confirming that Europe is not a "closed shop" even in high-tech fields. The quality and the extent of its clientele, its order book, and its range of products are today essential for maintaining a competitive civil aircraft industry in Europe and for avoiding a monopoly situation, which would inevitably retard progress in air transportation.

NOTES

1. This work force is about a third of that of the U.S. industry.

2. Other activity includes regional aircraft, business aircraft, and tourist aircraft.

3. The mystery behind the accidents was solved after tremendous work. The problem was structural fatigue of the pressurized cabin, a phenomenon that was poorly known at that time.

4. At that time, the U.S. airlines represented more than 50 percent of the world market.

5. The studies of a competitive version had nevertheless been conducted as far as defining the modifications required, but application was not decided on.

6. Production of the Caravelle would be subcontracted in the United States to Hughes (then the main shareholder in TWA) in its Culver City facilities.

7. This led to the designation "A300" (retained for tactical reasons in spite of later changes).

8. Rolls-Royce wanted to continue to benefit from state funding.

9. Rolls-Royce also knew that there was little chance of beating General Electric and Pratt & Whitney, which had taken a serious lead in the development of the versions of their engines intended for the long-haul DC-10.

10. BAC had not been retained by the British government at the start of 1967.

11. BAC had since merged with Hawker-Siddeley Aviation, hence the acronym HSA.

12. There were 205 Fokker 27s produced under license in the United States under the designation of Fairchild 227.

13. *Groupement d'intérêt économique* (Grouping of economic interests under French Law).

14. The twin could fly the transcontinental route in the United States.

15. HSA had since become British Aerospace (nationalized).

BIBLIOGRAPHY

Bogdan, Lew. *L'Epopée du Ciel Clair*. Paris, 1988.
Gunston, Bill. *The European Triumph*. London, 1988.

Marck, Bernard. *Dassault, Douglas, Boeing et les autres.* . . . Paris, 1979.

Mueller, Peter. *Airbus, der flüsternde Europäer.* Vienna, 1983.

Muller, Pierre. *Airbus, l'ambition européenne.* Paris, 1989.

Newhouse, John. *The Sporty Game.* New York, 1982.

Picq, Jean. *Les ailes de l'Europe.* Paris, 1990.

Quittard, Jean-Pierre. *Airbus ou la volonté européenne.* Paris, 1979.

Reed, Arthur. *Airbus.* London, 1991.

 **PART ONE**

History of Airports

A Contextual Approach

Emmanuel Chadeau

Introduction

The evolution of airports is a fascinating new field of study in the history of aeronautics. In the beginning (ca. 1918–20 in Europe), an airport consisted of a grassy takeoff and landing area and a few wooden or iron hangars. Located close to large cities, it handled only a few small planes each day. Airline companies had their headquarters downtown, where the few passengers who traveled by air assembled for their journey. They were taken to the airfields by a special car. They walked across wet grass to reach their plane, shook hands with the pilot, then—as air travelers—became heroes of a new age of mankind. The largest airfields of the early 1920s were Croydon, near London, and Le Bourget, three miles north of Paris.

By the mid-1930s, as air traffic grew, these early airfields evolved into airports. There were separate areas for passengers, freight, and maintenance. Control towers handled the increasing number of airplanes. Passengers, now numbering in the hundreds of thousands at the main airports, could find lounges, bars, and dining rooms. They could buy newspapers, hire taxis, and rent cars. A hierarchy among airports appeared, both in Europe and in North America. Airports became symbols of modernity—and were even used for propaganda, such as Berlin's Tempelhof Airport, intended as a monument to a search for worldwide power.

The years after World War II brought a new phase to the development of airports. Large airports became big business, as services offered to travelers multiplied. Ground transportation systems were developed between cities and airports. Large hotel chains and car and office rental companies invested in airport areas. Freight and maintenance areas expanded. The number of skilled employees increased. Airport authorities, their powers greatly enlarged, had to face environmental and security problems.

The 1970s saw the age of the "wide bodies." The annual flow of passengers at major airports now numbered in the tens of millions, with a corresponding increase in freight. Airport areas became centers for business gatherings. A service industry developed around airports, providing numerous jobs. New towns grew up around the airports. As railroads had done a century before, airports created a new economic, social, and geographical reality.

Historians need to describe and analyze the evolution of airports. The three chapters that follow take a major step in that direction. Let me suggest other areas that should be examined:

1. The rise of airport authorities (like the Port of New York Authority in the United States or Aeroports de Paris in France)

2. The development of skills, jobs, and social organization in the airport economy

3. The competition between airports in a national and/or international perspective

4. The development of airport security systems

5. Airports and their relationship to surrounding areas (including the connection to nearby cities and to other means of transportation)

6. The integration of airport landscape and daily life through architecture and esthetics

These studies could be conducted in various ways: through monographs and case studies of airports, national and international comparisons, institutional or corporate studies, legal or social studies.

As historians trace the path from the pioneering age to the modern times, it is well to keep in mind that the state of airports has been in constant change. Commercial aviation is still an open frontier, and the future will see new kinds of airports and new relationships between airports and the people surrounding them.

 Robin Higham

A Matter of the Utmost Urgency

The Search for a
Third London Airport, 1918–1992

Once an idea has been announced as an immutable assumption, it tends to bifurcate into twin conceptions.

On the one hand the idea becomes an ideal and goes on driving research and planning until estimate costs are challenged by the reality of potential returns on investment. The ultimate solution may be the adoption and development of items long available but often scorned.

On the other hand the pursuit of the ideal delays real decisions about existing items or facilities. Only grudgingly is action taken to retain their usability in the face of ongoing demands that cannot be ignored.

In the case of national airports, attitudes to planning, the democratic process, and decision making all play their part, as does the availability of money.

What makes the study of London's airports so fascinating in the years 1918–92 is that their creation, development, and uncertainties reflect not only the growth curve of commercial civil aviation but also the slow recognition of the importance of air transport. More than this, the subject of airports reflects also the slow understanding of the connections between passenger and cargo growth, facilities, technical development, ground access, urban sprawl, preservation of the countryside, and agricultural and residential noise concerns. Furthermore, historical analysis, present concerns, and prediction of the future all have to be melded in planning and development.

However, the conception of the complete picture did not appear until computers were developed by the airlines, primarily in the United Kingdom by the British Overseas Airways Corporation (BOAC). And it took from the mid-1960s to 1978 to rationalize the whole planning process and link it with governmental understanding of the centrality of air transport to British economy and life. And that too, as in the past with shipping and aviation, had an international dimension that had moved, as did the Plimsoll Line, from mere access to destinations to technical regulation for the commonweal.

The subject of the growth of London's airports is double-barreled. On the one side is the entire process of choosing a third London airport with all its regional surface and air complexities. On the other is the constant interfacing at a specific airport—such as Heathrow or Gatwick—of political, economic, social, and ideological pressures with the technical realities of international and internal air services, aircraft, passengers, and cargo.

One of the truths of air transport has been that productivity has increased enormously due to advances in technology, causing employment to grow relatively slowly in comparison as companies have striven to lower labor costs, in contrast to civil-service bureaucracies, which according to Parkinson's Law grow at 6 percent a year. This has directly influenced airports, which have been compelled to get more and more use out of a limited area, a task requiring vision, volume, and "vinance."

The story of the search for a third London airport is a tale of technology and process in modern civilization. It is also a history of prediction, adaptation, and construction against a background of growth. A critical peak came with the realization that the solution would exceed the sensible investment of national funds. It also involves a subhistory: the contrast between locally owned enterprises and those belonging to the state. And this scenario places concepts of planning and executive freedom in juxtaposition.

The title of this chapter is taken from *Cmd. 9296* of 1954, "The matter is, therefore, one of a good deal of urgency." This was a theme that would be repeated in advice to the governments of the day on several occasions thereafter, for it was not until 1985 that a decision was made, and that one, as will be seen later, was still flawed by lack of a full comprehension of the patterns of aeronautical and technical history.

In 1918 *Cd. 9218* had laid out a plan for postwar British aviation. Immediately after the war ended there were three London airports—Hounslow Heath (close to modern Heathrow), Cricklewood, and Croydon. By 1920 the last one had become the London airport. It opened a new terminal and airport hotel in 1928, but by 1938 the Cadman Committee (*Cmd. 5685*) was recommending that a new site be found, since housing had encroached around this grass airfield. Moreover, in 1934 a second London airport had been developed at Southampton with the inauguration of the Empire Air Mail Scheme and the utilization of flying boats on these long-haul routes.

At this time the concept of new airfields with concrete runways was just beginning to appear. This "Airfield Revolution" coincided with the "Technical Revolution" in aircraft construction and with the beginnings of the "Electronic Revolution." Altogether between 1935 and 1945 there were four dramatic changes—the last being the "Jet Revolution"—that would affect the development of London's airports.

Between 1934 and 1944, new airfields built in Britain numbered 444, most with a three-runway layout in place of the standard grass airfield, with operations always into the prevailing wind. From this standard plan in 1944 evolved a super postwar transport aerodrome begun at Heathrow on the west side of London next to the Staines' reservoirs. The idea was that this should be for both landplanes and flying boats. In the end the dramatic increase in size and range of landplanes won the day, in part because airfields had been built all over the world with military funds.

Construction of Heathrow was slow because it was under the hands of the ministry and its bureaucracy at a time of much change in government and of a lack of appreciation of the important economic role that civil airlines would play in the British economy. Moreover, though Winston Churchill, as secretary of state for air, had decreed in 1920 that civil aviation had to fly by itself, it would not be able to do so until the later 1960s when traffic growth made it self-supporting. Investment was restricted in the post-1945 years not only because competing demands were placed on the Exchequer but also because Victorian-educated civil servants did not understand modern business. It was only gradually, in the decade 1957–67, that the House of Commons Committee on Nationalized Industries came to realize this and forced a change. At about the same time that BOAC was given its magna carta in 1964 to act strictly as a commercial concern, the British Airports Authority was created to be a self-supporting establishment controlling Heathrow (LHR), Gatwick (GAT), and Stansted (STD). By then the other London airports such as Croydon and Heston had been phased out as inadequate or in conflict with LHR's traffic patterns or, like Luton, were privately owned and so not of much interest to the powers in London.

The development of LHR was slow. It opened in January 1946 with its passenger terminal in tents and huts on the north side next to the Bath Road. It had over 2,700 acres, of which an area north of the Bath Road was subsequently sold off, though this area would have been useful later for a cargo or other terminal or for commuter and short-haul runways. Not until 1962 was the short-haul terminal in the Central Area opened, and not until 1966 was a long-haul terminal completed so that international traffic could all be moved into the Central Area, where congestion in the access tunnel and a shortage of car-parking space were already creating new demands.

One solution to the access problem, envisaged in the original plans, was a London Underground (Tube) connection from Hounslow West to the Central Area, a distance of two miles. This was finally completed in 1984. The high-speed rail line from Victoria Station Airways Terminal to LHR via Feltham was, in the end, never undertaken. Instead, in 1985 the Thatcher government laid it down as a matter of urgency that to relieve road congestion, such a rapid

3.1. Looking from the eastern end of the BOAC headquarters and maintenance complex, about 1970. In the foreground is a working party for scale, two 707s, a Super VC-10, a VC-10, and a newly arived 747. In the background across Runway 27L is Central Area, Heathrow. (Author's collection)

service was to be developed from Paddington regardless of whether it might break even. It was expected to be completed in 1996. Such a connection to the London Airport, then Croydon, had been suggested in 1937.

In contrast, when Gatwick opened in 1936 it was sited on the London-Brighton main line and had its own station. And in 1958 when the new GAT opened, sited just north of the original field, it too had a main-line railway station, now incorporated into its terminal building. And in contrast to Croydon's grass and Heathrow's two main 12,000-foot runways, GAT had a single 7,000-foot one.

The problem with Gatwick serving as London's second airport was interlining, a subject that, curiously, hardly appears in any of the many reports on the subject of a third London airport, though by 1990 half of the people using LHR were in transit. Because automobile ownership came late to Britain, very little attention had been paid to developing a highway system similar to the German prewar autobahns. As a result, there was no rapid road route from Gatwick to Heathrow, and helicopters had to be used until that portion of the new London Ring Motorway, the M-25, was completed in 1984. And this roadway was out of date by 1993.

In addition to road access, noise was a problem in any consideration of London's airports. Studies of it had been begun by the Aeronautical Research Council as far back as 1920, but noise came into prominence only in the 1960s with the advent of the big jets such as the Boeing 707 and the Douglas DC-8 and the necessity for night operations if these jets were to be used with maximum efficiency across many time zones east and west.

Noise problems were technical and psychological. The early jets of all sizes had unmuffled engines with a noise footprint far larger and somewhat different from even the largest piston and, especially, the new turbo-prop aircraft. Moreover, both on climb-out and especially on landing, they operated at close to full power. And on the approach to LHR they started 14 miles away at Marble Arch and with wheels and flaps down needed 90 percent power for a safe approach.

Meanwhile, housing for the more than 40,000 workers employed at Heathrow had spread out around the airport and filled in the vacant spaces. Hotels too had been built to serve passengers. People owning and renting property in the area began to complain and to use not only lobbying organizations but also public inquiries to express their feelings; many of them also developed an irrational fear of an accident in their own back gardens. Moreover, the big transatlantic jets affected a much wider area of the country than had their predecessors, for they began their letdown from roughly 30,000 feet at Fishguard, 198 miles to the west of LHR.

To have some scientific grounds to consider noise complaints, the government installed measuring devices that could allow the fining of particularly loud aircraft. It also undertook psychological studies, such as *Cmnd. 2056, Noise* (1963), which came to the interesting conclusion that whenever a new aircraft was announced as going into service, complaints rose. But by careful logging of noise measurements and phone calls it was possible to show that most complaints were related to aircraft that had been in use for some time and also that many complaints originated from homes directly connected with employment at the airport itself. The subject was reexamined in 1977 in Department of Trade, *Night Disturbance from Aircraft Noise at Heathrow and Gatwick,* and in the 1980 CAA Paper 78011 *Noise and Sleep.*

A solution to airport noise was the protection of houses through noise insulation grants, as evidenced by statutory instruments for Heathrow (1972 No. 1291), Gatwick (1973 No. 617), Heathrow (1974 No. 2051), and Gatwick (1975 No. 916). It was the Swiss, however, who got everyone's attention in 1964 by banning the new Vickers VC-10 from Zurich because of its loudness. Thereafter, great progress was made in noise abatement, so that the trend was already downward in the jumbo 747 and the wide-bodied DC-10 and Lockheed L-1011, which came into service in the late 1960s and early 1970s.

Airports had always been what lawyers call an attractive nuisance. The fact that people came to watch airplanes created traffic problems and airport profits even at Croydon. Shops, restaurants, viewing areas, and carparks all became paying propositions. In 1990 Heathrow handled 12,000 passengers an hour and employed 53,000 persons, not counting visitors. British Airports Authority (BAA), Plc, was such a highly profitable venture that in 1992 it won the contract to run the mall and the concessions at the new airport at Pittsburgh, Pennsylvania, in the United States.

In addition to the people employed there, each airport attracted a cluster of businesses either ancillary to the airlines and airport activities, such as catering services, or in the import/export business, where accessibility to the airport is an asset. This terrestrial side of airport development is not nearly as well known as is the air side. Nevertheless, it was important for planning and siting considerations because of its impact on any area in which an existing or new airport was to be located.

Traffic growth was also an important factor. Up to the 1960s London area traffic grew at a consistent 15 percent a year and thereafter at between 7 and 8 percent. Moreover, a rough idea of the impact of growth in aircraft can be gleaned from multiplying their full load of passengers by their cruising speed for one hour to provide a measure of work. A DC-3 such as was widely used in 1947 had a value of 3,360, whereas a 747-400 in 1992 had a value of 299,880. The DC-3 weighed 26,000 pounds, and the 747-400 weighed 870,000 pounds.

The search that had begun just before World War II for other London airports resulted in the selection of a number of sites—Lullingstone, Fairford, Langstone Harbour, and Luton. In the recommendations of the 1937 Maybury Report (*Cmd. 5351*) and of the Cadman Inquiry (*Cmd. 5685*), Gatwick was seen as a reliever for Croydon, which would have to be replaced because it could not have a high-speed rail link and was being surrounded by housing.

After World War II, as the Ministry of Civil Aviation (MCA) took over the civil functions of the Air Ministry, the Labour government said that since so many airfields had recently been built with public funds, they should remain in public ownership if they were to be developed. Moreover, the International Civil Aviation Organization (ICAO), which had just been founded at Chicago in 1944, would provide standards for designated international airports. At the same time the MCA acquired Stansted as a diversionary and training airport. In 1948 the experimental radar unit at London Airport (LAP until 1960) was starting to advise aircraft within its coverage in order to improve air traffic control, and in 1949 uniform airport control facilities were provided with gridded maps to direct fire and rescue operations, with Air Traffic Control (ATC) logbooks, and with pictorial display of the airport for directing aircraft on the ground.

From 1946 to 1950, air transport movements (ATMs) grew from 2,046 to 25,450 and passengers handled from 63,151 to 523,351. Concerned with this growth, a committee reported in 1953 (*Cmd. 8902, London's Airports*) that the number had again tripled and would probably double again by 1963 to 3.5 million. Already ATC was being swamped. MCA's answer was to close four of London's seven airports (Heston, Northolt [reverted to the RAF], Croydon, and Baringdon, with Blackbushe being shut in 1960). *Cmd. 8902* called for immediate action to provide two alternate airfields needed because of construction time and pointed out that these new facilities would need the same access to London as LAP and should not create insuperable ground traffic problems or disturb property, amenities, or agricultural land. The report considered a number of options, including making Stansted the third London airport, and opted for a rebuilding of Gatwick, but not before there had been a local inquiry. This latter action set a precedent that has often bedeviled airport expansion worldwide. The cost would be £6 million over seven years, but it was required, since all the sites north of the capital were in the wrong places.

Nothing was done with Stansted at this time because the Royal Air Force took it over as part of the cold war buildup. After considering the public inquiry results (*Cmd. 9215*), the minister in *Cmd. 9296* accepted the Gatwick idea with 7,000-foot runways, which, however, were recognized as unsuitable for outbound Stratocruisers on the North Atlantic. These would have to refuel at Prestwick or Shannon. As to noise, it was inevitable that some people would be affected. Since BOAC and BEA had agreed to use GAT, the project would go ahead. The minister noted, "The matter is, therefore, one of a good deal of urgency."

Because no revision of the LAP master plan had taken place since it had been drafted in 1946, in 1955 the minister appointed a new panel, advised by the director of aviation from Zurich. This body reported (*CAP 145* of 1957) that there had been a 16.4-fold increase in passengers served and an 8-fold increase in ATMs and that the size of aircraft had gone from the 21-passenger 158-mph DC-3 to the 91-seat, 356-mph Britannia 102. Nevertheless, looking ahead, the committee believed that LAP could still handle 12 million passengers until just before 1970. Although it felt development was necessary, the committee added, "It seems impossible to forecast with any degree of realism much beyond 1970." Therefore, with jets on the horizon (the Comet I had just been withdrawn after a series of disasters), the committee argued for flexibility for "the foreseeable future." At the same time, it felt that LAP's three pairs of parallel runways were "long enough and strong enough to serve any transport aircraft likely to be operated in the foreseeable future." Nevertheless, with a 9 percent anticipated growth rate, a rising standard of living, and falling airfares with the coming introduction of Tourist class and a more sophisticated ATC, which would allow an increase from 40 movements an hour to 40 takeoffs and 40 landings per hour with a passenger throughput of 6,000 per hour, the stage two terminal at Gatwick needed to be developed at once so that London would not lose its status as the world's busiest airport.

To the committee the crucial question was whether all operations should be crowded into the LAP Central Area or should be developed around the periphery. Part of the problem was that cargo went on passenger aircraft and so could not be loaded until the last minute. Approving centralization, the committee noted that the Central Area would have to be expanded from 140 to 264 acres and that this would mean closing several runways. Moreover, as the big jets came into service, it would no longer be practicable to march passengers to and from the aircraft or safe to do so with jets on the tarmac. This meant, then, that jetways similar to those in use in America would have to be installed. However, what that would do to terminal layout was uncertain, since very little information was available on the ground-handling of the new big jets.

These jets posed other problems, from disgorging 150 or more passengers at a time to each needing 21,000 gallons of fuel. Moreover, as the use of the airport skyrocketed, car parking would need to be developed on the periphery, the entrance tunnel would need to be doubled in capacity, and serious consideration would have to be given to traffic exiting the airport onto the Bath Road as well as to a high-speed rail link. So another £17 million would be needed, to bring the total investment in LAP to £47 million.

In 1961, the year after LAP became London Heathrow (LHR), a study of air traffic control and navigational facilities (*Cmnd. 1457*) noted that although the government had in 1946 been willing to subsidize civil aviation until it could fly by itself, Heathrow would in 1961 break even, including covering the interest on its debts. In fact the London Group of airports now had a revenue of £7.5 million and could offer careers to "able men."

At the same time, *The Fifth Report of the Estimates Committee of the House of Commons* (1961) was highly critical of the management of London's airports, chastising the government for limited capital expenditures. The committee noted, "The fundamental problem facing planners of Heathrow was that the capacity and weight of aircraft were becoming more important factors than the number of movements." Moreover, since the new big jets coming across the Atlantic had a high fuel consumption at low altitudes, ATC tried to bring them in directly. The problem for the future was not money but air space. Yet finances were, nevertheless, an issue that BOAC raised and the committee supported.

The national airline rightly complained that it paid not only landing fees based on weight but also a 100 percent surcharge because its flights were international, whereas BEA's were considered European and thus BEA paid only by weight on smaller aircraft. This forced the Ministry, now of Aviation, to agree to a working committee to restructure the fees. The Commons Committee concluded, "Although the inflexibility of the present system may make for simplification in administration, your Committee consider the disadvantages to outweigh the advantages." The minister agreed but blamed the failure of BOAC and BEA to agree on a formula. Moreover, the matter was complicated by several factors including the fact that LHR had become a North Atlantic hub-and-spoke system, to use modern terminology, whereas Gatwick suffered from the difficulties of interlining. BEA particularly complained that its aircraft using GAT had to be flown to LHR for maintenance and that it paid two extra landing fees as a result. Moreover, BEA was using the same Comet IVs as BOAC and was poaching in the latter's Middle East, so what was the difference between European and intercontinental flights?

This landing-fee problem was related generally to the need of the Ministry to make money on its airports. Thus the matter of office rentals, duty-free shops, and Customs and Excise all became entwined, and of course, all of these things affected how soon the space at LHR and GAT would be consumed. As to the matter of freight facilities, the Ministry said that it had to be guided in its policy of expansion by what the customers were willing to pay.

On the matter of the extension of the runway at Gatwick to take fully loaded long-range jets, the Ministry felt it was not justified in this action, considering how few jets would use the runway and the little use made of LHR's long runways. Nevertheless, the minister was considering lengthening the runway to be able to handle short- and medium-range jets. And although GAT was not intended to be a replica, he was having a study done to determine if a second runway and terminal and other facilities should be developed to handle the rapid growth of the inclusive-tour business.

As for Stansted, now released by the RAF, the minister felt that this care-and-maintenance-only airport should be studied as the third London airport and that a firm decision should be treated as a matter of urgency. But the study would have to be of a wider nature to look at all sites for a possible third London airport in view of the coming of the Concorde supersonic transport (an aircraft that did not, in the end, enter service until 1976). The study was to be thorough and urgent.

So in 1964 an interdepartmental working committee was established which later reported in *CAP 199*. It concluded that even if Gatwick had two runways, neither it nor Heathrow would be able to handle London's traffic after 1972; thus a third airport had to be available by 1973 or London's traffic would be diverted to Amsterdam and Paris. Such a new airport would need to be of LHR's capacity with two parallel runways able to handle everything from short-haul aircraft to the coming supersonic transport (SST). Since this new airport would have to be far enough away from LHR and GAT so that all three could operate at full capacity, it posed problems: 80 miles was too far out, a maximum ground transport time of no more than one hour being mandatory. In view of the unreliability of a high-speed rail link being available (British Railways having just recently been "Beechinged" to make it profitable), this meant reliance on road access alone. The only areas in which these requirements could be met were due east of the city, bringing them into conflict with the Ministry of Defence (MOD) primary weapons research establishment at Shoeburyness. Stansted thus had to be chosen, The committee recommended, "The planning of the airport should be part of a comprehensive scheme embracing housing and industry and taking particular care to avoid noise problems: any new residential development planned for the area should be made compatible with the airport."

Moreover, the question of whether and where a fourth airport should be located needed to be considered in about four years' time. There followed a ministerial inquiry by the inspector of airports, who heard only matters bearing on local issues. He reported (in *Cmnd. 3259* of 1967) that Stansted was not a suitable location. This led to a very acrimonious debate in Parliament on June 29,

1967, and finally to the appointment of the inquiry under Mr. Justice Roskill (Sir Eustace Wentworth Roskill, QC) of the High Court, whose report and eight volumes of appendices were published in 1971.

In the meantime the estimate of the growth of civil aviation had proven to be about half the real 1960s growth rate of 17 percent a year, resulting in a more than doubling every four years, as seen in the BAA's annual reports. Moreover, the new 747s just coming into service in 1969 had five times the capacity of the Comet IVs, which had started jet transatlantic service only 11 years earlier in 1958.

The Roskill Inquiry was the climax of the planning process for London's airports. Because it made use of consultants, computers, and simulated scenarios (all then the rage), it cost £1,130,000 as opposed to £5 19s. 9d. plus £128 printing costs for the 1938 Cadman Committee report.

Mr. Justice Roskill pointed out that by 1969 the 1964 estimates for London's airports had already been exceeded and that although the 1964 committee had looked at 100 sites and selected 18, its report had been classified and so languished under the 30-year rule. He also noted that in spite of clear reports and urgent pleas since the investigation of 1953, the government had failed to act on Stansted. Moreover, in the 23 years since the end of World War II, Britain had failed to develop a national airport plan, a matter that he did not remedy because it was not part of his instructions. Just as Wolfe before Quebec in 1759 had said that war is "an option of difficulties," so Roskill noted, "Every solution has its price." The dilemma was that an airport needed to be near enough to be accessible yet far enough not to be a nuisance. There were only two possible sites, one inland and one coastal. Clearly, there was "no ideal site for a new London airport."

The Roskill consultants had looked at market and planning approaches, both of which aimed to consider the social welfare of society, but all the results had problems with margins of error. These lay in the costing and valuation of property, including the noise factor, and in estimates of passenger traffic and airport capacities, as well as in cost-benefit analyses of particular sites. Perhaps the most experienced member of the committee, Professor Colin Buchanan of the Imperial College of Science, entered a vigorous dissent against both the inland site at Cublington and the coastal one at Foulness (later tactfully renamed Maplin). He saw the main issue to be whether a small and densely populated island such as Britain could plan centrally with social purpose, taking into account both commercial and environmental needs. He claimed that in recent years too many decisions had favored the economy over the environment—but that the economy had not improved. On the other hand, the majority of the

Roskill Inquiry took the view that choosing Foulness would show that Britain was willing to take a stand. Roskill concluded: "The painful and difficult choices which have to be made arise from the attempt in a democratic society to find an acceptable balance between conflicting interests. We have viewed our work as part of that process." In April 1971 the government accepted the idea of Foulness, and a Maplin Development Authority was established in early 1973. But then the Arab Oil Embargo hit.

In 1972 the Civil Aviation Authority (CAA) published *Airport Planning: An Approach on a National Basis,* in which it pointed out: "Aviation is an industry of rapid technological change. . . . Airports are very large and not easily adaptable pieces of investment; mistakes can be very expensive." Moreover, the CAA noted that since the new quiet aircraft needed shorter runways, in some cases only one-third of the available length, perhaps this would change current assumptions.

In July 1974 BAA issued the *Gatwick Master Plan.* This pointed out that the runway had been lengthened to 3,100 metres (9,920 feet), that the terminal was the first in Europe with a pier, baggage conveyor belts, and new railway and coach stations, and that a doubling in size of the terminal was under way. In addition four automatic noise-monitoring systems were installed and their data independently transmitted to the Board of Trade in London. Noise insulation grants were under way for the inner and outer noise zones. And the local authorities were represented on the consultative committee along with travel agents and airlines. Moreover, in 1973–74 Gatwick Airport had contributed £575,000 to local rates.

In view of the decline in air travel as an instant reaction to the Arab Oil Embargo, the advent of the jumbos and wide-bodies, and the increased use of the regional airports around London, in March 1974 the minister of the environment ordered a review of the Roskill Inquiry on the basis of revised projections of air traffic in the 1980s and 1990s. At the same time, the chancellor of the Exchequer announced that there would be no funding for Maplin in his new budget and that this followed on the July 1973 cancellation of planning authority for Maplin and its New Town. Even though the governments had changed party, the 1973 Inquiry was pursued and issued as *Maplin* (1974).

Maplin announced cancellation of the plan to open in 1982. Instead it went over the forecasts again, consulted with the International Air Transport Association (IATA) airlines, and looked at LHR, GAT, STD, and LUT (Luton) again and the probable influence of the Channel Tunnel, then moving toward approval. *Maplin* considered a slower growth of incomes and predicted lowered holiday travel figures, the impact on ATMs of the higher-capacity jets, the effect of the prices and incomes policy, and the International Passenger Survey, which, however, was deficient in that it did not cover transit (interline) passengers, military and airline personnel, passengers traveling to take up employment, government charter flights, or traffic to and from the Irish Republic. (It would seem that once again whatever statistics had been collected were not the ones wanted.) Having taken these and other factors into account, *Maplin* concluded that the 31 million passengers of 1973 would become 90 to 132 million in 1990. "It was therefore difficult to select a figure assessing the noise, planning, cost and surface access consequences of various patterns of airport development."

The *Maplin* group tried to estimate runway and terminal capacity and concluded that the various changes in process would cause ATMs to be less than the Roskill figure of 470,000 a year for the four London airports. What was surprising was that whereas in the estimates LHR stayed at Roskill's estimated 338,000, Gatwick climbed from 110,000 to 168,000 ATMs. By spreading demand over more hours and days and considerably increasing the use of Stansted and Luton, the combined total of acceptable ATMs could rise to 620,000 and 114 million passengers a year, averaging about 225 passengers per aircraft versus 112 in 1960.

Maplin also looked at each of the four airports. At LHR it recognized the need for the fourth terminal that BOAC had been seeking for years and that its successor (as of 1974), British Airways, was in a strong position to demand. Moreover, *Maplin* pointed out that once Terminal Four reached capacity, the only other site left (since significant acreage north of the Bath Road had been abandoned many years before) was the Perry Oaks sludge farm. BAA estimated that with a fifth terminal in place, LHR would be able to handle 50–55 million passengers a year. Gatwick could be increased from 16 to 25 million passengers, Stansted needed 4 million to be viable, and Luton, which had processed 3.5 million in 1973, should be able to handle 10 million. So if Heathrow had five terminals, the system should be able to handle 104 million passengers annually, and there would be no need for the horribly expensive Maplin.

What was needed was an immediate decision about Perry Oaks, since it would take 10 to 15 years to move the sludge farm and create a new terminal on that site. Gatwick, Stansted, and Luton needed five to seven years lead time, owing to the statutory planning process.

As to noise, *Maplin* pointed out that the new Airbus A-300B registered only 90 EPNdBs as compared with 114 for the 707s. It was expected that by 1990, of the aircraft using London, 94 percent would be noise-certificated versus only 2 percent in 1971. As a result of this action and of the development of the Noise Number Index (NNI), the number of people affected around Heathrow would drop from 2,092,000 in 1971 to 450,000 in 1990 with the Perry Oaks terminal in use.

Maplin was also concerned about employment, since airports attracted people and industries. Allowing Gatwick to grow to 16 million passengers a year would bring 60,000 additional persons into the area, and that would radically change its ambience.

The problems with Maplin as a site were not merely fiscal. There were the expected four to five years needed to dig out all the buried ordnance in the area, as well as the cost of moving the MOD weapons-development facility to other parts of the United Kingdom and dredging the sands to create an island on which to place the airport and the road and rail access. Altogether the investment would be over £1 billion, compared with only £125 million to expand facilities at LHR including moving Perry Oaks and only £70 million to bring Gatwick to a 25-million capacity. The big problem was at Heathrow, where the roads then in the planning stages would not be available until the 1990s. (Luton and Stansted presented no real problems, since they had adequate sites.) British Rail noted that it could not put in a high-speed link from Victoria Station; thus a line would have to be developed from Paddington at a cost of £80 million, with another £60 million needed to upgrade the London-Brighton line for Gatwick.

Consulted on all this, the scheduled airlines, which feared compulsory dispersion of their operations, thought Maplin was premature. They wanted a second runway at Gatwick. The charter airlines, on the other hand, liked the idea of moving to Stansted and Luton, where there was far less congestion.

As for the public on the ground, *Maplin* noted that their fears were highly exaggerated. In the decade 1959–69 there had been only six landing or takeoff incidents out of 15 million flights. Actually, the only significant difference between the five sites was that Maplin had a greater likelihood of bird strikes.

Compared with the Roskill Inquiry, *Maplin* was a model report—short and concise. But it delayed once again a decision on a third London airport, even though by 1990 the 61 million passengers to be handled every year would be the equivalent of the entire British population.

In 1976 the government published a two-volume study, *Airport Strategy for Great Britain,* the first volume dealing with London's airports and the second, issued somewhat later, with regional airports. These studies benefited from the comments of some 1,000 organizations, which gave bureaucrats a better idea of who was interested in airports and why. Specifically emphasized were the role of air transport in the national economy, environmental and land-use implications, consumer demand, more effective use of existing airport, road, and other infrastructure resources, and affirmation of the decision to cancel Maplin.

In 1978 the Labour government published *Airports and Policy (Cmnd. 7084)*. It argued that changing economics, improved technology, and slower rates of growth had altered the options for such major public investment. *Cmnd. 7084*, after reviewing the past, refocused attention on the fact that the air transport system was vital to a country that lived by trade. It proposed that the four London airports, as well as the airlines, should be given "the maximum scope for commercial decisions." Relief for the gateway airports should be sought by encouraging more direct flights from regional airports such as Birmingham, Manchester, and Prestwick. And, since with the jumbos and wide-bodies half the cargo went on passenger airliners, a separate cargo airport was no longer feasible. However, even though a balance had to be struck between airport expansion and local authorities, the taxpayer should no longer pay for airport expansion, since the industry had now reached the stage at which it could be self-supporting. Essential to the proposed new order were forecasts (such as the airlines had long been doing) for 10 and 15 years ahead. These needed to take into account everything from family size to the expected vast rise in tourism from 5 million in 1977 to 32 million persons in 1990, a figure that London's hotels were not in 1978 able to handle. More noise studies would be undertaken, and road building would be limited by the rules laid down in the White Paper *Transport Policy* (1974) on access to ports, industrial areas, and airports. BAA would now have to get specific planning permission to build the Perry Oaks terminal.

Cmnd. 7084 went on to say that the main lesson learned from Roskill was "the need for caution in the planning of airports' capacity, yet there would still have to be another study of the long-range future of London's airports and more co-operation with local bodies to do so." *Airports and Policy* concluded that LHR was too cramped for a fifth terminal, which would create a hazard. BAA's master plan for Heathrow had been completed in March 1976, and consultation with local authorities was, in 1978, taking place, to be followed by a public inquiry. As to Gatwick, BAA was confident that 25 million passengers could be handled on the single runway, and so the £10–12 million needed for the second runway would not be made available. As far as the government was concerned, it would not be opposed to a BAA plan for a two-terminal international airport for 25 million passengers in the 1980s.

Owing to the airline recession after the 1973 oil embargo, it was envisioned that Stansted would be able to develop, within its existing boundaries, to a passenger capacity first of 4 and then of 16 million and would not need the four-runway layout for 50 million passengers as earlier envisioned. Thus it would rank with Gatwick. The report continued, "The Government considers the principal criterion should be the number of people expected to be affected by particular airport developments." With this in mind the government proposed that BAA take over Luton from the Luton Borough Council but that, in order not to conflict with Stansted, its development be limited to 5 million passengers using a single terminal. Overall it was envisioned that with a slower movement into wide-bodies and with air traffic control imposing longer separations between aircraft, total ATMs would be limited to 550,000 in 1990. So the present 1978 strategy was to use existing airports.

In 1979, with a newly elected Conservative government in power and not bound by *Cmnd. 7084, The Report of the Advisory Committee on Airports Policy* (November 1979) appeared. The Steele Committee was a group of civil servants told to work with the Study Group on South East Airports, which published the Dick Report in December 1979. The Steele Report noted that Gatwick had, by compact with the local authorities, lost the site for the second runway, which had been converted into a cargo and a second passenger terminal area, and that new off-site buildings now obstructed the former intended approaches. This meant that GAT would not reach the capacity of its two terminals until 1990, when the newer, larger airliners would allow passenger numbers to rise again still using the single runway. What happened to Luton and Stansted would depend on a decision as to a third London airport. Given the uncertainties in forecasting, the new policy should be as flexible as possible. The question was whether the government should take steps to meet demand or instead to suppress it by a pricing mechanism. But Steele found the latter unacceptable because of the loss both to airlines and to the national economy— British Airways alone brought in £2,000 million and produced £350 million in visible earnings. Steele concluded, "In the end the decision will be one of political judgement in the light of the Government's view of national priorities." Moreover, Steele noted that the Study Group on South East Airports had looked at six sites for a 4,972-acre two-runway airport and had concluded that what was needed was "a clear and rapid decision," for a new airport would cost £2,000 million plus another £1,000 million to remove MOD establishments.

Unhelpfully, in 1980 the CAA issued *Noise and Sleep (CAA Paper 78011)*, which concluded that a survey of the literature provided no useful guidance. Between 1981 and 1983 the inspector of airports carried out the "Stansted Inquiry," but Mr. Eyre's report was not completed until December 1984, when it was incorporated into the new Conservative government's *Airports Policy (Cmnd. 9542* of June 1985). Eyre concluded that LHR was saturated and that, therefore, Stansted should be developed. The White Paper noted that air transport had grown phenomenally from 2 million passengers in 1950 to 67 million in 1984 and that 20 percent of the British population now vacationed abroad. Moreover, civil aviation was vital, for it provided 85,000 well-paying jobs and contributed £100 million to the balance of payments. More than 66 percent of the travelers to the United Kingdom came by air and spent some £6 billion a year while some £27 billion of visible exports left Great Britain by air, two-thirds of it through LHR. It was, therefore, vital for British airlines to have the infrastructure they needed. It was time to balance environmental concerns against jobs, demands for housing, and other facilities and services with widespread benefits. Although planning bodies would still have to work within the law, the government favored airport expansion. With the new fourth terminal coming into operation at LHR in 1986 and the second one at Gatwick in 1987, it was clear that London still needed additional capacity.

Invited to plan for the expansion of Stansted, the local district council had in 1979 suggested instead that a fifth terminal be built at Heathrow and that other traffic be diverted to airports in the Midlands. Thus Eyre had been sent to hold his inquiry. He recommended that Stansted be expanded to a capacity first of 15 million and later of 25 million passengers, but at the same time he said that the government should "unequivocally disallow" a second runway there, even though BAA had acquired the land, which the government now ordered it to sell. He also accepted the Stansted suggestion that a fifth terminal be studied for LHR. So the government accepted the idea of moving the Perry Oaks sludge farm. If, said the inspector, these two developments took place, London's needs would be met well into the 21st century.

In the meantime the problem facing planners had not improved as the mix between wide-bodies and commuter aircraft using the airports kept changing. On the other hand, the Thatcher government noted that once Perry Oaks was moved, LHR might be expanded all the way west to the new M-25 Motorway. At the same time an urgent study would be commissioned to develop a high-speed rail link to LHR, even though it might be uneconomical, in order to relieve congestion on the roads. Since Gatwick would reach its 25-million capacity in 1990 as the world's fourth-busiest airport, traffic would have to be diverted to Stansted, where the BAA was being encouraged to engage in a £400-million expansion. However, ATM limits would be imposed to provide a balance between the airport and the local community. BAA and British Rail (BR) were being encouraged to develop better rail links from Stansted to London. The government felt, however, that the 17,000 new houses that would need to be built around the airport would not pose a problem to agriculture. And the White Paper also announced the impending privatization of BAA.

As a spinoff from *Cmnd. 9542* the CAA published a series of studies on planning: (*CAP 510*), on air traffic distribution in the London area; (*CAP 522*), on runway utilization at LHR and GAT; (*CAP 534*), which made the first mention of the value of "slots" to the airlines—about £1 million each; (*CAP 546*), advice to the secretary of state on the use of air space; and (*CAP 559*), on traffic distribution in the London area, as well as *CAP 548*.

In the meantime, in 1986 London had opened the new London City Airport on what had been the London Docks and was soon providing jet service to places as far away as Zurich. That had come about when the London Docks had gone virtually bankrupt due to the development of supertankers and container ships, which needed newer and cheaper facilities on navigable waters. By the 1980s the London Docks were on their way out when a Thames Barricade to control the river began to become reality, in effect closing the Thames River, about which there already was much concern with the elimination of pollution.

By 1990 the Boeing 747-400 had immensely changed the map of the world. London was now within nonstop distance of Singapore to the East. The world was ever shrinking while the planners' headaches kept growing. Or had the development of airliners reached a plateau?

3.2. London City Airport, looking toward the city of London. The Canary Wharf Tower is just upriver from the single runway from which flights depart for places as far away as Zurich. (Courtesy London City Airport)

In contrast to the search for the third London airport is the story of Luton, eventually picked as the fourth London airport. From its founding in 1936, Luton was owned and operated by the borough council. It was and is a successful "private" airport, which not only has attracted industry to Luton but also has contributed heavily to the rates, so that local taxpayers have seen their assessments reduced. It had grown post-1945 to the point that it was handling 2.5 million passengers yearly, and for 40 years, until told it was creating a bird-feeding hazard, it had used the borough's garbage to level the airport. In 1959 it began the construction of a concrete runway—5,432 by 150 feet at a cost of £225,662—just as the new M-1 Motorway from London to York passed nearby, making access to London easy. Commercial success was so swift that the runway was extended in 1961 to 8,000 feet, and two new terminals were built in the next five years, always with the idea that when they were replaced, they could be converted to other uses.

In 1963 both noise monitoring and a five-year plan were instituted, and parking was increased to handle 450 cars. In 1966 Luton was designated "international" (becoming LIA) but was told its expansion would be limited because its

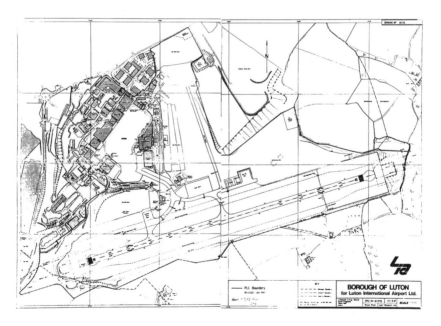

3.3. Borough of Luton. (Courtesy Borough of Luton)

operations conflicted with those at Heathrow. In 1967 traffic forecasts were for a 4-fold increase by 1971; the reality was a 7.25-fold jump. Finding that no permission was needed from London, the airport again expanded the terminal. And in spite of noise complaints as jets began to operate, the Airport Committee decided to go for a major expansion so that Luton could handle wide-bodies. In spite of Board of Trade inquiries, all went well until the minister in 1973 denied permission to expand on the grounds that Luton would interfere with the proposed new airport at Foulness. This caused airlines to pull out from what had become Britain's busiest airport. The same level of activity and passenger throughput was not achieved again for 15 years. The minister of the environment's decision was, of course, vitiated in 1974 by *Maplin*. Nevertheless, Luton went ahead with a £70-million expansion scheme only to be hit by the Arab Oil Embargo and the collapse of the inclusive-tour business as a consequence of high fuel prices.

In 1978 the government again included Luton among London's airports, and plans were at once made to make LIA capable of handling 5 million passengers by the 1990s. By 1979, in spite of the 1973 reverses, Luton was profitable, and the taxpayers knew it. In 1985 the government approved the expansion to 5 million passengers, and in 1986 Luton's catchment area was vastly enlarged due both to the opening of the M-25 London Ring Road and to the new British Rail Thames Link, which provided direct service to Brighton.

Why did Luton do so well? There seem to be three basic reasons. First, it was not a national airport and so did not need permission from London for many of its commercially driven actions, only from the local planning authority. Thus it had to accommodate only its own taxpayers. Second, and equally important, the airport was a capital asset paying visible returns. And third, it was managed by its own local Airport Committee headed by a member of the borough council. (Its story is chronicled in Jamie Glass's history.)

What lessons and conclusions are to be drawn from this urgent tale of indecision bordering on the classic British image of muddling through? The modern civil airport is the focus of political, diplomatic, military, economic, scientific, technological, medical, and ideological factors. The search for a third London airport reflects these, even if not all of them have been visible in this chapter. It is also obvious that the fitful search since 1937 supports my barbed-wire-strand theory—as facts become evidence and are placed before management, by the time a decision is made, the facts have changed. Yet success is always anticipating uncertainties.

Historical analysis, present concerns, and future forecasts all have had to be included in the planning and development process. With airlines constantly at war, forecasts and estimates were based on normal activities and perceived variables as well as occasionally being forced to react to crises. The most successful forecasters, however, have been those who have taken a long-term view with an allowance for periodic unforecastable events.

But the public planning process carries as well the danger that the democratic process brings with it the seeds of its own destruction. The nature of reaching and staying in power in democracies—indecision, perfection, and the accommodation of pressure groups—leads to a "teatimetable" of progress.

One of the interesting fallacies that emerges from the history of aviation is that because much attention is paid to state-of-the-art aircraft, such forward thinking also applies throughout both civil and military aviation. For instance, cost accounting was used by the Ministry of Munitions in England in World War I but was not adopted by BOAC until the late 1950s and by the Ministry of Aviation until the early 1960s. After BOAC took over airside transport at Heathrow, it took 10 years to discover that the main reason aircraft departed late was that no one was in charge of motor vehicles; there was no maintenance schedule for these vehicles, and so when they broke down, they were simply abandoned in situ.

The impact of the computer on the aeronautical world has not been much assessed, if at all. But one explanation for both the complexity of fares and the great indecision in selecting a site and building another London airport appears to be the arrival of the computer. This BOAC had programmed and sold in the United Kingdom using IBM mainframes to provide a major impetus in the aviation and other industries.

By the time of the 1971 Roskill Inquiry report with its eight volumes of appendices, it is evident that the number of scenarios, the beautifully contoured noise maps, and the "garbage in, garbage out" nature of results—all based, like economics, on assumptions—were driving the decision-making machine. Not that the process of selection, second-guessing the minister, and political anticipation had not been present, as in the case of the Orion-Britannia versus the 707 in the late 1950s. The data base appeared full of base data.

Thus the Maplin Committee of 1974 simply pumped in different assumptions to prove its point that Maplin was not needed. And in 1978 the Committee on London's Airports did the same. Sixteen years and one terminal at Heathrow later, the problem of a site remains unsolved, but the momentous decision had, by 1992, been taken to erect a fifth terminal on the Perry Oaks sludge works acreage, due to be completed in 2016. It seems a suitable final solution for an airport that, thanks to the Channel Tunnel, the Train de Grande Vitesse (TGV), and French foresight in developing Charles de Gaulle Airport and earlier Orly, is likely now to lose its place as the primary transatlantic gateway. In March 1993 the British government announced it would invest £2–3 billion to link the nearly completed tunnel to St. Pancras Station in London, not to the airport. But operation is still years in the future.

Forecasting has always been difficult, yet Roskill and others have made no reference to either railway or shipping development. Neither was tidy, but the major decisions were made in the days before democracy in the United Kingdom impinged on decision making, especially when the facilities were private or the pressure groups were limited by a stratified, respectful society.

Before World War II one major estimate of the future was made: the Air Staff air war calculations, which proved inadequate, if not badly flawed as well, when war came in 1939. It was not merely that the statistical machinery available was not common knowledge, but that interpolations were made from inordinately narrow data. National planning was a subject largely resisted outside of war. And not even the Cabinet was charged to or willing to do it except under a mercurial Prime Minister Winston Churchill.

For people brought up in the declining Victorian era or, even worse, in the long depression of the interwar years, the growth of air transport at a compound rate above 10 percent a year was incomprehensible. The very small coterie of airline planners consisted of largely shy, professional types who worked safely hidden within the airline bureaucracy. Yet they made sophisticated, worldly predictions for 5, 10, 15, and even 20 years ahead. And it was on their expertise, in part, that airlines based plans, purchases, and prospects. The danger always has been that a short downtime will lead to the abandonment of long-term programs, resulting in chaos because of inadequate responses to the pressures of progress.

In looking at the transformation of the ownership and management of London's airports, one should note that civil aviation both reflected and led in the program, generally pushed by Conservative governments, to denationalize, first under public corporations in the 1960s–1980s and then under privatization, as the *Parliamentary Reports on the Nationalized Industries* reveal. The shift was from government ownership, in order to manage public funds better, to privatization on a fully commercial basis. The process was also a reflection of an increasingly sophisticated knowledge of financial and commercial techniques and milieu.

In days of inflating costs, airports and other highly visible technological enterprises have used constant modernization as the way to force expenses down and reduce employment. In fact employment has remained stable, but productivity has shot up. At airports the "employed" have been the runways and terminals. But it has been primarily runway capacity that has driven the step-by-step move to bigger aircraft, and it has been environmental concerns and residential pressures that have forced the search for quieter machines. The 1973 Arab Oil Embargo, a necessary shot in the arm, focused attention on fuel economy, though it can be argued that about the same time span elapsed in the development of steam engines before fuel efficiency came into play as an economic factor.

It is also interesting to observe that in aviation and other high-technology fields, the sophisticated can be made functional in a calculable time, but it can take forever to get the mundane accepted, especially when a vocal minority have their say. However, Parkinson's Law of Great Decisions applies—no one wants to put his or her neck on the table in deciding on the unknown, but everyone has an opinion about the well-known.

Airport development was hampered after World War II by a continuation in Britain of the dichotomous attitude that there were Empire air routes and transatlantic ones. This, coupled with the failure to recognize that with Tourist and then Economy class fares, tourism and holidays abroad would grow exponentially, resulted in a lack of comprehension of the gateway nature of international airports for both passengers and cargo and a failure to see the importance of interlining-transit passengers. This was also linked to the lack of understanding of the planning process and to the long delay in setting out a national airport policy.

At the same time it should be noted that Maplin and Concorde were both examples of the plateau theory in which technological development was stopped for political, economic, social, and ideological reasons. Yet airport development was driven by the increasingly larger aircraft, computers, electronic air traffic control, and ground access. The past shows a Malthusian pattern of passenger and cargo demand versus airport facilities, including air traffic control.

Several lessons may be drawn from the London airport search.

1. The British always muddle through.

2. Local borough councils and locally controlled airports plan and act more quickly than large national ones because in the former case, decision making is among friends and parochial voters much less impressed than are distant politicians with outlandish arguments. Moreover, local ratepayers can see the profits of an airport in their rates.

3. However, decision making appears also to depend on the society. The French have been decisive and farseeing with Charles de Gaulle on its 7,670

acres, as have Coloradans with the new Denver airport on its 21,000. But in Germany 29 years, from 1963 to 1992, were needed to decide on and build Munich II, yet already the airlines have said it is too expensive.

4. In Britain ministers have shown a grievous lack of foresight in spite of being told that airports had rates of growth roughly averaging 10 percent a year, meaning a doubling every seven years. LAP was allowed to dispose of land north of the Bath Road, Gatwick was allowed to dispose of its second-runway land, and Stansted was ordered to get rid of its similar acreage. And privately owned Luton was badly damaged by a casual ministerial approach to Foulness-Maplin at a time when history had already shown that immensely expensive projects such as the TSR-2, the Blue Steel, and the British space program could not be brought to reality. By the 1970s airports had reached the plateau, in part because the politics of the planning process made them extremely slow, costly projects.

5. On the plus side was the way in which advanced technology constantly met the challenge, making aircraft larger and quieter while staying within runway and terminal limits.

6. Terminals themselves inevitably grew, as Robin Higham and C. C. Bonwell have shown, in arithmetic steps while traffic grew geometrically and runways remained constant.

7. At the same time technology provided air space by better radar control, variable separations between aircraft, and education of all concerned. Indeed the development of the simulator both trained ATC personnel and reduced training flying to a minimum, thus relieving runway and airspace and allowing aircraft to be used more productively. The development of jet engines and their ground silencers stopped the need for air tests. And jet engines not only extended time between overhauls from 1,800 hours of piston-engines to beyond 15,000 hours between full inspections on today's jets but also made impressive gains in noise abatement and thus, coupled with noise insulation of homes, reduced the political and social opposition to airports. And all these technological developments have helped make the London airports into both economic and urban enterprises in their own right.

8. Also a part of the process of the indecision and lack of a sense of urgency was the politicians' and the civil servants' failure from 1945 onward to comprehend the growing importance for Britain of airlines and airports to the balance of trade and to the earning of dollars, even if much of the equipment was American. Typical of this was the long failure to capitalize airport development properly until BAA was able to fly by itself, nearly 45 years after Churchill in 1920 had wanted civil aviation to do so.

3.4. A Crossair BAe landing at London City Airport. History was made on February 18, 1992, when a BAe 146 operated by the leading Swiss regional airline, Crossair, became the first foreign-registered jetliner to visit the airport, which is situated only six miles from the city of London. The skyscraper is due west, halfway to the city. (Courtesy British Aerospace)

9. Moreover, this self-sufficiency came at the same time as the modernization of the merchant navy and the collapse of the London Docks in the 1970s. The double irony of this was that no one seemed to link these events, whereas at the same time phoenix-like London City Airport arose from the heart of the rubble almost on the doorstep of Whitehall. This fall and rise, and the final admission of Luton to status as the fourth London airport, have given a new lease on life to the London airports.

10. Complicating the development of and rational decision making about the London airports was the equally slow realization that Britain was becoming a nation of car owners and of road transport. As a result, the government was equally slow in providing the surface motorway infrastructure so necessary to the success of air travel. By the time it did begin to complete a basic road traffic system, the Channel Tunnel was in process, and the threat of the ascendancy of Charles de Gaulle (Paris) and Schipol (Amsterdam) through TGV high-speed rail connections to Europe and Britain again challenged London's primacy as the hub-and-spoke airport of international air transport. And that posed a challenge also to the premier world international airline, British

Airways, on the eve of the European Community's dogfight expected to follow the birth of the single community on January 1, 1993, a market into which the xenophobic island politicians have been sullenly advancing like Shakespeare's schoolboy.

11. The story of indecision making on the third London airport, and indeed on the fourth, makes the word *urgent* appear to be the plea of a tortoise.

BIBLIOGRAPHICAL NOTE

Permission to use official documents has kindly been granted by the Comptroller of Her Majesty's Stationery Office (HMSO). Papers by Command of the House of Commons have run in three sequential series in the 20th century—*Cd.* to 1919, *Cmd.* to 1956, and *Cmnd.* since then. Any librarian familiar with British government documents can locate them; HMSO, their publisher, will also now supply photocopies. Most are also available on microfiche collections of parliamentary documents.

Apart from these works, the course of the story of London's airports may be followed in *Aeroplane* to 1967 and in the merged journal *Flight International* after that date. Neither of these journals is reliable where the publication of either official reports or books is concerned. For at least the last decade, *Flight International* has totally neglected to indicate important works. Some appear in *Aerospace* (London).

There have been numerous debates in Parliament, and these are to be found in *Official Reports,* along with questions and answers (PQs) in the House of Commons.

HMSO can provide limited numbers of printouts of aeronautical document titles and copies. But beware that although HMSO thinks the London Library is safekeeping all out-of-print documents, this is not so; some copies cannot be supplied. Finding older documents is not easy, especially now that libraries are computerized and such items as Command Papers are "unknowns." HMSO does not carry the publications of the Civil Aviation Authority and its Civil Air Publications (CAPs), nor does it carry the British Airports Authority works. Both sets must be sought, prepaid, from the publishers. Moreover, the BAA charges outrageously even for the *loan* of a slide. Somehow privatization has adversely given these public relations departments a civil-service attitude. Luton was much more helpful, whereas the Uttersford Borough Council supplied some materials on Stansted.

The Times of London contains a plethora of information, especially regarding parliamentary activities, but since each airport is indexed separately, it can be time-consuming to locate the needed items.

Hans-Joachim Braun

The Airport as Symbol

Air Transport and Politics at Berlin-Tempelhof, 1923–1948

Without good airports, efficient air transport is impossible. Apart from this obvious fact, airports can also acquire symbolic meanings, reflecting the aims and aspirations of engineers, administrators, and politicians involved in their construction, maintenance, and use. Tempelhof, Berlin's major airport from the early 1920s to the 1960s, is an example. From a symbol of efficiency in air transport in the rationalization period of German industry in the latter half of the 1920s, it changed to a symbol of Nazi grandeur in the 1930s. Shortly after World War II, in 1948–49, it became the greatest pillar of the Berlin airlift and, as such, a symbol of freedom and democracy. Therefore, Tempelhof reflected not only the technical and economic development of aviation but also the dramatic changes in political, social, and cultural conditions, which were more extreme in Germany than in any other country during the first half of the 20th century.

Although Tempelhof was the most important Berlin airport, it was not the first to be founded. On September 4, 1909, Orville Wright made his first flight in Germany from the Berlin-Tempelhof airfield, which had earlier been used as a military parade grounds.[1] In the same year, however, Johannisthal, south of Berlin, began air service as Berlin's airfield. During World War I, Staaken, northwest of the city center, was added. Staaken also served as a major zeppelin and airplane production center. A third, small airfield, which also served Berlin, was situated near Potsdam.[2]

At that time, Johannisthal was the most important of all these airfields. At the air show during its opening ceremony in late September 1909, well-known flight pioneers like Louis Blériot, Henry Farman, and Hubert Latham took part. From early January 1910 onward, the airfield was extended, including new hangars, stands for spectators at air shows, and facilities for the construction of airplanes. During 1911 there were about 500 flights from Johannisthal per month. By 1914 that number increased to about 4,000. Johannisthal soon became the center of the German aircraft industry. The Deutsche Versuchsanstalt fuer Luftfahrt (German Testing Institution for Aeronautics) was based in nearby Adlershof.[3]

After the war, civil aviation was taken up again on February 6, 1919, with a series of flights from Johannisthal to the national assembly at Weimar. However, the Versailles Treaty of June 28, 1919, severely restricted the development of the German aircraft industry, which was to a large extent based at Johannisthal.

From Staaken, the other major Berlin airfield at that time, the first inland airship route to Friedrichshafen was established in August 1919 and serviced by the LZ 120 airship, the *Bodensee*. A few months later, however, in December 1919, the Interallied Control Commission interdicted the continuation of airship traffic, and the LZ 120 had to be handed over to the Italian government as a war reparation. At the end of the 1920s, departures of the LZ 127 *Graf Zeppelin* transatlantic and world operations took place at Staaken.[4] Also, from 1921 onward, the two German air companies, Aero Lloyd and Deutsche Luftreederei (DLR), established a limited air service to various places in Germany and, after 1922, to London and Amsterdam. A great disadvantage of the Staaken and Johannisthal airfields was their location a long distance from the city center.[5]

Airline managers and Berlin transport officials had for some time made plans to remedy this unsatisfactory situation. Leonhard Adler, Berlin's chief transport official, in collaboration with the Aero Lloyd and Junkers aviation companies, hit on the idea of developing Tempelhof into Berlin's main airport. Tempelhof had various assets, especially its favorable location just two miles from the city center and its excellent public transport links.[6]

Operations from Tempelhof began on a limited scale on October 8, 1923. From 1924 onward, the increase in passengers was spectacular. In 1926 the newly founded Luft Hansa airline started operations with Tempelhof as its central airport. In the late 1920s Tempelhof was, together with Croydon, regarded as a model airport. Its enormous hangars created a sensation among the air transport experts of the time. Also, a continuous concrete apron stretched along the entire front of the buildings, allowing passengers to embark or alight on these hard-surfaced areas.[7] An underground fueling system allowed the servicing of six airplanes at the same time.[8] Transport officials regarded the airport lighting equipment as exemplary. Night flights were soon introduced and rapidly extended.[9] In the context of the rationalization movement in German industry between 1924 and 1928–29, German and many foreign airport designers looked on Tempelhof as a symbol of efficiency. In addition, the great air shows that took place at Tempelhof at that time not only provided the airport authorities with additional income but also associated the airport with spectacular aeronautical achievements.[10]

Looking closer at Tempelhof as a symbol of efficiency and rationalization, one notices the central location of the airport. Fast roads and a well-designed public transport system added to this favorable impression. The constructional features of the main terminal building, which consisted of more or less uniform construction elements that could easily be extended, and the enormous hangars, with a floor space of about 12 square kilometers, were often praised by contemporary observers.[11] In winter, when services were suspended, these hangars

4.1. Tempelhof airport. (Courtesy Berliner Flughäfen-Gesellschaft)

4.2. Terminal building, finished in late 1928. (Courtesy Berliner Flughäfen-Gesellschaft)

housed about 60 percent of the entire German civil aircraft fleet.[12] Engineers and transport officials were particularly impressed by the electrically operated folding doors, 40 meters wide and 8 meters high, in the hangars. The architects who designed Tempelhof repeatedly made it clear that this should, in every respect, become the number-one airport in Europe.[13]

There was strong competition, however, among which Croydon and Le Bourget stand out. Croydon was founded in 1915 as a military airfield and, after extension and rebuilding for civil aviation during the years 1926 to 1928, reopened in May 1928. Tempelhof had always been keen on superseding Croydon. Le Bourget, used for both civil and military aviation purposes, was the other main rival.[14]

A strong point that favored Tempelhof was its excellent night flight facilities, which were installed in 1927. The huge searchlight tower was the starting point for the illuminated night air route from Berlin to Königsberg via Danzig. This flight took 14 hours, as opposed to 62 hours by train.[15] There was also a night flight route from Berlin to Hanover and Zurich. Reliability on these flights was generally high. Less than 10 percent of the scheduled night flights had to be canceled due to adverse weather conditions.[16]

At that time the main air routes touching Berlin-Tempelhof went from Scandinavia (Malmö, Copenhagen) in the north to either Munich and Zurich in the south or to Vienna and Budapest in the southeast. There was also the important London-Moscow route. Owing to its central location in the middle of Europe, Sefton Brancker, head of the International Air Transport Association (IATA), called Tempelhof "the crossroads of the air."[17]

Publications of that time stressed the efficiency, punctuality, and reliability at Tempelhof. During the latter half of the 1920s there was a steady increase in takeoffs and landings at the airport. The Great Depression caused stagnation and recession in air transport, which also affected Tempelhof, but after 1933 the number of passengers increased significantly.

There were problems, however. Spatial conditions at the airport became increasingly tight, requiring much improvisation.[18] Also, time and motion studies made it clear that much could be improved. As a result of these studies a German efficiency expert came to the conclusion that Tempelhof was highly overstaffed. He also found out that the location and the length of the runways were less than ideal. Besides, the comparatively long distances at the airport were mainly responsible for the fact that clearance time for airplanes at stopovers averaged 24 minutes. In comparison the Halle-Leipzig airport needed only 15 minutes.[19]

The National Socialists wanted to remedy all this. In 1934 Hermann Göring, Reichsminister of aviation, proclaimed that Tempelhof was to be redeveloped

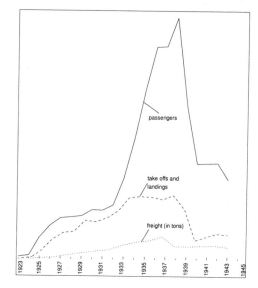

4.3. Number of passengers, takeoffs, landings, and freight (in tons) at Tempelhof, 1923–45. (From Helmut Conin, *Gelandet in Berlin: Zur Geschichte der Berliner Flughäfen* [Berlin, 1974], 225, courtesy Berliner Flughäfen-Gesellschaft)

and extended into the world's largest airport.[20] It did, indeed, become a symbol of Nazi grandeur. Ernst Sagebiel, the architect who had designed the Reich Air Ministry and surely understood the needs of the National Socialist government, undertook the reorganization of the airport buildings. His task—to combine the function of an airport with that of a gigantic stadium for the annual air shows (Reichsflugtage)—was not easy.[21]

In putting his ideas into practice, Sagebiel ran into another problem. Owing to a shortage of construction workers and building materials, which in the late 1930s were mainly used for armament purposes, the construction process at Tempelhof dragged along slowly and, under Nazi rule, was never finished completely. However, by the early 1940s the construction of the airport had progressed so far that the Tempelhof facilities could be used without too many restrictions. Something similar happened to the new airports at Munich and Stuttgart, which had also been designed by Sagebiel. Because of supply problems with workers and building material, the size of the main terminal buildings had to be cut down substantially.[22]

At Tempelhof, Sagebiel inaugurated an innovation in airport design: The main terminal building was constructed so that the flow of passengers, luggage, freight, and visitors could move on different levels. Mail and freight were transported from an underground railway station, whereas a nearby subway station facilitated passenger traffic.[23]

The Nazis took up the tradition of air shows, extending them to gigantic proportions. Celebrations on the First of May 1933 were combined with a grand air spectacle. Ernst Udet, World War I ace, amazed the incredible number of one million spectators with spectacular feats of stunt flying. Zeppelin airships came in all the time, and there was a lot of promotion activity for aviation.[24] At the opening celebration of the new main terminal building in December 1937, Göring gave a speech calling Tempelhof a symbol of the determination of the Third Reich to rise again after the years of shame following the "Versailles dictate." To him, Tempelhof was a symbol both of the audacity of the Reich, stretching out to other countries, and of its perpetuity symbolized by the everlasting, impressive main terminal building. So, the theme of inward security and outward aggression, popular with Nazi politicians, cropped up here too.[25]

In the late 1930s new Berlin airfields in Gatow and Schönefeld were built for military purposes. Gatow housed the newly founded Luftwaffe Academy; Schönefeld was mainly used as an airfield for the Henschel aircraft works. Another airfield at Rangsdorf served the Buecker aircraft company.[26]

During World War II, the Tempelhof buildings constructed in the 1930s and early 1940s experienced only minor damages, whereas the original part of the

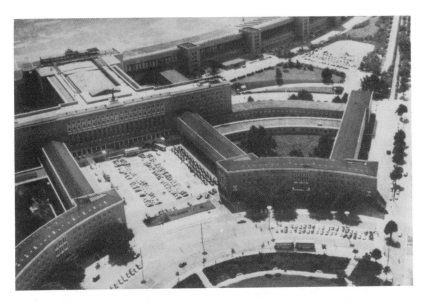

4.4. Main terminal building. (Courtesy Berliner Flughäfen-Gesellschaft)

airport built in the 1920s was severely damaged. After having been a symbol of efficiency and aeronautical prowess in its early days and of Nazi grandeur in the 1930s and early 1940s, Tempelhof, in the late 1940s, became a symbol once again. This time, it was the symbol of freedom and democracy, of the determination of the United States to assist West Berlin in an extremely difficult situation and of the will of the West Berliners to survive under adverse political conditions.

At the end of April 1945 Soviet troops had occupied the airport, which was taken over in July by the Americans. After July, Tempelhof served as the U.S. Air Force base in Berlin. As one of the first measures to improve facilities at the airport, the Americans built a hardened runway. It consisted of interlocking pierced-steel planks. On May 18, 1946, the first civil aircraft, an American Overseas Airlines (AOA) DC-4, landed on these rattling planks.[27] This flight inaugurated civil air services at Tempelhof, services that were at first available only for the relatives of American soldiers in Germany.

On November 30, 1945, the Western Allies had, by an agreement that created the Berlin-Hamburg, Berlin-Hanover, and Berlin-Frankfurt air corridors, secured the right to fly over the Soviet-occupied zone. This agreement was the basis for the great airlift starting in June 1948, by which goods were flown in for the 2 million West Berliners during the Soviet blockade. Although flights went to Gatow and Tegel also, Tempelhof soon became the mightiest pillar of this airlift. After a third runway was built, under good weather conditions an airlift aircraft, a "currant bomber," landed every 90 seconds. The affectionate and ironic term "currant bombers," which the West Berliners gave to these airplanes, expressed the dual-use character of aviation in a most striking way. During the airlift, Tempelhof became a symbol of freedom not only to Berliners but also to the whole Western world.[28] The airlift monument that was erected in front of the airport terminal served as a memorial for the 76 persons who lost their lives during the airlift, as well as a symbol of freedom for those many thousands of refugees who were flown to the West from Tempelhof.

About six months after the end of the airlift the Americans released a small part of the southern rim of hangars for general air transport. On July 9, 1951, civil air service to Western centers began from part of the airport. Passenger traffic to and from Berlin developed so fast that the 240,000-passenger annual capacity of the main terminal building was exceeded by more than 80,000 by the end of the year. As in the late 1920s the Berlin Airport Corporation had again to resort to improvisation. In 1959 the Americans released other parts of the airport, including the main terminal building, for civil air services. The Berlin Airport Corporation started construction work, and after three years of building and rebuilding, the new facilities began operation in July 1962.[29] By that time, however, jet aircraft had come into use for civil aviation. For the jets, Tempelhof was too small. Already in early 1960 Air France, using the Caravelle jet, moved its services to the Tegel airport.[30] Gradually, Tempelhof's role in aviation decreased, being superseded by Tegel to the west and Schönefeld to the east. With the increase to and from Berlin after the unification of Germany in 1990, however, Tempelhof's importance has been on the rise again, providing takeoff and landing facilities for numerous turboprop and small private aircraft. As in the 1930s and 1940s, the fate of Tempelhof Airport is closely linked to political developments.

NOTES

I should like to thank W.-D. Schultze of the Berliner Flughafen-Gesellschaft, Dagmar Rasmussen, Berlin, and Deborah Douglas, National Air and Space Museum, Washington, D.C., for providing me with contemporary material on Tempelhof.

1. Stedman S. Hanks, *International Airports* (New York, 1929), 10.

2. For this and the following, see Helmut Conin, *Gelandet in Berlin: Zur Ges-*

chichte der Berliner Flughäfen (Berlin, 1974), and idem, "Tempelhof: Geschichte eines Luftkreuzes" (Tempelhof: Story of a Crossroads of the Air), *Airport Forum*, no. 3 (1975): 27–42.

3. Werner Treibel, *Geschichte der deutschen Verkehrsflughäfen: Eine Dokumentation von 1909 bis 1989* (Bonn, 1992), 51.

4. Ibid., 52.

5. Heinz J. Nowarra, *60 Jahre deutsche Verkehrsflughäfen* (Mainz 1969), 7.

6. Conin, "Tempelhof," 30.

7. Conin, *Gelandet in Berlin*, 74.

8. Otto F. Sauernheimer, *Zeitschrift des Vereins Deutscher Ingenieure* 70 (1926): 1549–57.

9. "Nachtflug-Veranstaltung der Deutschen Luft-Hansa," *Illustrierte Flugwoche* (1928), 94–95.

10. Treibel, *Geschichte der deutschen Verkehrsflughäfen*, 57.

11. Edwin P. A. Heinze, "Tempelhof: Germany's Premier Airport," *Aero Digest* 13, no. 4 (October 1928): 836–39; "The Great Tempelhof Field: Berlin's Airport," *Airports* 1, no. 4 (August 1928): 17–18, 30–33; Paul Engler and Klaus Engler, "Empfangsgebaeude des Flughafens Berlin-Tempelhof," *Deutsche Bauzeitung* 63, no. 39 (1929): 345–48.

12. Sauernheimer, "Der Zentralflughäfen Berlin."

13. Rudolf J. Schmeisser, "Europas groesster Lufthäfen," *Der Bosch Zuender* (1927), 282–84.

14. W. Hanuschke, "Die bedeutendsten europaeischen Flughäfen," *Technische Blaetter: Wochenschrift zur Deutschen Bergwerks-Zeitun*, no. 3 (1931): 38–40.

15. Treibel, *Geschichte der deutschen Verkehrsflughäfen*, 55.

16. Leonhard Adler, "Der neue Berliner Flughafen auf dem Tempelhofer Feld," *Verkehrstechnik*, no. 2 (1924): 11–13.

17. Treibel, *Geschichte der deutschen Verkehrsflughäfen*, 58.

18. Conin, "Tempelhof," 34.

19. Leonhard Adler, "Rationalisierung der Flughafenbetriebe tut not," *Berliner Wirtschaftsberichte*, February 2, 1929; Carl Pierath, ed., *Forschungsergebnisse des Verkehrswissenschaftlichen Instituts fuer Luftfahrt an der Technischen Hochschule Stuttgart*, vol. 2 (Munich, Berlin, 1930). See particularly the contribution by Richard Brandt, "Die betriebswirtschaftlichen Grundlagen fuer die Anlage und Ausgestaltung von Verkehrsflughaefen," 41–75.

20. Ansel E. Talbert, *Famous Airports of the World* (New York, 1953), 74.

21. Ernst Sagebiel, "Die Bauten des Weltflughäfens Berlin-Tempelhof," *Baukunst und Staedtebau*, no. 3 (1938).

22. Nowarra, *60 Jahre deutsche Verkehrsflughäfen*, 64.

23. Hanks, *International Airports*, 10.

24. *Voelkischer Beobachter*, May 1, 1933; *Berliner Morgenpost*, May 2, 1933.

25. See, in a different context, Barton Hacker, "Imagination in Thrall: The Social

Psychology of Military Mechanization, 1919–1939," *Parameters: Journal of the U.S. Army War College* 12, no. 1 (1982): 50–61.

26. Nowarra, *60 Jahre deutsche Verkehrsflughäfen,* 23.

27. Conin, "Tempelhof," 38.

28. On the airlift, see Magistrat von Gross-Berlin, ed., *Luftbruecke Berlin: Ein dokumentarisches Bilderbuch* (Berlin-Grunewald, 1949); Lucius D. Clay, *Entscheidung in Deutschland* (Frankfurt am Main, 1950) [*Decision in Germany* (Garden City, N.Y., 1950)]; W. Phillips Davison, *Die Blockade von Berlin: Modellfall des Kalten Krieges* (Frankfurt am Main, Berlin 1959) [*The Berlin Blockade: A Study in Cold War Politics* (Princeton, 1958)]; Klaus Scherf, *Luftbruecke Berlin* (Stuttgart, 1976); Geunther Gerhardt, *Das Krisenmanagement der Vereinigten Staaten waehrend der Berliner Blockade (1948/1949): Intentionen, Strategien, Wirkungen* (Berlin, 1984); Uwe Prell and Lothar Wilker, eds., *Berlin-Blockade und Luftbruecke 1948/49: Analyse und Dokumentation* (Berlin, 1987).

29. Conin, "Tempelhof," 38–41.

30. Treibel, *Geschichte der deutschen Verkehrsflughäfen,* 66.

■■■
■■■
■■■■ Deborah G. Douglas

Airports as Systems and Systems of Airports

Airports and Urban Development in America before World War II

Wherever an airplane takes off or lands, there is an "airfield." The invention of commercial aviation required the creation of a network of specialized facilities—"airports"—dedicated not just to takeoffs and landings but also to the larger purpose of the efficient transfer of people and goods from air to ground, from one geographic area to another. The idea of commercial aviation began to gain momentum during that early era of unabashed enthusiasm for aviation immediately following World War I. Likewise, the idea of airports also developed.

During the next two decades both the facility we have come to know as an airport *and* a national system of airports were developed. This was the formative period in the history of American airport development and is the subject of this paper. The airport is a key component in a technological system that is a means of both transportation and communication. In simpler terms, most Americans of the period came to believe that the airplane was unable to achieve its potential without that elaborate network of facilities. The commercial value of the airplane was not its potential to go "anywhere" but rather the fact that it went "somewhere"—somewhere individuals already wanted to go.

Unlike other types of large technological systems, airports are not the subject of secondary literature describing their history. The basic framework of this analysis thus draws on the ideas of the regional scientist Brian J. L. Berry. In the early 1960s, Berry suggested an urban model in his seminal article entitled "Cities as Systems within Systems of Cities."[1] Berry proposed a dual approach that involved scrutiny of the specific artifact (the city) *and* of the spatial relationships among the artifacts. This approach is particularly useful for the study of airports, hence the title of this paper.

The political, economic, and technological history of the airport unfolds over three distinct phases of development. These phases are demarcated by several key events—the conclusion of World War I, the passage of the Air Commerce Act of 1926, the election of Franklin D. Roosevelt, and the passage of the Civil Aeronautics Act of 1938. The study of airport as system focuses sharply on the question of who controlled (and therefore who funded) the airport. From the start, there was a shared assumption among aviation advocates that primary control belonged to the federal government.

But stating in 1919 that the federal government should take the leading role in the development of commercial aviation and assume the mantle of fiscal responsibility for airports meant something quite different than it would two decades later. The development of airports both mirrored and contributed to the development of the nation's cities and industries. The history of airports, then, is an important case study of some of the critical patterns and dynamics of institutional relationships in the early 20th century. In my conclusion, I hope to suggest that the "large technological systems" model described by Thomas Hughes and the "modern industrial enterprise" model described by Alfred Chandler should be viewed as complementary rather than competitive explanations. Further, I argue that even used in this fashion the two are incomplete, that urban development and the city represent a critical third area of study. Together, the three forms of analysis help describe those features of the historical landscape that characterize and differentiate Western industrial society from its predecessors.[2]

The earliest phase of airport development was the period before the passage of the Air Commerce Act of 1926. This was an era of unabashed enthusiasm. World War I had created an important legacy in the form of "aviation evangelists." Note the bold language of the 1919 opening editorial of *Ace,* a new aviation journal for southern California:

> We know the psychological moment when we see it, we Aces. There are things
> of the past; let them lay. There are things of the future; we will come to them.
> There is this one thing of the palpitating, pulsating present, this aviation, an ag-

gressive, vital thing. It was, it used to be said, the thing that would end the war. It was the warrior supreme. It is, we say now, a peace-engine, a re-builder, an on-looking progressive instrument of re-construction, and after. The war started aerial events; peace hurtles them forward at breakneck speed.

That is why we're here, we "The Ace." We couldn't possibly be persuaded that anything more wonderful than the conquest of the air has happened in the last thousand years. It isn't a thing to be conservative about. It's young,— breathlessly expectant of all the things it will do.[3]

Hundreds of pilots, mechanics, and others who worked directly with airplanes during the war became the foremost advocates for the development of commercial air transport. The inauguration of airmail service by the U.S. Post Office in the spring of 1918 gave critical encouragement to such ambitions. The National Advisory Committee for Aeronautics (NACA) made the most important statement concerning the development of commercial aviation in general and airports in particular. In its report for 1919, the committee pointed to the fact that the governments of many European nations had aggressively pursued a policy of subsidy of commercial aviation. It deemed such "material encouragement" from the U.S. government essential if this new transportation technology was to be successful. Central to the success of commercial aeronautics, however, was the development of airfields. NACA did not mince words; this was the major recommendation concerning civil air transport both in the 1919 *Annual Report* and in a special statement issued in August of that year.

The greatest need at the present time is the proper location and maintenance of suitable landing fields in every city and town. These landing fields should be established and maintained by the municipalities as part of park systems. The Government should cooperate at the beginning by assisting in laying out the fields according to approved specifications and by the erection of at least one airplane hangar on each field. The fields should be made available for use alike by Government and private aviators. The initiative in this matter properly rests with the people, under our principles of Government.[4]

From the beginning there was an expectation that the federal government could and should play a role in commercial aviation. However, in spite of the unity of expectation and the vigor with which all of the aviation advocates lobbied Congress, it took seven years to enact legislation. The questions of control and constitutionality proved to be major bottlenecks, with the latter being the less difficult of the two. As for control, a rancorous debate soon developed between those who wanted a single, separate aviation department, which would oversee both military and commercial aeronautics, and those who preferred the status quo, which left control of military aviation with the War and Navy departments. Once the commerce clause was accepted as the constitutional basis for a federal role, the control debate was effectively concluded. The Air Commerce Act specified separate federal jurisdictions over the two branches of aviation.[5]

Civil aviation was put under the control of the secretary of commerce. The Air Commerce Act of 1926 mandated the federal government to be a promoter and regulator of aeronautics. A new division within the Commerce Department was set up. The Aeronautics Branch would coordinate the work of several other government agencies, license pilots, inspect and register aircraft, control air space, and establish civil airways. What the Air Commerce Act specifically did not authorize the government to do was build airports.[6]

The reason for the exclusion was twofold. First, the drafters of the legislation relied on precedents in maritime law and the manner in which the federal government had provided aid to maritime transportation. In an influential statement in September 1925, then Secretary of Commerce Herbert Hoover made explicit reference to commercial waterborne navigation: "I am convinced that the time has arrived when the airport will be a necessary adjunct to each important town. It has been our national policy in the past that the docks and terminal facilities for water borne traffic should be supplied either by the municipalities or citizens of our cities and not by the Federal government."[7]

The other major reason for excluding airports was that the cost was expected to be prohibitive. Highly publicized hearings led by New York's fiery Republican representative, Fiorello La Guardia, immediately after World War I had revealed the extraordinary costs associated with constructing airfields for the military. Congress and the president were willing to commit to aviation legislation to the extent that the costs could be dispersed among multiple agencies. This precedent was critical because it became the means for justifying to the public which things the government would pay for and which things it would not.

Aeronautical experts and the staunchly Republican administration feared not just the exorbitant cost associated with building an airport but also the quagmire of pork-barrel politics that would inevitably result if the federal government became the chief patron of airports. In addition, Hoover shared the mindset of the technocrats who feared not only a waste of public money but also the failure to create a truly efficient system of air transportation.[8]

The law that was passed reflected these political concerns. But so too did the landing fields of the period. Without financial support, the airports of 1926 were still little more than grass fields, and apart from the tiny network estab-

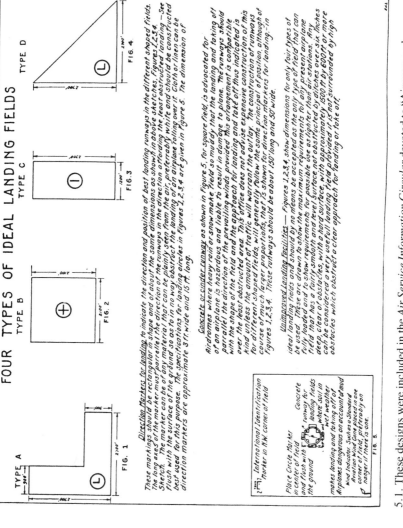

5.1. These designs were included in the *Air Service Information Circular* devoted to "Airways and Landing Fields." In the early 1920s, the military shared much of the aviation expertise it had cultivated during the war. (From "Airways and Landing Fields," *Air Service Information Circular* 5, no. 404 [March 1, 1923]: 4)

lished by the U.S. Air Mail Service, there was no meaningful airport network. The military shared the limited expertise it had cultivated during the war, but airport design technology remained static. The same advice was given throughout the period preceding the Air Commerce Act. A plot of land of about 100 acres with a level surface, good drainage, and no high obstacles was the norm throughout this time.[9]

Aside from the political and financial constraints there were other obstacles to airport development before 1926. One was that aircraft technology did not undergo significant changes. With only the U.S. Post Office and a handful of wealthy individuals interested in buying nonmilitary aircraft, manufacturers paid scant attention to aircraft for commercial application. Most planes were modified military vehicles, adapted for carrying sacks of mail or an extra passenger or two. For the majority of aircraft, takeoff and landing speeds ranged between 45 and 60 miles per hour. This meant the runway length was about 2,800 to 3,000 feet.[10]

Some early "airports" were also the local fairgrounds, racetracks, or parklands. There were four basic types of landing field layouts: the square, the rectangle, the "L" shape, and the triangle.[11] Because aircraft had limited abilities, they were forced to take off heading directly into the wind. The square represented the field of choice because the direction of takeoff or landing could be adjusted in any direction. The other field shapes limited the number of angles of approach and takeoff but had the advantage of requiring significantly less land.[12]

One aspect of airport technology that did develop at this time was the recognition that airplanes required comparable takeoff and landing sites. The establishment of standards and ratings of airports became one of the most important tasks assigned to the Commerce Department under the Air Commerce Act of 1926.[13]

Archibald Black, one of the earliest engineers to specialize in airport design and construction, was among the first to develop such standards. One of his first iterations was a fourteen-item checklist published in 1923 in *American City,* a journal for city administrators and the new city planning professionals.[14] Black's rationale for planning was quite simplistic. He, like others, believed that transportation was critical to the development of the nation's commerce. He assumed a causal role, meaning that a major factor contributing directly to the economic development of a city was the existence of transportation networks. In an article Black wrote for *Aero Digest* in 1925 there is a not-so-subtle threat that the town that failed to build an airport would share the same fate as the town that had rejected the railroad.

WHY SQUIRRELVILLE NEVER HAD A RAILROAD

THEY ARE STILL WITH US ONLY THEY DON'T WEAR SUCH LONG WHISKERS

5.2. It was an article of faith that building an airport would result in economic development for a city. Civic leaders were warned that the city that failed to build an airport would suffer the same consequences as the town that refused to grant the railroad a right-of-way. (From *New York Herald Tribune*, 1930; © New York Herald Tribune Inc. All rights reserved. Reprinted by permission.)

There are people who don't take this landing field business seriously. They can't see why their town should have one—no "need" for it, they say. . . . If Pudunk, U.S.A. waits until it "needs" a flying field, it's liable to have a nice, long wait. Long before Pudunk "needs" its flying field, its neighbor Squedunk, twenty miles away, will have discovered that it "needed" one. And, once the Squedunk field is in operation, there never will be any "need" for one at Pudunk. . . . Perhaps you see no lineup of airplanes waiting for your city to layout its landing field? What of that? You buy your fire extinguisher before the fire? When you need either, you're going to need it badly. [15]

This attitude was shared by those staffing the new Aeronautics Branch of the Commerce Department. As this agency began to exercise its authority, as municipalities built facilities, and as investment in commercial aviation expanded, the character of the airport underwent a steady change. The passage of the Air Commerce Act, even though it had "excepted" airports, had a substantial impact on their development.

The passage of the Air Commerce Act signaled the start of a new phase in the development of airports. Although the federal government was prevented from actually building or operating airports, the vigorous program of airport promotion and the establishment of the first ratings guide for airports generated enormous interest. Several airport engineering textbooks appeared, and new journals such as *Airports: Construction, Equipment, Administration and Financing* were started. [16]

William MacCracken, a young Chicago lawyer, veteran World War I pilot, and key lobbyist for the Air Commerce Act, became the new assistant secretary of commerce for aeronautics. In 1928 in the opening editorial for *Airports* he wrote, "The establishment of an airport would benefit the city concerned in several ways—in a general increase of business; in more satisfactory connections with the rest of the world, and in acquisition of a reputation for service which would be carried to all parts of the country by air visitors to that city." [17]

MacCracken's appeal needs to be remembered in the context of Charles Lindbergh's epochal solo crossing of the Atlantic in May 1927. That flight galvanized public attention and made aviation the most potent metaphor for progress in the United States. It also fueled a phenomenal sale of aviation securities. The massive infusion of cash, the transfer of airmail operations to private contractors, and the federal government's commitment to promoting safety had a salutary effect on manufacturers. This optimism was sustained throughout the bleak years of the depression and affected the development of airports and air transportation. [18]

After Hoover's election as president, Walter Folger Brown, who had served

5.3. This editorial cartoon illustrates the kind of boosterism that was used to encourage municipalities to build airports. (From the William P. MacCracken Papers, Herbert Hoover Library, West Branch, Iowa, courtesy E. W. Scripps Company)

as Hoover's assistant secretary of commerce, became the new postmaster general.[19] From this new post, Brown began work on his dream of building a coherent air transport system that would move the mails and passengers. His was to be the dominant articulation of how airports and airways should be ordered.[20]

The influence of Brown's conception was noticeable in the literature of the period. The Harvard City Planning Studies devoted its first volume, published in 1930, to the subject of airports. The authors argued that there were now three significant factors that determined the optimum site for a new airport. The first was simply a restatement of practices that had been instituted beginning with the siting and construction of airfields for the military during World War I. The second and third factors represented novel concerns. Airport planners were asked to assess a site according to the functional relationship between the airport and the city or region, as well as determine its relationship to the national transportation network.[21]

These were the ideals expressed by Brown. What neither Brown nor the authors of the Harvard study conceded was the complexity of the newly emerging relations between federal, state, and local governments, the aircraft manufacturing industry, and the public. One 1930 article in *Airport Construction and Management* stated bluntly, "Of all the various enemies that beset the struggling young airport, both before and after it is born, none is quite so insidious, or so dangerous, as Politics."[22] Later that year an editorial stated: "There will come a time when state and federal governments will join forces to provide the country with a system of airports comparable to the highway system that now spreads its network over the land. Just when that time will arrive it is difficult to predict, principally because of the complications that beset the financing of such development. The source of the funds for establishing airports is quite a knotty problem."[23]

Brown viewed the solution to such seemingly intractable problems from the perspectives of a Progressive and a technocrat. Yet he was limited, by his position as postmaster general, in the ways in which he could change policy and effect change. Brown saw the need to create an oligopoly among service providers. With the passage of the Watres Act in April 1930, Brown believed he had at least a partial license to fulfill his dream.[24]

Brown created a new map of the airway system and then arranged for a "spoils" conference among the biggest airlines to divide up the routes. The weak spot in Brown's plan was airport development. Although Brown believed that one of the most important features of his new plan was its emphasis on connecting the majority of the nation's metropolitan regions, he was unable to change the official policy banning government financing of airports.

This meant that one of the major problems in implementing the Brown system was the fact that airport development did not proceed at the same pace as changes in airway route structuring. The Commerce Department was sympathetic to Brown, and the Aeronautics Branch dramatically intensified its efforts.

The government was imploring communities to invest in new facilities, but there was a basic, and usually unstated, problem. Airports were not sound propositions; they did not pay for themselves. This accounts for the flurry of articles about accounting techniques and the exhortations to build miniature golf courses, swimming pools, and anything else that might draw the public to new airport facilities.[25]

An article in the *Journal of Land and Public Utility Economics* in 1931 outlined in great detail the failure of municipal airports to be financially self-sufficient. Only those airports located in the nation's largest cities (over 1 million population) could be expected to break even. Still, the author concluded by attempting to assign a market value to the intangible value provided by an airport to its host community. The airport returned about $1.08 per capita in community benefit, according to the estimate. For a community of 10,000 whose airport was predicted to operate at a $10,000 loss, the implication was that the deficit was offset by the facility's intangible benefits. This was one of the earliest attempts to calculate a return on investment.[26]

The remarkable persistence of interest and investment in airports despite the stock market crash and the depression was a strong indication of the public's identification of aviation with progress. Even when the numbers clearly indicated that airport operations did not, and could not be expected to, pay for themselves, communities continued to build (albeit at a slower rate than suited Brown and the airlines).

The result was a hodgepodge of facilities, ranging from grass fields to expensive and complex infrastructures boasting the latest in electrical and radio technology. The technological challenge facing commercial aviation was to achieve both speed and reliability. The most significant hurdle was flying at night or when conditions prevented visibility. Two different but complementary systems were simultaneously developed. The first involved lighting the airways and was an extension of the principles of marine lighting.[27] Lines of large electric beacons placed at fifteen-mile intervals stretched from one airport to another. The first beacon was installed in August 1923, and by 1933, some 18,000 miles had been lighted.[28]

A system of lighted airways and airports had important limitations. It was a fair-weather flying technology, and it ignored the fact that airplanes, unlike other transportation vehicles, moved in three dimensions. Further, it offered little latitude for deviation from a fixed course in case of an emergency. Many aviation experts began to identify the new technology of radio as holding the solution to the problems of "blind flying." At first most of the research involving radios and commercial aviation focused on two-way communication. Although the U.S. Air Mail Service had experimented with radio navigation in 1920, the Bureau of Standards began serious investigation in the late 1920s. It installed a series of radio beacons and ran tests with the Aeronautics Branch and National Air Transport in 1928. The tests were successful, but radio technology was slow to be adopted because maintaining radio beacon stations was costly and because flying by beacons required cognitive and piloting skills substantially different from those needed for contact flying.[29]

Airports that were on these new "high-tech" airways varied greatly from those that were not. Secondary or intermediate fields acquired a distinction from primary fields, one that they had not previously had. Managers of primary fields began to use other technologies, such as paved runways. The development of new types of aircraft such as the trimotors, the Vega, and various all-metal low-wing monoplanes lessened the need to construct fields with multiple unpaved runways that looked like giant asterisks.[30] Attention was being given to the problems of traffic control. The Aeronautics Branch began developing field rules and air rules to speed up plane movements in and around ground facilities.[31] Finally, there was a new consciousness that it was essential to view the airport as a point of transfer whose fortune was intimately tied with both the economy of the local city and that of the nation.[32] Still, the idea of passenger transport remained mostly a dream.

The election of Franklin Roosevelt and the subsequent personnel turnover in the Aeronautics Branch had a profound effect on airport development. The federal government began a complete revolution in its policy toward airports. In response to the drastic unemployment caused by the depression, Roosevelt and the New Dealers adopted the view that airport construction represented a worthy target for federal relief dollars. The intention of the new administration was not to undermine the traditional "dock" concept; FDR's plan was to incorporate large construction projects into the various programs of relief work.[33] In 1936 W. Sumpter Smith, the principal aeronautical engineer for the federal Works Progress Administration (WPA), stated: "The WPA program is strictly a relief program, and the first rule and order that we have to carry out is the relief angle, and that is putting men to work. . . . Frankly, our job is to salvage from the depression as much useful work on airports as we possibly can, in the use of labor from relief roles."[34]

Airports received federal aid under two pieces of legislation approved in the late spring of 1933: the Federal Emergency Relief Act (FERA) and the National Industrial Recovery Act (NIRA). The former, which created employment opportunities for the jobless, assigned workers to projects created by the Aeronautics Branch. The latter, which created the Public Works Administration (PWA), included airports on its list of public works projects that would support American industry. Even before these programs began, however, work on airports had been initiated by the Civil Works Administration (CWA) in late 1933.[35]

Within six months, construction work had begun at more than 800 airports and landing fields. Of those projects, 60 percent represented the building of new fields or the reopening of abandoned facilities.[36] Eugene Vidal, the director of the newly reorganized Bureau of Air Commerce,[37] had announced the planned allocation of $10 million dollars. It was expected that the projects would employ 50,000 unemployed individuals and pump $8 million dollars of wages into the ailing economy. The bulk of the federal contribution was in the form of wages; municipalities were still expected to acquire the land, and the cities and states were required to loan the necessary construction equipment. An average grant for a single community was $5,000, of which only 10–12 percent was to be used for materials.[38]

When the CWA closed down in the spring of 1935, it had spent nearly $11.5 million dollars on airports.[39] In its place, the PWA and FERA continued to funnel money through the Bureau of Air Commerce until July 1935, when these programs were consolidated under the WPA. The bureau quickly set up the Division of Airways and Airports to work under the chief engineer of the WPA. The mission of the Airways and Airports Division was to expand the scale and scope of the national air transport system.[40]

The WPA program built on Brown's idea, completing many of the projects he had proposed, but it also went beyond his goal. Flush with cash, the Division of Airways and Airports focused considerable attention on the development of sites that would support feeder systems. The second major goal of the division was to upgrade the entire airport system to a new minimum standard. *Aviation* magazine reported in 1936: "The present Works Progress Administration plan has undertaken to improve further certain of these fields to a status sufficiently developed to permit their being termed 'airports.' During the past five to eight years a great many landing fields were called 'airports' even though they were principally undeveloped pasture land or other clear fields."[41]

The urgency for the upgrade and expansion of airport facilities was in part a consequence of the introduction of the Boeing 247. Although it could not transport as many passengers as the Ford Trimotor, the 247 was 50 percent faster.[42] In those early stages of development when most airlines flew at 50 percent capacity anyway, the reduction of seats proved to be of little concern to the airlines. Increased speed, however, was a very different matter.[43]

Because of the alliances that had formed between airlines and aircraft manufacturers, Boeing, a member of the United Aircraft group, refused to sell 247s to Transcontinental and Western Air (TWA). TWA then turned to Douglas, which responded with its famous DC-1, 2, 3 trilogy. The DC-1 was introduced in late 1933. The production version, the DC-2, could cruise at 170 mph (20 mph faster than the 247) and carry 14 passengers. Later in 1936, Douglas introduced the DC-3. With a significantly enlarged cabin, the DC-3 could seat 21 passengers and had a greater range than either the DC-2 or the Boeing 247.[44]

The three aircraft not only made passenger operations economically viable but also helped salvage the pieces of an industry that had been ripped asunder by the cancellation of the airmail contracts in 1934. The unethical sleight of hand of Brown's "spoils" conference (which had defied the Watres Act's intent of opening airmail contracts to free and competitive bidding) had finally come to light. The early years of the Roosevelt administration were shaped by the powerful influence of the antitrusters. The cancellation of the airmail contracts was intended to punish the architects and participants of the spoils conference.[45] The goal was to break up the large holding companies and allow competition among all operators, instead of among only a handpicked few.

Simultaneously, there was an equally strong, contradictory impulse that manifested itself among legislators and the public. This was the demand that transport industries, especially air transportation, be granted the status of a public utility. Public utilities were "an inherently monopolistic industry providing essential public services, one in which the nature of the service, the large amounts of capital required, and the presence of high fixed costs all combine[d] to produce large economies of scale and make any competitive duplication of facilities wasteful and inefficient."[46]

As early as 1925, there had been calls for commercial aviation to be considered a public utility.[47] During the depression, such calls intensified as aviation leaders joined others in the transport industry pleading for help. In each case the claim was the same—public safety and national defense demanded the federal government do more than regulate. The historian Ellis Hawley has described the result as "a mixture of controls, protection, subsidies, and publicly sponsored cartels, in which the government became not only a regulator, but a protector, supporter, and provider as well."[48]

During the spoils conference investigation and hearing, the "public utility" appeal was temporarily squelched. However, it was resurrected in the brief period during which the U.S. Army Air Corps took over the Air Mail Service in 1934. As is well known, the air corps effort was an unmitigated disaster. Three pilots lost their lives in a training flight, bad weather canceled operations on the first day, and then two more pilots died in successive crashes. The nightmare continued as the death toll from crashes rose precipitously during the following weeks. The public pressure to end this tragedy was both enormous and unstinting. There was a strong demand to return to the old system. Roosevelt was unwilling to make that concession at first, but by the time the Air Mail Act of 1934 was passed into law, the federal government was once again committed to the roles of protector and supporter. This was to be Roosevelt's first major policy defeat.[49]

In late April 1934, Postmaster General James Farley convened a meeting for the newly reorganized airlines, and the bidding for routes began anew. With new contracts let and new types of aircraft, airport technology also underwent a period of innovation and development. The DC-3 was at least twice as heavy as the majority of its competitors. Heavier aircraft required longer runways with a more stable surface than sod or cinders. The growth of passenger traffic (500,000 in 1933 to 1.2 million in 1938) put enormous pressures on existing terminal facilities. New passengers demanded more efficient transfers between air and ground transport. New airports required all operations to be scaled up to accommodate the new demands of commercial air transport.[50]

Airport technology now encompassed careful studies of traffic circulation and ground movement of aircraft. New designs featuring parallel hard-surfaced runways allowing simultaneous takeoff and landing operations were proposed.[51] Zoning laws became much more strict as airport managers became increasingly vigilant over any obstructions. Unlike in previous periods when the assumption was that aircraft technology would remain at a constant size, everyone now expected aircraft to gain in size and speed. "The heavier the aircraft, the longer the runway" was the maxim. This affected assumptions about airport size and location. Planners argued that additional land should be purchased and held in reserve.

Despite developments in airport planning, air transportation was beset with problems. Airports remained insolvent operations, and the Air Mail Act of 1934 did not work particularly well. The new system was not as profitable as expected, and the airlines began pressuring government officials for change. The Bureau of Air Commerce convened a National Airport Conference in December 1937 to study the problem of "the gap between airport resources and air commerce needs."[52] The unanimous conclusion was "the need for a national system of public airways and airports."[53] Each of the participants also made a commitment to work for a change in the stated policy of the Air Commerce Act of 1926. An Airport Advisory Committee was appointed by the secretary of commerce, and this group played an active role in the negotiations that would lead to the Civil Aeronautics Act of 1938. The committee gave vigorous testimony arguing that all previous federal investment in aviation would be wasted if a comparable commitment to and investment in airports was not also made. In the end, Congress capitulated, and in the Civil Aeronautics Act of 1938 the phrase "except airports" was deleted. The federal government was now committed to the concept that its role was, in fact, regulator, protector, supporter, and provider of airports.[54]

These airports had become large technological systems. Historian of technology Thomas Hughes has developed a heuristic model to describe such artifacts. The interwar period was a time of innovation and development. At first the airport—or, more accurately, the airfield—was simply a geographic site. Within 20 years, however, the airport was a highly planned entity with a large number of interacting technical components. From radio and electrical technology to the creation of new architectural forms and civil engineering techniques, the physical airport came to reflect the political and economic concerns of the newly urban America.

Given the domineering presence of the federal government, it would be easy to assume that these facilities were simply installed in American communities. This was not the case. Two forces were especially potent in the development of a national system of airports. First were the municipalities, which footed the bill for airports. Second were the executives and managers of the new "modern business enterprises," who were the primary consumers of commercial air transport and, therefore, of airports.

The advocates, builders, and operators of airports were able to marshal the requisite resources to give initial life to the earliest dreams of commercial aviation. These individuals were sustained in their efforts, despite meager capital, by an abiding faith in the commercial value of speed. In article after article, book after book, it was speed that was identified as the motive for developing air transportation. One editorial put it succinctly, "Speed must always be the merchandising factor in aeronautics."[55] Speed, as we know from the physical sciences, is a phenomenon of movement relating time and distance. In the 19th century, speed acquired cultural significance as well. Historians have given us ample descriptions of how industrialization both changed and was changed by Western society's new understanding of speed.[56]

The significance of speed was not its aesthetic expression but rather its economic value acquired during the late 19th century. The development of the modern industrial enterprise—the multiunit business with its own supply, sales, and distribution networks, with operations of unprecedented scale and scope—was premised on the ability to schedule a high-volume flow of goods from the suppliers of raw materials to the ultimate consumer. The revolutions in transportation and communication were important for two reasons: One, they

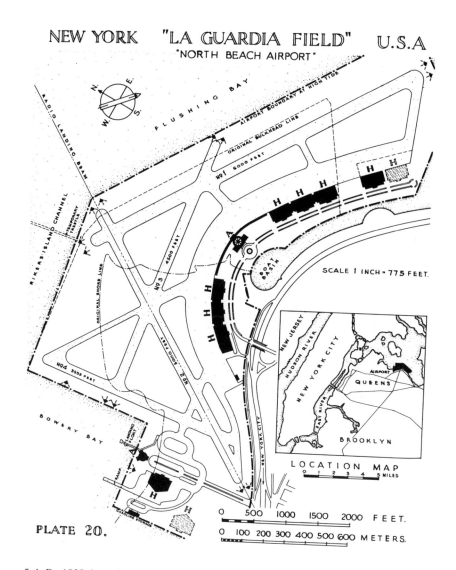

NEW YORK "LA GUARDIA FIELD" U.S.A
"NORTH BEACH AIRPORT"

SCALE 1 INCH = 775 FEET.

LOCATION MAP

PLATE 20.

5.4. By 1938 the technology of airport design and construction had changed considerably. This plan for La Guardia Airport was state-of-the-art in 1938. (From John Walter Wood, *Airports: Some Elements of Design and Future Development* [New York, 1940], 112) made possible changes in distribution, production, and marketing; and two, these enterprises (especially the railroads) were structured so differently that they became a paradigm for other industries to emulate.[57]

The managerial class about which Alfred Chandler writes so eloquently gained in efficiency to the extent that it recognized speed as a means to increase productivity. The minute and the mile became unyielding and universal arbiters of "efficiency." Production meant the movement of goods through time and space; the faster goods moved, the greater the profit. In short, the most basic definition of an industrial revolution was the dramatic increase in the amount of output relative to input, especially in the form of capital.

Most contemporary observers viewed commercial air transport as a logical extension of developments begun by the railroad and the telegraph. Quoting from a letter sent to the Aeronautics Branch, *Domestic Air News* reported in 1928: "The past generation was born to steam; it accepted the steam engine as an accomplished fact; the present generation accepted the automobile as the common means of travel. In the same manner, the rising generation accepts the airplane."[58]

Compared with other forms of transport, the airplane was a much more expensive means of travel. For example, a federal government survey of 26,000 intercity travelers in 1933 compared the average cost per mile of the various modes of transportation. The average cost of driving between two cities was 1.37 cents per mile; the train cost an average of 2.01 cents per mile; the airplane cost 5.90 cents per mile.[59]

So whereas the "rising generation" may have accepted the idea that air transport was an improved form of travel, only a small handful of individuals were able to directly achieve the benefit of speedier movement. That same 1933 survey made this point in two ways. First, it collated data from the Interstate Commerce Commission, which stated that there were 138 million intercity passengers in 1933, of which 420,000 (or 3 percent) traveled by air.[60] Second, the 187 million travel miles reported by the respondents were distributed as follows: 60 percent to private automobile; 34 percent to rail; 4 percent to airplane; and 2 percent to bus.[61]

The fact of limited access was, for the most part, accepted by Americans. Most presumed that eventually the price would drop and the system would carry vastly greater numbers of passengers. In fact, this was one of the concerns of rail carriers. Rail passenger traffic had declined steadily during the 1920s, and even though most in the business saw their primary competitor as the automobile (as has been borne out by the statistics), they did not discount the potential of air carriers to have a substantial effect on long-distance travel.[62]

However, the fact that air travel was not yet universally available did bother certain individuals. Eugene Vidal's abortive autogiro project—touted as the airplane for everyman—was one such attempt to remedy the situation. Vidal's program was influential in that it sustained hopes among those who envisioned an airplane in every garage. Still it failed, in large part because Vidal had thought that the solution to increasing air traffic was to use the automobile model. The capital required to build a system of airports and airways was substantially greater than that needed for roads and highways. The aviation industry did its best to ignore Vidal's airplane program and concentrated on increasing the size, range, and speed of aircraft and on designing airports to support this kind of vehicle.[63]

The fact remained, however, that in this early period, air transport could be used only for sending high-value goods, such as the mail, that had little physical mass. When the airlines received an incentive from the federal government to transport passengers, it became affordable for certain firms to send employees to distant locations. (In 1933, of all air carrier travel miles, 85 percent were flown by business and professional men.)[64] This proved remarkably appealing, in large part because of the importance of human interactions in the conduct of business.

The massive industrial enterprises were originally cemented together through human contact. Close and constant communication was necessary to coordinate and maintain these complex and vast empires. Although these firms used several technologies, one of the airplane's touted features was that it had the potential to rival the speed of the various communications technologies, with the significant advantage of allowing an individual to make physical contact.[65]

In a lengthy document on the value of air transport to business, one corporate executive noted:

> There is, of course, the factor that ofttimes business is gotten because of local offices, closer contact with people and the desire on the part of customers to deal with local individuals because of our natural tendency to provincialism and to do business with those whom we know and trust. Just as we have seen the gradual growing away from provincialism all over the country, so with the greater ease of travel on the part of all people, shall we see an ever-increasing tendency to know and understand the people with whom we do business, even though they may be located one thousand or three thousand miles from us.[66]

The image of the traveling businessman was well ingrained in the public mind. The airport builders were quite cognizant of this, but few appreciated the fact that business travel was not random movement. All cities were not equal, and the movement from one point to another was less a function of the quality or caliber of a locality's airport than of the nature of that community's economic base. Thus, although one could not fly to a place without an airport, all of the places to which the existing air transport customers wanted to go did have such facilities.

Michael Conzen's influential work on bank capital flows shows how the movement of money parallels patterns of urban development. In his study of the Midwest, Conzen shows how cities such as Milwaukee, which exerted regional dominance, were in fact closely linked to the capital markets of New York. Using Conzen's work, William Cronon mapped out the relationships between major American cities and lower-order cities based on the patterns of correspondent banking.[67]

By 1917 the majority of America's largest and most significant business enterprises had been established. The top managers of these firms were not arbitrarily selecting destinations for travel. The airline routes that coincided with the most important business destinations were well traveled.[68]

The financial community dominated the market. Banks, investors, securities traders, and insurance companies had been the first to use airmail. As part of the most rapidly growing sector of the economy, financiers readily experimented with this newest mode of travel. This group, along with the upper echelons of the largest American industries, embraced the belief that "time is money."[69] The ideas of Frederick Taylor and scientific management had assigned monetary value to the most minute movements of the worker; likewise, the executive began to measure his time in increasingly smaller units.[70] Air travel became identified as the premium means of transportation. It should be noted, then, that during the interwar period, the size and profitability of a given firm, as well as its end product, determined the likelihood of air travel, and the location of that firm's subsidiaries and suppliers indicated the overall patterns of travel.

Apart from the pragmatic appeal (which was limited due to the cost) there was a romantic appeal. The titans of business were not immune to the dramatic imagery of aviation. The cult of the ace, first developed during World War I, received increasingly fuller expression during the 1920s and 1930s. Lindbergh's flight and the public's subsequent adulation of that accomplishment reveal just how potent the image of the ace was in American society. Further, aviation was being run by actual World War I aviation veterans. To fly was to literally come close to that archetype.[71]

This made flying very attractive. To fly was to identify with the modern. Airports became a means for communities to invest in progress and to display their commitment to the future.[72] The realization that this sort of investment had limited value unless a national air transportation system, including a network of airports, was established evolved slowly and was expressed in different ways during the interwar period. One common feature that was shared by all airports and that transcended each of the historical periods was the importance of speed. Speed was the dominant value, and it guided decisions from site location to passenger amenities. The more easily recognizable this fact was, the more highly prized the airport was as a civic monument.[73]

By 1938, airports achieved the basic form that would sustain them through the era of deregulation in the 1980s. The most important discovery was that municipalities alone could not create a national air network, just as the raw material suppliers alone could not forge a modern business enterprise. A singular centralized authority was needed to make each viable, which in the case of air transport was the federal government.

Local and federal governments made vital contributions to the development of a national system of airports. Of even greater influence was the "consumer" of these facilities. In her influential essay "The Consumption Junction," Ruth Schwartz Cowan wrote, "I focus on the consumption junction, the place and the time at which the consumer makes choices between competing technologies, and try to ascertain how the network may have looked when viewed from the inside out, which elements stood out as being more important, more determinative of choices, than the others, and which paths seemed wise to pursue and which too dangerous to contemplate."[74]

The "consumer" who was making the choices among competing transportation technologies for intercity travel was the "modern business enterprise" described by Alfred Chandler. The government's 1933 passenger traffic study noted that there were "two great divisions into which travelers may be grouped—those who travel through necessity and those who travel through desire. Among air travelers the great expense of flying minimized the total number of the latter."[75]

Air travel ranked equivalent to deluxe rail service in terms of speed but was plagued by higher fares, greater hazards, the separate expense of baggage transportation, and the general inaccessibility of airports.[76] Still, these conditions had been consistently improving, and by 1933 (certainly by 1935) there was a substantial shift in public opinion. The rhetoric of speed had become commonplace. Distance had come to be referred to in terms of time rather than miles. Although that change had, in fact, been precipitated by the railroads, popular perception gave greater credit to the airplane. Speed as a cultural value was embedded in popular conceptions of air transportation.[77]

As noted earlier, Chandler has argued that the central characteristic that differentiates the modern business enterprise from its predecessors lay in the processes of production. The new firm was different in its "potential for exploiting the unprecedented cost advantages of the economies of scale and scope."[78] What Chandler does not fully describe is the significance of location to the development of the firm.

One of the most important locational theorists of the interwar period was Alfred Weber. Weber argued that the study of industry location was a vital part of understanding the local distribution of economic activities. "In each economic organization and in each stage of technical and economic evolution there must be a 'somewhere' as well as a 'somehow' of production, distribution, and consumption."[79] For Weber, transportation costs were the most basic element determining location. He also believed that for the most part, the location of consumption was subordinate to the location of production and distribution.[80]

Weber's thinking influenced those city planners who had begun to define the process of planning an airport in the language of systems. In 1930 Jacob Crane wrote "Reflections of a City Planner on His Profession." He argued that airports, zoning, and subdivision control were the three most influential factors in shaping the planning profession. "The exciting topic of air travel supplies one of the most interesting new influences in city planning," Crane wrote. "Is there a man with a soul so dead that he has not enthusiastically supported the idea of more and more 160-acre airports? Probably not."[81] These city planners believed that by planning transportation networks, one could influence the location of industry and the quality of life within the city and could ultimately expand the nation's economy.

In 1938 the American Society of Planning Officials and the American Municipal Association published *The Airport Dilemma: A Review of Local and National Factors in Airport Planning and Financing*.[82] The report reflected and amplified the sentiments of many city planners: Airports needed to be planned, built, financed, and operated according to a national plan. The authors concluded:

> I have endeavored to point out that we are now giving a national service paid for by local taxpayers. The advantage afforded the city is nil in so far as our airports increase commerce and trade for respective merchants of our cities. There is nothing left but prestige and you know very well, as I do, that taxpayers are not interested in the prestige. They may have been enthusiastic when the airport was first developed but that enthusiasm has waned to a point where they do not want the burden, preferring to have it rest upon the federal government and the state government where it rightfully belongs.[83]

The basic issue was that airports were not serving specific communities but rather the operations of large national business enterprises. Although this fact was slowly gaining recognition, the federal government, to ameliorate the effects of the depression, had in fact started a program of national funding for airports. Experience with federal funding strongly suggested that the federal government and *not* the municipal governments should shoulder the burden of planning. Nonetheless, there were two competing visions for how such a system of airports might be organized—one with a local orientation, the other with a national perspective.

The reason for this duality of perception becomes clear if one examines the patterns of urban development. Urbanization means both the changes that take place within a specific city and the changing relationships among all cities.[84] In the United States before World War II there were significant changes in the character, shape, and size of cities. In 1910, the U.S. Census Bureau recognized the existence of a new type of urban area, one that extended beyond the traditional boundaries of the central city. These "metropolitan districts" were defined on the basis of population density. Urban areas were expanding throughout the interwar period. In particular, the rate of growth was highest in the satellite areas that ringed the central city.[85] A demographer of the period noted: "The development of trade and service industries in the larger metropolitan districts . . . probably accounted for much of their population growth in the 1930s. . . . The larger metropolitan districts are becoming trade and service centers and centers of financial and industrial control in an increasingly complex system."[86]

The assessments of the Census Bureau demographers correspond with a type of urban development called a "network system." In network systems, cities were linked together through patterns of trade. Cities were nodes of distribution that created demand for goods and services. In particular, they coordinated the flow of goods from one region to another. The principal economic players were merchants and bankers, who benefited from the constant movement of resources, goods, and capital from one place to another.[87]

This new pattern of urban relationships in the United States was being superimposed on an older image that viewed the relationships among cities as hierarchical. This was the idea that the city was a "central place" that performed administrative services and whose primary function was to consume the surplus goods produced by the surrounding hinterlands.[88]

How contemporaries viewed the significance and character of urban development during this period was clearly reflected in the competing visions of air transportation technology. Those that understood cities as central places thought air transport would be used as was the automobile; those that identified cities as links in a network looked to the railroad. From the perspective of hindsight, it is clear that air transport could have developed along either line. The omnipresence of "speed," the lack of sufficient local capital, and the fact that the consumer of airports was the national business enterprise, however, resulted in the dominance of the national system builders.

I have titled this paper "Airports as Systems and Systems of Airports" as a way of suggesting the bifurcated nature of air transportation as a type of large technological system. As I have tried to indicate in the first section, the individual airport facility was itself a technological system. Its design, construction, and operation involved a myriad of complex relationships. The "airport" evolved from the landing field of sod. By the end of the interwar period an "airport" had come to mean a geographic site with multiple acting and interacting technological subsystems. Its purpose was to be a point of fast transfer in the movement of people and goods.

But what made an airport valuable was the fact that there were many others. The airline companies, which were responsible for coordinating the movement of airplanes (and payloads), made choices of routes based on their best assumptions of consumer demand. In the second part of this paper I have suggested who that "consumer" was. The airlines were aware that the patterns of business travel affected the use of their services, but this knowledge was derived empirically and not from any specialized analysis. The principal actors in the world of commercial air transportation slowly identified the symbiotic relationship between transportation networks and the economic geography of American business. The airlines' primary means of stimulating customer demand, however, was through the development of special aircraft dedicated to carrying passengers. Only secondarily did attention refocus on the airport and its role in speeding the transfer of capital from one destination to another.

The major obstacle to the development of air transportation was the problem of finance—who was going to pay for the airports. For Europeans the answer was simple—the government was responsible. But in the United States the problem was seemingly intractable. In the era of the "red scare" and a visceral fear of Bolshevism, the idea of government subsidy for airports was philosophically unpalatable. In addition, the potential cost seemed well beyond the acceptable limits of federal spending, especially in light of the depression that had followed World War I.

On the surface, airports seemed to be local institutions, and municipalities seemed to be the immediate beneficiaries. The airplane itself was of limited range and capacity, so few imagined that air transport would ever mimic the scale and scope of the railroad. Besides, the reasoning went, airplanes were

different from trains. The image of the airplane was one of freedom of movement in any direction and dimension. This image eclipsed the reality that in
order for aviation to serve a commercial purpose—in order to merchandise
speed—it had to conform to schedules and routes and have convenient points of
interchange with surface transportation.

The small local enterprise still loomed large in America's consciousness. Big
businesses were disliked and feared by the general public. The response to in-
dustrialism, as Samuel Hayes so eloquently put it, was one of fear—fear of the
changes that industrialization had already wrought in every aspect of American
life. There was a degree of ambivalence about support for the infrastructure that
would enhance and support the expansion of big business, ambivalence that had
to be overcome if a commercial air transportation system was to be constructed.

The rise of commercial air transportation began as the Populist-Progressive
period was losing steam. The war had changed attitudes. The city planning profession that emerged during this time was imbued with optimism and the belief
that it was possible to mitigate the negative consequences of industrialization
and urbanization while retaining the positive aspects such as economic and material gain.

City planners seized on the airport as a way to prove their point. Here was a
transportation system that, by virtue of its newness, could be "rationally"
planned. They began by using the symbolism of flight—"man's oldest dream"—
and proudly trumpeted the triumph of heavier-than-air flight. By defining airports as a symbol of a community's commitment to the future and prosperity,
city planners and other aviation advocates were able to secure the necessary
funds to start construction.

As the historian Eric Monkkonen has noted: "Aggressive, highly conscious
local action created technologies and their subsequent adoptions. Ports, railroad rights-of-way, roads, and finance—all had to be effectively implemented
before any technology could be invested in and perfected."[89] Still, even as the
city planners focused on the airport as one important means to achieve their
dream of the "rational" city, they were acutely conscious of the fact that air
travel emphasized *intercity* movement. Airports had to share comparable technologies and be designed according to common standards. Taking this into account forced the recognition that the airport primarily served the new national
corporate interests. In other words, Ford may have been headquartered in Detroit, but it was part of a vast enterprise that connected businesses and resources
throughout the nation.

By 1938 and the passage of the Civil Aeronautics Act, these developments
had come to be identified by both local and national planners. Local planners

and municipal residents had become disenchanted with the rhetoric of progress. At that point the fundamental shape and purpose of the airport was fixed. The question of finance was resolved, and the responsibility rested squarely on the shoulders of the federal government. This was to be one of the important means by which the new national economy was regulated.

In closing, I would like to reiterate the idea that although the airport can be studied exclusively as a type of large technological system, one's understanding would be diminished without Chandler's analysis of the modern business enterprise. Further, it should also be clear that neither explanation is complete without first acknowledging the intimate connection between the airport and the city. An airport was considered an integral part of the city. Thus there are three important perspectives a historian must consider when studying modern American society. Each form of analysis informs and enriches the others. This particular case study, a history of airports, has explored the rich patterns and textures of the true impact of aviation on American society.

NOTES

1. Brian J. L. Berry, "Cities as Systems within Systems of Cities," *Papers of the Regional Science Association* 10 (1964): 147–63.

2. See Thomas P. Hughes, "The Evolution of Large Technological Systems," in Wiebe E. Bijker, Thomas P. Hughes, and Trevor J. Pinch, *The Social Construction of Technological Systems: New Directions in the Sociology and History of Technology* (Cambridge, Mass., 1987); Thomas P. Hughes, *Networks of Power: Electrification in Western Society, 1880–1930* (Baltimore, 1983); Alfred D. Chandler, *The Visible Hand: The Managerial Revolution in American Business* (Cambridge, Mass., 1977); Alfred D. Chandler, *Scale and Scope: The Dynamics of Industrial Capitalism* (Cambridge, Mass., 1990); Eric H. Monkkonen, *America Becomes Urban: The Development of U.S. Cities and Towns, 1780–1980* (Berkeley, 1988); and M. Christine Boyer, *Dreaming the Rational City: The Myth of American City Planning* (Cambridge, Mass., 1983).

3. "We Talk of Ourselves," *Ace* 1 (August 1, 1919): 20.

4. National Advisory Committee for Aeronautics, *Fifth Annual Report* (Washington, D.C., 1920), 17–18.

5. Charles C. Rohlfing, *National Regulation of Aeronautics* (Philadelphia, 1931), 16–19.

6. *Air Commerce Act, Statutes at Large* 44, secs. 568–76 (1926).

7. "Statement of Secretary Hoover on Commercial Aviation," Department of Commerce, Washington, D.C., for release September 24, 1925, Herbert Hoover—Commerce Papers, Box 40, Herbert Hoover Presidential Library, West Branch, Iowa.

8. National Advisory Committee for Aeronautics, *Twelfth Annual Report, 1926* (Washington, D.C., 1927), 11.

9. George Seay Wheat, comp. and ed., *Municipal Landing Fields and Air Ports* (New York, 1920).

10. U.S. War Office, Office of Chief of Air Service, "Airways and Landing Fields," *Air Service Information Circular* 5, no. 404 (March 1, 1923): 3–4.

11. Ibid.

12. Aeronautical Chamber of Commerce of America, "Airports in the United States and Possessions," *Aviation* 14 (January 15, 1923): 68.

13. Laurence F. Schmeckebier, *The Aeronautics Branch, Department of Commerce: Its History, Activities, and Organization* (Washington, D.C., 1930), 57–58; "Has Your Town a Landing Field? Aeronautical Safety Code Lists Necessary Requirements," *Aviation* 15 (August 13, 1923): 186.

14. Archibald Black, "Putting the City on the Airline: Why Your City Needs an Air Terminal—How It Can Be Created—Selecting the Site—Keeping Down the Cost by Planning Ahead While Providing Essentials," *American City* 29 (August 1923): 130.

15. Archibald Black, "Have You a Landing Field in Your Town?" *Aero Digest* 6 (April 1925): 186.

16. See, for example, the following: Archibald Black, *Civil Airports and Airways* (New York, 1929); Donald Duke, *Airports and Airways: Cost, Operation, and Maintenance* (New York, 1927); Stedman S. Hanks, *International Airports* (New York, 1929).

17. William P. MacCracken, Jr., "Your City, a Port of Call," *Airports* 1 (April 1928): 5.

18. Jacob A. Vander Meulen, *The Politics of Aircraft: Building an American Military Industry* (Lawrence, Kans., 1991), 92, cites Paul A. Dodd, *Financial Policies in the Aviation Industry* (Philadelphia, 1933), 3–5, 35–41.

19. Given the prominence of the U.S. Air Mail Service, the postmaster general was considered to one of the most influential posts in commercial and civil aviation.

20. Nick A. Komons, *Bonfires to Beacons: Federal Civil Aviation Policy under the Air Commerce Act, 1926–1938* (Washington, D.C., 1930), 197.

21. Henry V. Hubbard et al., *Airports: Their Location, Administration, and Legal Basis* (Cambridge, Mass., 1930). See especially the first section of the book, "The Airport in the City Plan."

22. Robert J. Pritchard, "Politics and Airports," *Airport Construction and Management* 2 (August 1930): 10.

23. "Editorial," *Airport Construction and Management* 2 (October 1930): 5.

24. Komons, *Bonfires to Beacons*, 197–201.

25. For example: Preston Sneed, "The Problem of Revenues at a Municipal Airport," *Southern Aviation* 2 (July 1931): 10–12; George C. Merkel, "An Airport as Social Center," *Western Flying* 11 (March 1932): 29; W. Sanger Green, "A Profitable Airport: Sales and Revenue as Viewed by the Privately Owned Airport," *Airway Age* 12 (April 1931): 362.

26. Ernest P. Goodrich, "The Economics of Municipal Airports," *Journal of Land and Public Utility Economics* 7 (November 1931): 341–42.

27. The Airways Division was placed in the Lighthouses Bureau of the Department of Commerce.

28. Komons, *Bonfires to Beacons,* 125–45.

29. Ibid., 147–63.

30. C. N. Connor, "Effect of Airplane Impact on Airport Surfaces," *Aviation Engineering* 7 (December 1932): 18–21.

31. A. Pendleton Taliaferro, Jr., "Traffic Control: An Approaching Problem," *Airway Age* 12 (August 2, 1931): 476–78.

32. Richard J. Neutra, "Terminals? Transfer!" *Architectural Record* 68 (August 1930): 99–104.

33. Ellmore A. Champie, *The Federal Turnaround on Aid to Airports, 1926–1938* (Washington, D.C., 1973), 4–5.

34. W. Sumpter Smith, "The WPA Airport Program," *Journal of Air Law* 7 (October 1936): 495.

35. Champie, *The Federal Turnaround,* 4–5.

36. "Airport Construction Progress," *Journal of Air Law* 5 (July 1934): 470.

37. "Recent News from the PWA and the CWA," *American City* 49 (January 1934): 72.

38. Champie, *The Federal Turnaround,* 5.

39. The Aeronautics Branch had become the Bureau of Air Commerce on July 1, 1934. This represented more than a name change. Hoover had deliberately structured the organization so that its activities would fall under the jurisdiction of existing bureaus within the Department of Commerce. For example, as noted earlier, the Airways Division was under the Bureau of Lighthouses. In 1933, all of these divisions were transferred to the Aeronautics Branch. The reorganization was completed with the new name of Bureau of Air Commerce in 1934.

40. "W. P. Airports," *Aviation* 35 (July 1936): 15–16.

41. Ibid., 16.

42. The average cruising speed of the Boeing 247 was 150 mph. The average cruising speed of the Ford Trimotor was only 100 mph.

43. Ronald Miller and David Sawers, *The Technical Development of Modern Aviation* (London, 1968), 18–19.

44. Ibid.

45. F. Robert van der Linden argues, in volume 2 of this book, that the cancellation was also intended as another dig at the much maligned Hoover administration and as a coverup for Roosevelt's lack of success in turning around the fiscal crisis of the depression.

46. Ellis W. Hawley, *The New Deal and the Problem of Monopoly* (Princeton, 1966), 226.

47. See, for example, "Making Aviation a 'Public Utility,'" *Ace* 6 (July 1, 1925): 10.

48. Hawley, *The New Deal*, 226–27.

49. Komons, *Bonfires to Beacons*, 260–62.

50. See, for example, "Our Airports Must Be Enlarged," *U.S. Air Services* 22 (December 1937): 26.

51. John S. Wynne, "Let's Have a Look at Tomorrow's Airport," *Aviation* 35 (July 1936): 13.

52. Champie, *The Federal Turnaround*, 14.

53. Ibid.

54. Ibid., 14–21.

55. "Speed . . . the Merchandising Factor," *Aviation Engineering* (January 1932), 7.

56. See, for example, Stephen Kern, *The Culture of Time and Space, 1880–1918* (Cambridge, Mass., 1983), and Michael O'Malley, *Keeping Watch: A History of American Time* (New York, 1990).

57. Chandler, *The Visible Hand*.

58. *Domestic Air News,* no. 25 (March 31, 1928): 34.

59. U.S. Federal Coordinator of Transportation, *Passenger Traffic Report,* January 17, 1935, 147.

60. Ibid., 115.

61. Ibid., 113.

62. Ibid., 7, 21, 32; Security Owners Association, *A Study of Transportation by Airway as Related to Competition with Rail Carriers in Continental United States* (New York, 1932), 27–58.

63. Joseph J. Corn, *The Winged Gospel: America's Romance with Aviation, 1900–1950* (New York, 1983), 97–104.

64. *Passenger Traffic Report,* 113.

65. Ralph L. Woods, "Merchandising . . . Study Your Social Register: The Social and Financial Leaders of the Country Are Important Factors in Selling Aviation to the Public," *Airway Age* 12 (May 2, 1931): 479–80.

66. R. L. Putman, "How Airplanes Will Affect Marketing and Production," *Domestic Air News,* no. 30 (June 15, 1928): 5–6.

67. Michael Conzen, "Metropolitan Dominance in the American Midwest during the Later Nineteenth Century" (Ph.D. diss., University of Wisconsin, 1972), 290–94; idem, "The Maturing Urban System in the United States, 1840–1910," *Annals of the Association of American Geographers* 67 (1977): 88–108; William Cronon, *Nature's Metropolis: Chicago and the Great West* (New York, 1991), 306.

68. Chandler, *The Visible Hand,* 498–500.

69. "Business Aspects of Air Transportation," *Domestic Air News,* no. 25 (March 31, 1928): 34–36; "How the Air May Be Used," *Domestic Air News,* no. 28 (May 15, 1928): 17–19.

70. Robert Wiebe, *The Search for Order, 1877–1920* (New York, 1967), 145–63.

71. See "Legend, Memory, and the Great War in the Air," Exhibition at the National Air and Space Museum, November 1991; George L. Mosse, *Fallen Soldiers: Shaping*

the Memory of World Wars (New York, 1990); Lee Kennett, *The First Air War, 1914–1918* (New York, 1991). See also chapters 2 and 3, "'A New Sign in the Heavens': The Prophetic Creed of Flight" and "'Let Your Airmindedness Be Shown Forth among Men': Evangelizing for Aviation," in Corn, *The Winged Gospel*.

72. This theme was also exploited by advertisers. An advertisement for *The Official Aviation Guide of the Airways* peppered its copy with phrases such as "modern achievement," "march of progress," "progressive business executive," and "leaders of modern civilization." See also Roger Bilstein, *Flight Patterns: Trends of Aeronautics, 1918–1929* (Athens, Ga., 1983), 147–63.

73. One of the most vivid illustrations of this point was the famous Lehigh Portland Cement Company's national airport design competition. See Lehigh Portland Cement Company, *American Airport Designs* (New York, 1930).

74. Ruth Schwartz Cowan, "The Consumption Junction: A Proposal for Research Strategies in the Sociology of Technology," in Bijker, Hughes, and Pinch, *Social Construction of Technological Systems*, 263.

75. *Passenger Traffic Report*, 38.

76. Ibid., 46.

77. Carol Aronovici, "Space-Time Planning and Airmindedness," *American City* 42 (April 1930): 104.

78. Chandler, *Scale and Scope*, 21.

79. Alfred Weber, *Theory of the Location of Industries*, trans. Carl J. Friedrich (Chicago, 1929), 1.

80. Ibid., 4.

81. Jacob L. Crane, Jr., "Reflections of a City Planner on His Profession," *Journal of Land and Public Utility Economics* 6 (February 1930): 47.

82. American Society of Planning Officials and the American Municipal Association published *The Airport Dilemma: A Review of Local and National Factors in Airport Planning and Financing*, publication no. 62 (Chicago, 1938).

83. Ibid., 24.

84. Berry, "Cities as Systems."

85. Donald J. Bogue, *Population Growth in Standard Metropolitan Areas, 1900–1950: With an Explanatory Analysis of Urbanized Areas* (Washington, D.C., 1953), 2–4.

86. Warren S. Thompson, *Population: The Growth of Metropolitan Districts in the United States, 1900–1940* (Washington, D.C., 1947), 24.

87. Paul M. Hohenberg and Lynn H. Lees, *The Making of Urban Europe, 1000–1950* (Cambridge, Mass., 1985), 62–69. See also Cronon, *Nature's Metropolis*.

88. Hohenberg and Lees, *The Making of Urban Europe*.

89. Monkkonen, *America Becomes Urban*, 164.

PART TWO

Technical Developments in Civil and Commercial Aviation

Holger Steinle

Introduction

As noted by Hans Degen, a Swiss architect and descendant of Jakob Degen, his ancestor was a talented clockmaker and inventor. Inspired by a balloon ascent, Jakob began a series of experiments in flight techniques. In 1807, Degen made his first public attempt to fly with his "oscillating wing flying machine." Later, he used a gas balloon as compensation for the missing motive power. After several successful "flights" in that manner, his economic situation forced him to abandon his flying experiments. Besides his models of helicopters driven by clockwork motors, his most famous and important invention was the technique of printing colored bank notes. A forgotten aeronautical pioneer, Degen died in 1848.

William M. Leary, of the University of Georgia, points out that in the number of passengers and passenger-miles, the air transport industry in the United States made enormous progress during the 1930s. Within a decade travel by air had become—for affluent Americans—a speedy alternative to the train. Simultaneously, air travel was growing safer. As Leary makes clear, there were technological advances in airframes and engines; however, equally important was the development of instrument flying techniques, which together with the application of radio enabled airlines to navigate from point to point in all kinds of weather with regularity and safety. The change from emphasizing the "glamour" of air travel to focusing on safety and reliability, together with falling costs, finally brought about the rapid expansion of civil aviation.

John Wegg, a well-known aviation writer and editor, illustrates the evolution of air traffic control. The problems of weather, navigation, communication, collision avoidance, and the expedition of air commerce all led to the development of a sophisticated system to control air traffic. By the beginning of World War II, fully controlled airspace with sophisticated landing aids had been introduced in Europe and the United States.

Virginia P. Dawson, associate historian of the Winthrop Group, contends that the transfer of the turbojet was probably the most important technical development in commercial aviation after World War II. She emphasizes the importance of the Lewis Flight Propulsion Laboratory of the National Advisory Committee for Aeronautics in stimulating American turbojet development. British engines as well as the engines of Pratt & Whitney, General Electric, and Westinghouse were tested. This federally funded laboratory promoted competition and technical innovation among American companies in two ways: by acting as a clearinghouse for British turbojet technology and by distributing its research findings. By the mid-1950s, Pratt & Whitney and General Electric had both succeeded in building engines superior to those of the British.

 Hans Degen

Jakob Degen and the Art of Flying

Jakob Degen developed and built, in the first decade of the 19th century, an apparatus with flapping wings. His flying experiments in Vienna in the presence of the emperor and the court made headlines throughout Europe. Later, his attempts to fly with various helicopter models did not find the same resonance among the general public and were largely forgotten. His revolutionary system of printing bank notes remains current technology today but, outside the field of specialized literature, is practically unknown. In present-day German textbooks one can find mention of his aeronautical work, but it is all very fragmentary. In French writings his name crops up, but only with reference to the flapwing machine. Thereby, the malicious pleasure taken by French writers over his unsuccessful experimental flight in Paris is allowed to obscure his very real successes. Reference books of the English-speaking world hardly mention him at all. Practically all the sources cited in German-language technical literature can be traced back to the Swiss aviation expert Dr. E. Tilgenkamp. His series "Swiss Aviation" was published in 1942. Because of the war in Europe it was impossible to carry out research on the spot, and there were important lacunae in the information as well as mistaken interpretations (e.g., concerning Degen's origin). These omissions and errors have been rectified here.

7.1. Jakob Degen. Watercolor by
Adalbert Suchy in the Historical
Museum of the City of Vienna.
(Courtesy Museum of the City of
Vienna)

Jakob Degen was born in 1760 in Liedertswil, then part of the old canton of
Basel, Switzerland. The Degen clan in Liedertswil were all silk-ribbon weavers. This was a craft that was both a main and a secondary occupation, since the
people could not live adequately merely from pasturage in the high Jura
Mountains.

Silk-ribbon weaving had been brought in by religious refugees, the so-called
Huguenots, from the south of France. The Basel silk-ribbon weavers made considerable improvements in the loom design and not only were masters of their
craft but for a long time were the unchallenged masters. The Empress Maria
Theresa wanted to introduce the craft into Austria, and a number of silk-ribbon
weavers from the Basel hinterland were persuaded to emigrate to that country,
taking their looms with them. Among them were the parents of Jakob Degen
and two of his uncles. Jakob Degen was 11 years old at the time, and besides
attending school he also had to work part time, as was customary in those
days—in this case at the weaving looms. Living in Vienna, he remained faith-
ful to the craft of silk-ribbon weaving until he was 19. In his spare time he re-
paired the watches of his comrades. Thanks to his exceptional technical and
craftsman's skill he was allowed to become an apprentice clockmaker and, at

the age of 32, obtained his master's certificate. Various sources indicate that already during this period he had made several inventions in the fields of weaving techniques and clockmaking.

Moreover he was, for 17 years, the organist in the Protestant church, which had a Helvetian or rather Zwinglian character and a strongly national propensity. This church, together with other religions, was officially permitted in ultra-Catholic Vienna only from 1784 on. Yet this ghetto-like crowding together of the silk-ribbon weavers in their own street, the Bandgasse (Ribbon Alley), and in their own church and school explains why Jakob Degen's obituary stressed that to the end of his life Degen remained true to his "Swiss way."

Jakob Degen was so fascinated by the spectacle in the Vienna Prater when the famous French balloonist Jean Pierre Blanchard made his ascents that Degen decided also to experiment in flight techniques. In his theoretical studies and practical tests he was strongly supported by the Jesuit scholar Dr. Stelzhammer, who later became dean of the University of Vienna. Degen attended the lectures on mathematics, mechanics, and experimental physics. In the memoranda of these later years he described how he wanted to accept "the challenge of flying." He observed the flight of birds and analyzed their body and wing structures. In these memoranda also he included practically everything that concerned human flight, starting with the myth of Daedalus and Icarus and concluding with the balloonists of his own time. It is interesting that Leonardo da Vinci is nowhere mentioned. This confirms the historians' view that Leonardo's sketches and notes on the subject were unknown at that time. Degen, with his connections, would surely have known about them.

The practical consequence of his studies was the construction of a flap-wing apparatus. Degen was 45 when he made this machine, whose wings contained 3,000 flaps that closed on the down-stroke. By means of striker rods connected to the wings, he could include leg kicks as an additional motive force. The material for the wings consisted of varnish-impregnated paper on a framework of reeds. The wings had a surface area of 12.2 meters and a span of 6.7 meters. In the Spanish Riding School he installed a device to provide the drive power. He discovered that although he indeed obtained drive, it was insufficient to enable lift-off using his physical strength alone. The following calculation is taken from the data given at the time: "He weighed 119 pounds, the flying machine 25 pounds and the friction of the roller 9 pounds. The necessary counter-weight to compensate for the motive power lacking, was 75 pounds."

He made up this power deficiency with a self-constructed gas balloon, and with a further development of the flap-wing machine he achieved flight movements in any desired direction. Before starting with the flight movements, he balanced the balloon with lead-shot ballast in order then to obtain lift-off by means of flapping the wings. To calculate the air currents, he built a special, absolutely innovative wind-gauge. On September 10, 1810, in the presence of the Emperor Francis I and the whole court, he demonstrated what was for him the most important ascent in Vienna. The flight was successful and lasted a full four hours. Jakob Degen received, apart from the costs of the flight, an imperial gift of 4,000 guldens. The emperor wanted to make sure, however, that he was not going to be the victim of a hoax, and beforehand he had ordered everything checked and a test flight made under scientific supervision. Weight, capacity, wind velocity, and temperature were exactly determined both at the start and at the landing. Surveyors ascertained by means of theodolites the actual altitudes reached and the number and direction of movements. This successful flight experiment, witnessed by the emperor, was subsequently chronicled in detail by Degen's teacher Dr. Stelzhammer. This record was published in the Munich *Annals of Physics* for the benefit of the scientific profession.

His reputation spread to the Western world, principally in the gutter press, which introduced him to a wide public but in a much less sober and scientific approach. Wonders were told in connection with him, and soon businesspeople approached him with the proposal to come to Paris, where he would be a great public attraction. Arriving in Paris, accompanied by his 12-year-old son, he found that he was supposed to make an ascent almost immediately, his manager having already announced the first flight. But the arduous, bumpy journey by coach had damaged his machine, and one of the wings had been broken by too eager spectators, so he had to postpone the ascent. The next day the weather was unfavorable, but the impatient public refused to accept a further postponement. There was such a strong wind, however, that he was unable to fly in the direction he wanted to. Promptly the first satirical drawings and prints appeared, poking fun at Degen. He was also the target of verbal attacks by some of the French balloonists, who saw in him a dangerous foreign competitor in what had been until then—worldwide—French supremacy in aeronautics. This campaign reached its peak in a disgraceful libel. Another, this time successful, ascent followed on July 7, 1812. But his luck soon deserted him again. A third flight on October 5, 1812, ended in a catastrophe. Again the wind was too strong, the public clamorous for action. To add to his misfortunes, an assistant mistakenly worked the cord of the safety valve instead of the mooring rope. The balloon lost gas during the ascent. It sank, and the strong wind drove it into the trees. The spectators, who felt that they had not got their money's worth, attacked him physically, until the police had to intervene. There was also an attempt to institute a police investigation of his case, but this was going too far even for the Paris balloonists. They signed and sent to the prefects a declaration that, to their knowledge, "no aviator would have attempted to make an ascent against such a violent wind and with a loss of gas, thereby seeking, like Degen, to defy the dangers."

But the mob had its victim: Jakob Degen became the most famous citizen of Paris in his day. Lampoons appeared; he was the main subject of the carnival; even two scurrilous plays had his mishaps as their subject matter. That Jakob Degen had a hard time of it in Paris was to a great extent the consequence of the exaggerated hopes and expectations of the so-called Age of Enlightenment. There had been a whole series of literary fictions dealing with the idea of human flight, first and foremost the work *Le Nouveau Dedal* by Jean-Jacques Rousseau, the most famous visionary of the 18th century, who himself had announced that he would fly like a bird and brooked no doubters.

Jakob Degen's last flight performance took place on August 15, 1813. He had been elected a member of the Committee for the Birthday Celebrations of the Emperor Napoleon, and his flight was the main attraction. With great pomp and accompanied by a fanfare, he began the ascent from a raft in the middle of the Seine. I quote from a contemporary journal, "With the aid of his wings he floated horizontally towards the Pont Royal, in order to rise from there to a height of 900 'klaftern' and, following the course of the Seine, to soar over the whole of Paris."

But his good fortune did not last long. Napoleon was on his way to defeat at the Battle of Leipzig. The Allied armies entered France in 1814 and again in 1815, after Napoleon's downfall. In the turbulence of 1815, Paris had other things to think about. When the Austrian emperor, about to return to Vienna after the conference of the Allied leaders, offered to take Jakob Degen back with him in one of the imperial coaches, the offer was immediately accepted. There is no record of any later flights with the flap-wing machine.

The long way to the development of the modern winged aircraft was led by the German aviation pioneer Otto Lilienthal. He repeated the attempts with a flap-wing machine similar to that used by Degen and confirmed that propulsion by manpower alone was not possible. In 1896, with his rigid-wing glider, he showed the way to the future. His first flight carried him all of 15 meters through the air.

Some 80 years earlier Jakob Degen had been interested in the glider properties of his apparatus, but only in case he had to make a forced landing. He described these glider properties in detail and deliberately included them in his construction. Stelzhammer confirmed these glider properties in his accounts. It now seems clear that this was indirectly reconstructed by Degen's still better known epigone, the Ulm tailor Berblinger. Today historians are convinced that Berblinger successfully carried out short glider flights before his unfortunate plunge into the Danube (having been given a push into it). Jakob Degen's flap-wing apparatus can thus be described as a sort of hang glider.

Back in Vienna Jakob Degen was 55 years old, older than the average life expectancy at the time. In his luggage he had brought with him further new forms of flying machines that he had made in Paris. But he could no longer present them to the public. However, I discovered an announcement in the *Journal de Paris*. He describes them as his "small machines," the first helicopter models capable of flying. I assume that he knew of the airscrew produced in 1784 by the Frenchmen "Launoy and Bienvenue," who designed it as a toy made of birds' feathers. By means of a cord and the spanning of a bow it could lift itself into the air. Degen mentioned windmill wheels, among other things, as giving him the idea of the helicopter. Here too Leonardo da Vinci, at the beginning of the 16th century, had worked on the idea of an airscrew. But again he had gone no further than making a sketch of it.

Jakob Degen explained his helicopter as follows: "My intention was only to show that one could raise a body against the pull of gravity by means of fixed wings, (i.e. airscrews) set in motion by a clockwork motor. That my self-acting device can rise vertically, stand still in flight, descent and rise again is caused by a double (i.e. two-stage) clockwork, of which the one is always active when the other halts in its rotation." He tried first to use his adjustable airscrew in a horizontal position to the dirigible control of the balloon. For this he invented a vertical steering rudder, modeled on the tail fins of fishes. With this he had anticipated no less than the principle of the later airship. Subsequently he employed the airscrew as a vertical wing. In June 1817 one of his models, weighing six kilos, rose to the height of 160 meters in the Vienna Prater. Yet even people with a knowledge of physics could make very little of the experiments in those days. Probably the testing of models was too abstract, since they could not be directly related to human flying. In any case the general public was more concerned with immediate, important problems; a famine raged, the like of which has not been experienced since. Naturally the clock motors Degen had developed from the clockmaking techniques were not able to produce an adequate and long-lasting performance, either for the dirigible balloon (responsible for the later zeppelin) or for the helicopter.

One of his successful helicopter models was preserved in the Physics Institute of the University of Vienna. An assistant at the observatory later made a test of its capacities and in a written report noted that to lift a man weighing 130 pounds, this system would need to produce the united power of 20 men. "Thus the uselessness of the whole system for practical purposes is fairly proven." Looking back, one realizes that Weiss actually had delivered the proof of its usefulness. If his calculation is correct, today a two- to three-horsepower engine would be enough to lift these 130 pounds into the air.

It was not until the advent of the internal combustion engine some 60 years later that this precondition was given. Yet the first properly functioning helicopter was produced in 1920. Although many of the models constructed before this date bore a remarkable technical resemblance to Degen's helicopter principle, it was the Spaniard Juan de la Cierva who achieved the breakthrough in 1920 with his construction of a helicopter capable of flight. Meanwhile Degen, heavily in debt, gave up his flying experiments and resumed his work as a clockmaker.

From 1816 onward Vienna was plagued by the circulation of forged bank notes. Jakob Degen saw in this a new opportunity for one of his inventions. In 1810, before his stay in Paris, he had developed a "Wheel-cutting and stamp-engraving machine" (Guillochier machine), without, however, finding anyone interested in it. At that time bank notes were printed by using the wooden hand-press. So Jakob Degen improved his Guillochier machine until he had perfected

7.2. Jakob Degen's headstone.
(Hans Degen Collection)

it and devised a printing process, based on the Congrave printing method, for the production of multicolored bank notes. He etched rosettas and other patterns (the so-called guilloche) with the machine on every color support in the print forms. Together with an absolutely exact alignment, resulting automatically from the system and the two-color printing, it was possible to produce bank notes that were practically impossible to forge. Compared with traditional procedures, his invention was a quantum jump forward. And that caused him new difficulties. The officials of the Imperial Treasury were totally confused: The weird new machine aroused their mistrust. They had tests made, called in experts to judge it, and refused to come to a decision, "passing the buck" (and the relevant documents) to others—all this in spite of the fact that "His Majesty the Emperor himself commanded the Finance Minister to promote this object." Degen found it difficult to keep his head above water financially, and finally he was declared bankrupt. But the claims of the creditors were settled by the National Bank, and in 1825 Degen was given a post in the bank for life.

At last he was free of financial worries. At the age of 67 he made his last invention: He automated the process of numbering bank notes, until then done by hand. Gradually all the other national banks began to produce their bank notes using Jakob Degen's system. His revolutionary invention is still today, in every state, the basis of the printing process for bank notes and bonds. Thanks to him, Austria gained an international reputation in the production of Guillochier machines.

Jakob Degen died in 1848 at the age of 88, 10 years after the death of his talented son, Carl, who had accompanied him everywhere and had also become overseer of the bank note printing press after Jakob's retirement. Aviation remained Degen's secret passion, however. The following is written on his gravestone, which I eventually found in St. Marx Cemetery in Vienna, amid overgrown bushes not far from the Mozart memorial: "Jakob Degen 1760–1848, Aviation technician."

William M. Leary

Safety in the Air

The Impact of Instrument Flying and Radio Navigation on U.S. Commercial Air Operations between the Wars

For the airline industry in the United States to achieve its position as the prime mover of intercity passenger traffic, two things had to happen. First, air travel had to be made safe and reliable; and second, air travel had to be able to compete economically with other forms of intercity transportation. Safety and reliability came in the years before American entry into World War II and will be discussed in this paper; the economic revolution in airfares occurred after the Second World War.

The air transport industry in the United States made remarkable progress in the decade before American entry into World War II. In 1930 U.S.-scheduled domestic airlines carried 384,000 passengers and flew 85 million passenger-miles; by 1940 the count had soared to 2.8 million passengers and more than 1 billion passenger-miles.[1] At a time of severe economic depression, travel by air made the transition from a heroic individual adventure to a speedy alternative to travel by train—at least for the more affluent segment of the population.

Of all the factors contributing to the growth of air travel during the 1930s, the most important was the remarkable advance in safety that took place during the decade. In 1930 passenger fatalities occurred at the rate of 28.2 per 100 million passenger-miles.[2] Applied to 1980—the last year that the government used the

formula of fatalities per 100 million passenger-miles—that rate would have resulted in the deaths of more than 59,000 passengers.[3] Given these chilling numbers, it is hardly surprising that, as the historian Henry Ladd Smith pointed out
in 1942, "The greatest deterrent to air travel has been *fear.*"[4]

Happily for the industry—and, of course, the passengers—the situation improved rapidly after 1930. By 1939 the accident rate had declined to 1.2 fatalities per 100 million passenger-miles.[5] In 1940 the Equitable Life Assurance
Society of America informed the Air Transport Association (ATA)—the industry's trade organization—that it was removing all restrictions on life insurance
coverage for passengers flying on scheduled airlines. The ATA promptly
launched a nationwide advertising campaign, announcing that the airline industry had achieved "Safety in the Air."[6]

Although advances in airframes and engines contributed significantly to
"Safety in the Air," the key element that enabled airlines to navigate from point
to point, in all kinds of weather, with regularity and safety, was the widespread
application of the new technology of radio to air navigation. A small group of
government scientists, engineers, and officials, together with a few airline technicians and an intrepid band of pilots, civil and military, made this epic achievement possible. Most of these individuals have been long forgotten, but men like
J. Howard Dellinger, Francis Dunmore, Clarence Young, and Marshall Boggs
were at the cutting edge of the air transport revolution that took place in the
United States during the 1930s.

"The cornerstone of aeronautics is navigation," observed the radio expert
Henry W. Roberts in 1945. Looking back on developments over the previous
quarter-century, Roberts pointed out that Europeans and Americans had taken
different approaches toward applying radio to air navigation. Proceeding on the
premise that air and sea navigation were comparable, Europeans had emphasized a system of radio direction-finding (RDF) stations. An aircraft would
transmit its call sign in radiotelegraphy, followed by a long dash. The nearest
group of three direction-finding (DF) stations would take a bearing on the signal. A master station would triangulate the bearings, then notify the pilot of his
position. This process took about 10 minutes on average. Although the system
worked fine as long as aircraft flew at 100 to 150 mph in uncrowded skies, its
limitations became apparent as the speed and number of aircraft increased during the 1930s.[7]

Developments in the United States took a different path. Instead of relying on
ground-based operators for guidance, the American system emphasized the
cockpit interpretation of radio signals.

In May 1918 the U.S. Post Office inaugurated an experimental airmail service between Washington, D.C., and New York. Second Assistant Postmaster General Otto Praeger insisted that the mail be flown in all weather conditions, leading to experiments with compasses, turn indicators, and other instruments. It soon became apparent, however, that radio might provide the best answer to aerial navigation in bad weather.[8]

Experiments with radio direction finding began in February 1919. With assistance from the U.S. Navy, the post office installed direction-finding equipment on a Curtiss R4L biplane. One coil of rubber-covered aircraft wire—known as the "A" coil—was wound between the entering and trailing struts of the airplane, while another coil of wire—the "B" coil—was wound at a right angle to the A coil. The two coils were connected to batteries, a six-stage amplifier, a variable condenser, and a switch. Radio stations emitting a nondirectional signal on 1,050 meters were located at College Park (outside of Washington), Philadelphia, and Newark. The pilot, wearing a helmet with rubber ear cushions, kept the airplane headed in the direction of maximum signal strength by using the A or longitudinal coil. As he neared the station, he would obtain more precise directional information by switching to the B coil for minimum signal strength, or null.[9]

A number of flights took place over the next year, with mixed success. Pilots complained that the headgear caused considerable pain after an hour. Also, the airborne receiver proved temperamental. The major problem, however, centered on ignition interference. When attempts to shield the ignition and RDF circuits proved fruitless, the post office abandoned the use of the A and B coil system and installed a rotatable coil near the tail of a twin-engine Martin mail plane. A radio operator received directional signals by means of a trailing wire antenna. He also had a one-half kilowatt spark set for radiotelegraph communication with the ground.[10]

Tested in the summer of 1920, this new arrangement produced promising results. In late July James C. Edgerton, a postal official, reported to Praeger that the remaining problems with the system could be solved. "Future development must be toward successful utilization of adequate radio navigational instruments," Edgerton explained. "This is the only possible way in which long distance flights can consistently be made under varying weather conditions." Praeger approved, and Congress appropriated $87,000 for the development of radio aids to navigation.[11]

On August 20, 1920, Edgerton established and took charge of the Radio Division of the Air Mail Service of the U.S. Post Office. Experiments continued into the fall of 1920, but the work of the new division soon came to an end. In the winter of 1920–21, Praeger focused his attention on the development of a

8.1. Martin mail plane used for radio experiments by the U.S. Post Office's Air Mail Service, 1920. (Courtesy National Air and Space Museum [A-1983])

transcontinental air route and lost interest in the radio project. The new Republican administration of Warren G. Harding, which took power in March 1921, disliked government operation of the airmail service and cut its appropriations. The Radio Division disappeared.[12]

Just when the post office's experiments with radio aids to navigation were ending, the U.S. Army Air Service took the initiative in sponsoring important work with directional radio beacons. In December 1920 the army asked scientists at the U.S. Bureau of Standards, the government's research facility, for assistance in developing radio navigational aids. Francis H. Engel and Francis W. Dunmore, at the suggestion of Percival D. Lowell, began experiments with a crossed-field pattern of coil, or loop, antennas. Two single-turn coil antennas, each 40 by 150 feet, were placed at an angle of 135 degrees to each other. A two-kilowatt spark transmitter, operating on a frequency of 300 kHz, was used to impress the dot and dash of the Morse code letter "A" on one antenna and the dash of a "T" on the other. The signal was alternated from one antenna to the other every second. This produced an equisignal radiation path, or radio beam, at the bisector of the angles formed between the two coils. A Bureau of Lighthouses tender in the Potomac River detected the equisignal path of one and one-quarter miles in width—where the "A" and the "T" could be heard with equal strength—at a distance of 31 miles from the transmitter. This marked the beginning of the four-course, low-frequency radio range that would become the primary means of en route radio navigation by U.S. airlines during the 1930s—and after.[13]

Operational tests of the radio beam began in the fall of 1921, when the Bureau of Standards established an aerial navigation project at the Army Air Service's McCook Field, near Dayton, Ohio. The army equipped a De Havilland DH-4 biplane with a radio receiver and trailing wire antenna for the tests. Early flights revealed the need for a heavy weight at the end of the trailing wire so that it would hang in a nearly vertical position; this provided the best signal reception. When this was done, the pilot of the DH was able to follow the radio beam to McCook Field from a distance of 100 miles.

Despite the promising results, the army's work on radio aids to navigation received minimal funding over the next three years. The Bureau of Standards withdrew from the project, leaving a handful of army officers and civilian technicians to carry on the work. In 1923 experiments directed by Captain William H. Murphy led to two important improvements of the beacon system. First, building on the work of the Italian radio pioneers Ettore Bellini and Allessandro Tosi, Murphy's group developed a device—a goniometer—that eliminated the need to rotate the antenna array to change the direction of the beam. Second, the army experimenters changed the radio signals to the Morse code "N" (dash-dot) and "A" (dot-dash), then adjusted the transmission of the dots and dashes so that a pilot in the equisignal zone would hear a "T," or continuous dash.[14]

By 1925 the army not only was conducting flight tests on the improved beacon at McCook but also had assisted the Air Mail Service to install a beacon at a new experimental test facility at Monmouth, Illinois. The Air Mail installation contained one further improvement: instead of the spark transmitter used by the army beacon, the Air Mail beacon employed vacuum tubes.[15]

At this point, the federal government ended a lengthy debate and agreed both to subsidize and to regulate commercial aviation in the United States. In 1925 Congress laid the foundations for subsidy by passing the Air Mail or Kelly Act. This landmark piece of legislation led influential businessmen to develop a new commercial airline industry. The following year Secretary of Commerce Herbert Hoover took the lead in shaping the Air Commerce Act, which directed the federal government to foster air commerce by designating and establishing airways, operating and maintaining aids to air navigation, licensing pilots and aircraft, and investigating accidents.

On January 21, 1926, Assistant Secretary of Commerce J. W. Drake met with

J. Howard Dellinger, chief of the Radio Section of the Bureau of Standards, to discuss the implications of the proposed Air Commerce Act. Since the proposed legislation directed the Department of Commerce to assume responsibility for maintaining aids to aerial navigation, Drake wanted to be sure that the department was ready for the job. "He believes," Dellinger noted, "that a considerable research program should be undertaken—and hopes to obtain funds for it." Drake asked Dellinger to prepare a program of work on aircraft radio.[16]

Dellinger responded with a memorandum entitled "Radio in Air Navigation," which was sent to Drake on February 15 over the signature of George K. Burgess, director of the Bureau of Standards. Ground equipment, the memorandum noted, included transmitting and receiving equipment for voice communication with aircraft, a directional radio beam transmitter for en route navigation, and a localized radio system for assistance with landings. Aircraft radio equipment included a radiotelephone transmitter and receiver, plus receivers for the navigational signals. Dellinger went on to outline a research program to determine the best frequencies for communication and navigation, develop better antennas, eliminate ignition interference, improve the directional beam, and develop radio aids for landing. A vast amount of work would be necessary to place aircraft radio on an established engineering basis, Dellinger observed, but the results "should materially enhance the utility, safety, and success of air navigation." In his covering letter, Burgess informed Drake that preliminary research could get under way during the current fiscal year with the bureau's existing budget. Thereafter, the program would require special funding of about $50,000.[17]

On June 22, 1926, one month after President Calvin Coolidge signed the Air Commerce Act into law, Drake convened, at the Department of Commerce, a conference on radio aids to air navigation; it was attended by representatives of the Commerce, War, and Navy departments, the U.S. Post Office, the National Advisory Committee for Aeronautics, and three new airlines (Colonial, National Air Transport, and Robertson). Dellinger presided. The conference concluded that radio aids were "required for successful air navigation" and that the federal government was responsible for the ground installation and maintenance of such aids. Voice communication to and from aircraft was labeled "the most essential radio aid" to ensure safe flying and landing and should be given first priority. Also, directional radio beams, located about 200 miles apart, should be established as soon as possible on all flying routes. The development of radio aids for landing was given less pressing priority.[18]

Work at the Bureau of Standards got under way with the start of the new fiscal year on July 1, 1926. Arrangements were made to lease a former Air Mail Service field at College Park, Maryland, and contracts went out for construction of a wooden tower and house for the radio beacon. By the end of the year, flight tests were being made with the radio beacon and radiotelephone equipment. Six months later, a second radiotelephone and beacon system went into service at the Air Mail field at Bellefonte, Pennsylvania, on the New York–Chicago route. A third beacon at Cleveland followed shortly thereafter.[19]

The early months of 1927 saw two other radio beacons come on the air. The General Electric (GE) company built an experimental beacon station at Hadley Field, New Jersey, the eastern terminus of the transcontinental airmail route. Similar to existing beacons, the GE installation, according to Bureau of Standards observers, was intended to obtain technical data.[20] The second beacon went into service at Dearborn, Michigan, as property of the Ford Motor company. In fall 1926, when experimental work ended at McCook Field, Ford had hired Eugene C. Donovan, the civilian engineer who had largely been responsible for the technical developments achieved under Captain Murphy's direction. It was Donovan who had developed the automatic signaling system that produced the constant dash of the on-course signal and other refinements of the original Bureau of Standards equipment. He now continued this work at Ford, which later filed and received a patent for the automatic signaling device. The Ford beacon was a state-of-the-art system, using vacuum tubes and incorporating a nondirectional marker beacon of limited range. Stout Air Services, a Ford subsidiary, used the system on flights between Detroit and Grand Rapids.[21]

In August 1927 the post office's Air Mail Service—in its last month of operation before private airlines took over the government's airmail routes—outfitted a Douglas M-2 mail plane (#630) with radiotelephone and beacon receivers. Stephen T. Kaufman, the pilot, and Haraden Pratt, a Bureau of Standards radio engineer, flew between New York and Cleveland, testing the beacon system. "My first observation at night," Pratt reported to Dellinger, "revealed that the directive beacon interlocking gives erroneous courses when over 50 miles away—a serious defect."[22]

Bureau of Standards radio engineers placed major responsibility for the swinging courses at night on the characteristics of the trailing wire antenna used to receive the range signals. Over the next 10 months the bureau made substantial progress in resolving the problem. A shorter, simpler antenna was required, but this type of antenna needed a more sensitive receiving set, which in turn depended on the elimination of ignition interference.[23]

The bureau, assisted by the airlines, developed shielding techniques for magnetos, ignition cables, and spark plugs. This enabled Harry Diamond, a bureau engineer, to construct a 15-pound sensitive receiver, powered by a 15-pound, 6-volt battery. The trailing wire antenna could now be replaced by a 10-foot vertical pole-mast antenna. Test flights by National Air Transport—successor to the post office's Air Mail Service on the New York–Chicago portion of the transcontinental air route—revealed that the new antenna array went far to mitigate night effect. The problem, however, would not be solved until the development of a new ground transmitting antenna system in 1932.[24]

In early October 1928 Dellinger had an opportunity to assess the progress in developing radio aids to navigation. In a paper presented before the First Aeronautic Safety Conference in New York City, he observed that aviation had taken dramatic strides in recent years with the appearance of new aircraft, airports, and airways. Nonetheless, air travel had been slow to develop. The airplane would not become an important means of transportation, he argued, until passengers could rely "on a schedule service as regular as the railway trains, independent of weather or other contingencies." The solution to this problem lay in the application of radio to air navigation. Pilots could fly in fog by instruments, Dellinger said, but radio was needed to provide a course and find a landing field. Although the new radio beacon would provide the necessary course information, work was needed on a radio landing aid. "When this system is fully established," he concluded, "there is every reason to believe that the last great obstacle to safe flying will have been conquered, scheduled flight will be dependable, and passenger service can be considered established as a serious service."[25]

Three weeks after this speech, Dellinger informed Assistant Secretary of Commerce Clarence D. Young that the Bureau of Standards was contemplating experiments on radio aids for "blind" landing. Young replied that he would like to see this work pushed forward as rapidly as possible. Thus began the search for an instrument landing system.[26]

Operating on the premise that expensive, complex equipment should be on the ground, with inexpensive, simple equipment on the aircraft, Bureau of Standards personnel inaugurated the blind landing project in November 1928. The problem was to provide radio guidance that would enable a pilot to approach and land at an airport in limited visibility. A pilot had to have horizontal and vertical guidance, as well as an indication of the distance to the runway. To provide horizontal guidance, the bureau developed a low-power model of the radio beam that was used for airway flying. A reed indicator gave the pilot visual information on whether he was left or right of the proper course to the runway. A marker beacon, similar to the one used by Ford in 1927, was placed at the boundary of the airport. The major challenge came in developing equipment to provide vertical guidance. Early experiments with what was then termed "ultra-high frequencies"—100 MHz—led to a gently curved vertical radio beam, which showed promise.[27]

In January 1929, while work at College Park continued, the bureau joined the Daniel Guggenheim Fund for the Promotion of Aeronautics, which also was sponsoring a project to solve the problem of "fog-flying." At Mitchel Field, Long Island, bureau technicians installed localizer and marker beacons, which were used by James H. Doolittle when he made the first blind landing (with a safety pilot) on September 24, 1929.[28]

Doolittle's landmark feat is widely known but sometimes misunderstood. His work—together with the work of the Guggenheim Fund—was more important in developing new aircraft instruments than radio aids to navigation. From the perspective of the Bureau of Standards, Doolittle's flight had done little to advance its radio work—or certainly had accomplished nothing beyond the capabilities of its own pilots.

The real importance of the Guggenheim project came with the appearance of the Sperry artificial horizon and directional gyro—and to a lesser extent, the Kollsman sensitive altimeter. Until the development of the artificial horizon, pilots flying on instruments had to rely on their turn, ball-bank, and climb indicators to control the attitude of the aircraft. The artificial horizon greatly simplified the process. The directional gyro, which eliminated the northerly turning error of conventional compasses, permitted an instrument flying precision that previously had been impossible.

After Doolittle's flight, it took the Bureau of Standards two years to develop a three-element instrument landing system (ILS). On September 5, 1931, Marshall D. Boggs made the first blind landing without a safety pilot, using the ILS at College Park. The bureau system included a localizer, a glide slope, two marker beacons, and a cross-pointer indicator in the cockpit. In short, except for changes in frequencies and refinement of the glide slope, the 1931 system had all the elements of the ILS system that would become the international standard after World War II and that remains in use today.[29]

If Doolittle's flight on September 24, 1929, drew attention to the progress that was being made in instrument flying and radio navigation, an event that occurred four months later indicated that general acceptance of the new navigational techniques lagged far behind. On January 30, 1930, the front page of the *New York Times* featured a three-column headline: 16 PERISH IN PLANE CRASH, TRAPPED IN BURNING CRAFT ON BEACH IN CALIFORNIA. The accompanying story described in lurid detail the crash of a Ford trimotor transport, operated by Transcontinental Air Transport (TAT)-Maddux. The plane had been en route

from Agua Callente in Mexico to Los Angeles the previous evening when the
pilot, Basil Russell, encountered bad weather near Oceanside, California. He
flew lower and lower, attempting to maintain visual contact with the ground,
then reversed course. His wing clipped the ground on the turn; the plane cart-
wheeled and exploded. The 2 pilots and 14 passengers died in what the *Times*
described as "the worst aviation disaster in the annals of American commercial
aviation."

The TAT-Maddux accident revealed, with dramatic clarity, that the transition
from contact to instrument-radio flying was as much a human as a technical
problem. The first generation of airline pilots came out of a contact flying tradition. Skill was measured by the ability of a pilot to get to his destination with the
mail by flying low in bad weather. A few pilots on the eastern division of the
post office's Air Mail Service had developed the ability to climb and descend
through clouds by use of the turn, ball-bank, and climb (or airspeed) indicators;
but these pilots—and a few others—were a distinct minority.[30]

In 1928, as the first intrepid passengers climbed aboard the mail planes to
take their places amid the mail sacks, the old ways of flying continued to domi-
nate. There were 11 fatal accidents on scheduled air carriers in 1928, most involving night storms. In the same year, 14 of the 1,400 passengers carried by
the mail planes died.[31]

The next year, during which passenger traffic increased to more than 11,000,
there were 21 fatal accidents.[32] In July, Transcontinental Air Transport, an airline devoted exclusively to passengers, began operations. Two months later, on
September 3 (three weeks before Doolittle's blind landing), a TAT Ford trimotor was westbound out of Albuquerque in mountainous terrain when a sudden
storm caused the pilot, John B. Stowe, to lose sight of the ground. As he started
down to regain ground contact, he hit the side of Mount Taylor. Three crew and
five passengers died in the crash. "If this misfortune had a lesson," TAT general
superintendent Paul F. Collins observed, "it lay in insufficient intense pilot
training in instrument flying."[33]

The TAT accident occurred while airline pilots were engaged in a heated discussion over whether instrument-radio flying was feasible—or desirable. The
forum for this debate was the National Air Pilots Association (NAPA), the premier pilots' organization of the day. The controversy began in January 1929 in
the *NAPA Journal*, when Wesley L. Smith, a former post office pilot and superintendent for National Air Transport, published a lengthy description of the
blind, or instrument, flying techniques that had been developed by Air Mail
Service pilots. "Blind flying is still in its infancy," Smith concluded, "but it is
something that we must do one time or another if we are to operate air lines on

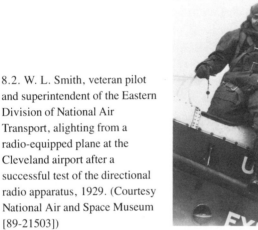

8.2. W. L. Smith, veteran pilot and superintendent of the Eastern Division of National Air Transport, alighting from a radio-equipped plane at the Cleveland airport after a successful test of the directional radio apparatus, 1929. (Courtesy National Air and Space Museum [89-21503])

regular schedules." Airlines that did not fly on a regular schedule, he warned, were "sure to fail in competition" with those that did.[34]

Smith's fellow pilots leaped into the debate in the months that followed. A few supported Smith, but most took a contrary view. Homer F. Cole, a Northwest Airways pilot, wrote in March: "All I can do is wonder and think. Wonder at how the hell they do it and think what a rotten pilot I turned out to be. The one and only thought I can express about present day fog flying is this: What's the use of it if it kills old, experienced pilots, burns up ships, burns up mail, and gives the mail service a black eye to the general public—our meal ticket."[35]

W. E. Larned, a Detroit pilot, agreed. "As far as I personally am concerned," he wrote, "I am staying under the stuff [weather] unless it is definitely local. It is a lot easier to put your passengers on a train than on an ambulance."[36] David L. Behncke, who would soon become the first president of the new Air Line Pilots Association, added his vigorous agreement in August. "Radio, beacons, blind flying and the like is, and I believe that practical men will agree," Behncke argued, "more or less hearsay, or I should say it is not practical." The best way to maintain communication with the ground, he concluded, was "by seeing it."[37]

Just as Behncke's letter appeared, the Department of Commerce placed three new radio beacons into operation. Beacons now were available on the airways from New York to Omaha and from New York to Boston.

As long as the airlines concentrated on flying the mail, the debate over instrument flying and radio navigation was not compelling. After all, a pilot could—and many did—simply bail out of his airplane when he encountered weather conditions that he could not handle. With the exception of Transcontinental Air Transport and Maddux, U.S. airlines carried few passengers. This changed in April 1930, when Congress passed the Watres Act. The new Air Mail Act substituted a space-mile formula for weight as the basis for compensating airlines. "Our government," Postmaster Walter Folger Brown announced, "has set out to develop an economically independent aviation industry by popularizing air transport and air travel." National Air Transport, American Airways, Boeing Air Transport, Transcontinental & Western Air, and other companies quickly entered the passenger-carrying business. [38]

The year 1930 was a difficult time for the emerging airline industry. U.S. airlines carried three times the number of passengers that they had in 1929—a total of 33,000. But 24 passengers died in 9 accidents. Passenger fatalities stood at 28.2 per 100 million passenger-miles. And the situation failed to improve in 1931. Over 59,000 passengers were carried by the scheduled airlines, but 25 died in 13 fatal accidents—or at the rate of 23.4 per 100 million passenger-miles. [39]

In July 1931 government officials met with airline operators and pilots in an effort to promote safer operations. The Department of Commerce proposed, among other things, that a special license be issued for pilots who were engaged in interstate passenger operations. After the pilots objected, the Commerce Department stated that this requirement, if adopted, would not be retroactive. Pilots currently employed by the airlines would not be forced to give up their jobs. [40]

By February 1932, however, the Department of Commerce had changed its mind. Assistant Secretary Clarence D. Young, encouraged by the progress made in instrument flying and radio navigation, drafted tough new standards for a proposed Scheduled Air Transport Rating (SATR), which would apply to *all* airline pilots carrying passengers. On March 1, 1932, Young announced that the new SATR license would become mandatory on January 1, 1933. Pilots, in addition to accumulating a minimum of 1,200 hours, would have to pass written and practical tests on instrument flying and radio navigation. [41]

Over the following months, Commerce Department inspectors worked with airline pilots to formulate the required test. The written portion involved questions on the theory of radio aids to navigation and on weather analysis and forecasting. In the practical test, a pilot (under a hood) had to make climbing and descending turns and steep banks to the left and right. On the final portion of the examination, the pilot had to recover from an unusual attitude, turn on his radio, and orient himself by radio range signals. He had to locate one of the four range legs, fly to the station, and pass over the cone of silence. He then descended to 1,000 feet on one of the range legs, reversed course, returned to the station, and simulated a low approach to the airport using the range leg that passed directly over the field. Between September 1 and December 31, 1932, of 725 airline pilots, 423 had passed the test for their SATR.[42]

It was no coincidence that the accident rate improved dramatically in 1933. Only 8 of the 74,000 passengers carried that year lost their lives in aviation accidents. The fatality rate had plummeted to 4.6 deaths per 100 million passenger-miles.[43]

Radio equipment improved considerably over the next seven years. The orig-

8.3. TWA "instrument ship," in which pilots were taught the technique of flying by instrument. The pilots are Arthur Burns, Howard Morgan, and Hal Snead, instructor in instrument flying. (Courtesy National Air and Space Museum [A-1797])

inal crossed-coil radio ranges were replaced by the superior transmission-line, or Adcock, ranges; simultaneous voice-beacon signals eliminated a dangerous problem; and automatic direction-finding equipment improved safety, as did a new generation of marker beacons.

Unfortunately, the administration of Franklin D. Roosevelt was slow to adopt these technical changes. Also, it took time for the airlines to realize the need for recurrent training for pilots. In the end, the airlines found it necessary to purge their ranks of the many first-generation contact fliers who refused—or were unable—to adapt to the new environment.

A series of accidents, beginning with the May 1935 TWA DC-2 crash that resulted in the death of Senator Bronson M. Cutting, called into question the safety of air travel.[44] Public scrutiny of the airline industry became intense during the winter of 1936–37, when five accidents—most involving radio navigation—killed 37 passengers and crew.[45] After an orgy of finger-pointing, the federal government in July 1937 announced a $7 million program of airways modernization. Improved Adcock ranges would replace the outmoded crossed-coil ranges; marker beacons, directional and nondirectional, would be installed throughout an expanded system of airways; and radio equipment in general would be updated.[46] By May 1, 1939, when the program was completed, the United States had 25,500 miles of airways, most equipped with the latest radio aids to navigation. Over 12,000 miles of these airways were covered by federal air traffic control.[47] In 1939 U.S. domestic airlines carried a record 1.5 million passengers. There were only 9 passenger fatalities during the year, at a rate of 1.2 fatalities per 100 million passenger-miles.[48]

Before the United States entered World War II in 1941, many of the major problems of applying radio to air navigation had been solved. Also, work was under way on the next generation of radio aids to navigation, including the higher-frequency visual omnirange (VOR), a three-element instrument landing system, and radar. However, even before these new radio aids appeared, the safety and reliability of air travel had been established. Still, air travel remained costly and was used primarily by businessmen. An economic, not a technological, revolution was required before air travel would become a commonplace means of intercity transportation.

NOTES

1. U.S. Bureau of the Census, *Historical Statistics of the United States: Colonial Times to 1957* (Washington, D.C., 1960), 467.

2. Civil Aeronautics Administration (CAA), *Statistical Handbook of Civil Aviation* (Washington, D.C., 1945), 55.

3. Federal Aviation Administration, *Statistical Handbook of Aviation* (Washington, D.C., 1981), 150.

4. Henry Ladd Smith, *Airways: The History of Commercial Aviation in the United States* (New York, 1942), 342.

5. CAA, *Statistical Handbook*, 55.

6. See *Life Magazine*, November 11, 1940, 19.

7. Henry W. Roberts, *Aviation Radio* (New York, 1945), 3, 11–13.

8. For a detailed account of the post office's flying operations, see William M. Leary, *Aerial Pioneers: The U.S. Air Mail Service, 1918–1927* (Washington, D.C., 1985).

9. James C. Edgerton, "Radio as Applied to Air Navigation in the Air Mail Service," *U.S. Air Service* 5 (February 1921): 12–14.

10. Ibid.

11. James C. Edgerton, "Horizons Unlimited," an unpublished memoir in the possession of the author.

12. Leary, *Aerial Pioneers*, 100, 102.

13. Wilbert F. Snyder and Charles L. Bragaw, *Achievement in Radio: Seventy Years of Radio Science, Technology, Standards, and Measurement at the National Bureau of Standards* (Boulder, Colo., 1986), 150–51.

14. William H. Murphy, "The Interlocking Equisignal Radio Beacon," *Aero Digest* 11 (August 1927): 172–75; F. H. Engel and F. W. Dunmore, "A Directive Type of Radio Beacon and Its Application to Navigation," January 5, 1924, *Scientific Papers of the Bureau of Standards, No. 480* (Washington, D.C., 1925).

15. Leary, *Aerial Pioneers*, 217–18; F. W. Dunmore, "Report on Trip to Inspect Crossed-Coil Equisignal Radio Beacon Development of the Air Mail Service at Monmouth, Illinois," July 25, 1925, in General Records of J. Howard Dellinger, Records of the National Bureau of Standards, Record Group 167, National Archives, Washington, D.C. (hereafter cited as Dellinger General Records).

16. J. Howard Dellinger to E. C. Crittenden, January 21, 1926, in Office Files of J. Howard Dellinger, Records of the National Bureau of Standards, Record Group 167, National Archives, Washington, D.C. (hereafter cited as Dellinger Office Files).

17. George K. Burgess to J. W. Drake, February 15, 1926, enclosing "Radio in Air Navigation," February 15, 1926, in Dellinger Office Files.

18. "Conclusions of Conference on Radio Aids to Air Navigation at Department of Commerce, June 22, 1926," in Dellinger Office Files.

19. Snyder and Bragaw, *Achievement in Radio*, 153–55.

20. Haraden Pratt and Carl B. Hempel, "Report of Trip of Investigation and Observation Relative to Radio Aids to Air Navigation," May 4, 1927, in Dellinger General Records.

21. Ibid.; Carl B. Hempel, "Report on Bureau of Standards Radio Tests Made in

Conjunction with the Stout Air Services and the Ford Motor Company on the Detroit-Grand Rapids Airline, January 4th and 5th, 1927," in Dellinger General Records; Owen Bombard interview with Charles Thomas, March 15, 1955, in Papers of Henry Ford, Edison Institute, Dearborn, Michigan.

22. Haraden Pratt to Dellinger, August 23, 1927, in Dellinger General Records.

23. George K. Burgess, "Aircraft Radio Beacon Development," *Aviation* 24 (June 18, 1928): 1764–65, 1798–1803; J. Howard Dellinger and Haraden Pratt, "Development of Radio Aids to Air Navigation," *Proceedings of the Institute of Radio Engineers* 16 (July 1928): 890–920.

24. Burgess, "Aircraft Radio Beacon Development"; Dellinger and Pratt, "Development of Radio Aids to Air Navigation."

25. J. Howard Dellinger, "Directional Radio as an Aid to Safe Flying," paper presented before the First Aeronautic Safety Conference, New York City, October 4, 1928, in Dellinger General Records.

26. Dellinger notes, "Blind Landing—Historical," n.d., in Dellinger Office Files.

27. *Air Commerce Bulletin* 2 (August 15, 1930): 79–87; H. Diamond and F. W. Dunmore, "A Radio Beacon and Receiving System for Blind Landing of Aircraft," *Proceedings of the Institute of Radio Engineers* 19 (April 1931): 585–626.

28. On the Guggenheim project, see Richard P. Hallion, *Legacy of Flight: The Guggenheim Contribution to American Aviation* (Seattle, 1977), 107–27.

29. Snyder and Bragaw, *Achievement in Radio,* 159–67.

30. Leary, *Aerial Pioneers,* 212–16.

31. U.S. Bureau of the Census, *Historical Statistics of the United States,* 470.

32. Ibid.

33. *New York Times,* September 3, 1929; Paul F. Collins, *Tales of an Old Air-Faring Man* (Stevens Point, Wis., 1983), 110–11.

34. Smith, "Blind Flying," *NAPA Journal* 2 (January 1929): 4–6.

35. *NAPA Journal* 2 (March 1929): 24–25.

36. Ibid., 31.

37. Behncke, "Flying the Night Airways," *NAPA Journal* 2 (August 1929): 15–17.

38. Walter F. Brown, "Air Mail and Passengers," *Saturday Evening Post* 203 (February 28, 1931): 23, 113–14, 118.

39. U.S. Bureau of the Census, *Historical Statistics of the United States,* 470.

40. *Air Commerce Bulletin* 3 (August 15, 1931): 87–92.

41. *New York Times,* February 17, 1932; *Air Commerce Bulletin* 3 (March 1, 1932): 415–17.

42. *Air Commerce Bulletin* 4 (December 1932): 264–66, and 4 (February 1933): 386–87; see also, Jack B. Jaynes, *Eagles Must Fly* (Dallas, 1982).

43. U.S. Bureau of the Census, *Historical Statistics of the United States,* 470.

44. See Nick A. Komons, *The Cutting Air Crash: A Case Study of Early Federal Aviation Policy* (Washington, D.C., 1973).

45. See "The Air Is How Safe?" *Fortune* 15 (April 1937): 75–80, 154, 158, 163–64, 166, 168, 170, 173–76.

46. *Air Commerce Bulletin* 9 (July 15, 1937): 1–3; Nick A. Komons, *Bonfires to Beacons: Federal Civil Aviation Policy under the Air Commerce Act, 1926–1938* (Washington, D.C., 1977), 337–46.

47. *Air Commerce Bulletin* 10 (October 15, 1939): 120–22.

48. U.S. Bureau of the Census, *Historical Statistics of the United States,* 470.

John Wegg

The Development and Emergence of Air Traffic Control in the United Kingdom and Europe, 1919–1939

When we use the term "Air Traffic Control"—or "ATC"—in Europe today, it conjures up a scene of dimly illuminated radar rooms, bustling control towers and en route centers issuing instructions by radio at a frenetic pace, hectic ramp areas, and absolute, total control of every movement of an aircraft, with all the associated restrictions and delays that are amply publicized. What is taken for granted is that the aircraft crews involved have few concerns with en route weather and navigation. It was a very different picture some 70 years ago.

Civilian air transport operations in Europe emerged in 1919 from the devastation of the Great War. Surprisingly, even though Germany was a defeated nation shackled by restrictions placed by the occupying powers, it was the first country to authorize civil airline operations, and flights started in early February 1919. But French companies were only a few weeks behind and—thanks to a farsighted and generous government—quickly established themselves on the callow air route map of Europe. In the United Kingdom, the government was slow to approve international flights, and regularly scheduled cross-Channel service by a British airline did not start until August 1919. The pilots, almost all with military experience, were a hardy lot, and the passengers they carried in mostly unreliable, cold, cramped, and noisy converted military aircraft must have possessed only a little less sense of adventure. Indeed, few travelers showed outward signs of fear.

Organization on the ground was described by one observer—with undoubted restraint—as "decidedly sketchy in nature." There was no wireless—or radio—which was later considered essential for regular operations, and weather forecasts were nonexistent. Aircraft instruments of the day consisted of a compass, airspeed indicator, tachometer, and fuel gauge, and navigation was strictly by visual contact with the ground. Pilots simply trusted in their own judgment and experience; they took off and pressed on, often in the most appalling conditions, in an effort to maintain a form of schedule. Forced landings, because of mechanical failure, impossible cloud ceilings, or visibility, were common.

This was not, it should be emphasized, an inconvenience to a particularly large number of people. Twenty cross-Channel passengers a week for an airline was considered good business in 1919, and there was a total of only 5,000 kilometers (3,000 miles) of organized air routes throughout the whole of Europe.

But improvements in aircraft equipment were rapid, and by the early 1920s relatively comfortable airliners were in service, such as the Farman Goliath, Junkers F-13, Vickers Vimy Commercial, and Fokker F-III. An enthusiastic press helped publicize anything concerning flying, and gradually film stars and other personalities began to travel by air. As aircraft were developed further and became larger and more comfortable, service in the air improved as well, with in-flight meals and drinks. And the airlines used their fleets for local joy-riding, which further encouraged public interest in flying.

As passenger traffic started to increase—cross-Channel passenger traffic exceeded 1,000 a week for the first time in August 1922—so did the demand for more reliable operations. Again, the French were quick to realize the commercial possibilities of this new form of transport and established a civil aviation ministry in January 1920, with departments for technical services, manufacturers, aerial navigation, and a national weather service. In the United Kingdom, an advisory committee on civil aviation was established in 1920, followed by passage of the Air Navigation Act later in the year. That same year an informal conference between French and British meteorological and wireless representatives decided that certain hourly weather observations should be made at several stations in each country. A "met" office was established at Croydon, the recently opened new London airport, although equipment was not installed until 1921.

Pilots could not always take early weather forecasts seriously. Expressions like "bolsons over the Channel" and "squaggy around Beauvais" were transmitted, and at the end of one bulletin was a note saying, "The cloud height given in yesterday's forecast as 3,000 meters should read 300 feet."

Attempts were also made at making navigation easier. In January 1920 the British Air Ministry announced that names would be painted on railway station roofs as an aid to pilots—who made good use of the railway lines as a visual aid. This was done at Redhill, Tonbridge, and Ashford on the cross-Channel route, and at Edenbridge the name was cut into the nearby chalk.

In addition, beacons, known as "aerial lighthouses," were installed at six points in England and nine in France along airway routes, each beacon flashing a distinctive identifier in Morse code. Of particular concern was the need to advise pilots en route of adverse weather conditions, particularly fog, and it was vital that the newly invented wireless be reduced in size and weight so that it could be carried by an aircraft. The Instone Air Line claimed it was the first airline to introduce wireless telephony between its aircraft and the ground. In August 1920 a wireless operator at Croydon connected a telephone call from the Instone offices with the company's Vickers Vimy Commercial *City of London*— nicknamed *Go Easy* after both its registration letters and cruising speed—en route from Croydon to Paris. This method of communication was called "line-switching," but it was not adopted for aircraft use because of the interference to more vital communications.

However, with the ever increasing number of flights, and the longer distances being covered, some form of effective communication with pilots was clearly essential. The Marconi Company first installed a wireless ground station at Croydon in 1920, consisting of a continuous wave and tone modulated telephone transmitter and a Bellini-Tosi direction-finding (DF) receiver. Early wireless telephony—more often referred to as radiotelephony or RT (that is, voice communication) to distinguish it from wireless telegraphy, or Morse code transmissions—left much to be desired in quality of reception, and misunderstandings were frequent. Radio was not always taken very seriously by the pilots either, since it was simpler—in good weather—to follow the railway lines or look out for landmarks than to go through a complicated procedure of flying the aircraft with one hand and operating the cumbersome radio with the other. On one occasion a pilot sang hymns into his radio all the way from Lympne to Sevenoaks, thus disrupting all communications from Croydon to other aircraft.

But air transport in Europe was coming of age. Britain and Germany consolidated several companies into national airlines; France eventually followed suit. Airliners also carried more passengers more reliably, exemplified by the great European trimotors: the Fokker F-VIIb-3m and Junkers Ju-52-3m. Steady improvements in the quality of radio equipment, with the weight of a set for avia-

9.1. Beacons, known as "aerial lighthouses," were installed along air routes in the 1920s as an aid to navigation. This is the light at Cranbrook, near London. (John Wegg Collection)

tion use reduced to less than 75 kilograms (165 pounds), and the pressing need for reliable air transport led to a widespread use of RT by the mid-to-late 1920s.

As air traffic grew and the use of radio became more common from 1922 to 1924, commercial flying became more organized. Three areas of the control of air traffic were recognized: the restriction of air traffic to certain areas because of military or security reasons or to prevent smuggling; the prevention of collisions either in the air or on the ground; and the provision of communications with aircraft in flight for navigation and safety reasons and to expedite transport.

In the United Kingdom, the Air Ministry prescribed civilian air corridors and entry-exit points, and prohibited areas, as well as aerodromes where aircraft had to make their first landing and departure—although this was more for administrative than for control purposes. In fact, the whole of the coast of Great Britain was open to air traffic. Holland had a similar open policy. France designated a corridor between Étaples, south of Boulogne-sur-Mer, and the Belgian

9.2. With a reduction in the weight of radio sets suitable for aircraft use, RT or radiotelephony (i.e., voice communication) became widespread in Europe by the mid-1920s. This radio operator is working in a Farman Goliath. (John Wegg Collection)

frontier as a point of entry from England and traced similar practicable routes from France into Belgium, Switzerland, and Italy. Other European countries were more restrictive, such as Turkey, where entry was restricted to two points.

Collision avoidance was founded on the articles of the International Convention for the Regulation of Air Navigation, signed in Paris in 1919, which was largely based on the older International Regulations for the Prevention of Collision at Sea. The articles contained General Rules for Air Traffic, divided into Rules of the Air, Rules as to Lights and Signals, and Rules for Air Traffic in the Vicinity of Aerodromes.

The world's first midair collision between two airliners occurred on April 7, 1922, resulting in seven deaths. A Paris-bound DH-18 of Daimler Airway collided over Poix, France, with a Grands Express Aeriens Farman Goliath bound for Croydon. Visibility had been poor, and both pilots had been following a railway line. The accident highlighted the need for proper organization of cross-Channel routes and adherence to the Rules of the Air. The Rules of the Air closely followed maritime practice, that is, east- and westbound sea lanes are separated. Officially recognized air traffic routes were defined by using prominent landmarks such as major roads, railways, rivers, canals, and stretches of coastline. Where there was heavy traffic, natural reference points were supplemented by light and radio beacons, and the course was defined in detail. Aircraft that elected to follow these routes had to fly at least 300 meters to the right of the routes, thus avoiding the danger of a head-on collision. Other aircraft had to remain clear of the routes or cross at right angles as quickly and as high as possible.

With the risk of collision generally the greatest near airports, special international rules were laid down, and aerodrome control was established to avoid collisions on the ground and maintain an orderly flow of traffic in the area. Very soon control towers, topped by glass "chart houses"—the contemporary term—appeared at major airports. For example, at Croydon, "The Official Air Terminus for London"—which in 1928 was able to boast the world's first "custom-built" airport terminal—the control tower was the nerve center for air traffic from the United Kingdom to the Continent. It was manned, on an outside platform, by a civil aviation traffic officer (the title was later upgraded to chief aerodrome officer), wireless (WT) operators, and aerodrome officers, who scanned for incoming aircraft. Wireless communications were possible with aircraft in flight, and the positions of all aircraft were recorded or calculated. Course instructions, weather information, and special traffic advisories could all be transmitted.

An improvement over the earlier tower was that the wireless operators were now on-site, instead of connected by land telephone line to the traffic officer from a remote station. The various offices in the tower were connected by pneumatic message tubes, and as little as five minutes elapsed between the transmission of a message from a station on the Continent and its reception at Croydon. Of course, aircraft were proceeding at a stately 160 kmh (100 mph). No aircraft was allowed to take off until it received an "all clear" from the traffic hand on the gallery, who was under the orders of the traffic officer. At Croydon, a flag was first waved for the all clear, borrowing from railway practice. Incidentally, the Soviet Union also used railway practice, and Germany adopted a similar method with a hand-held disc. Later, at Croydon, the tower displayed a panel or disc with the initial letter of the airline set in white against a green background—such as "I" for Imperial Airways, "K" for KLM, and so on. At this signal, the pilot was cleared to taxi out to the lee side of the aerodrome and turn into the wind (there were no designated runways), ready for takeoff. By day and night, takeoff permission was indicated by a white light from the tower. A swiveling telescope was attached to an Aldis lamp, whose beam could be accurately di-

9.3. Control towers, topped by glass "chart houses," appeared at major airports, where the risk of collision between airplanes was greatest. This is the original tower at Croydon. (John Wegg Collection)

rected at the cockpit of the holding aircraft. After takeoff, the aircraft circled the aerodrome once to test its wireless and to check that all was mechanically sound. All circuits were made anticlockwise, that is, with a left-handed turn— as they generally are today. A second airplane was not allowed to take off until the first was clear of the aerodrome. In foggy conditions, only one aircraft at a time was allowed to taxi from the tarmac in front of the tower. The pilot was then on his own and could take off whenever he chose—since there would be no other traffic in the vicinity. At Croydon, the pilot followed a white chalk line on the aerodrome's grass surface—first used in 1931. Previously, pilots had to rely on their meager instruments alone. The system was evidently most reliable and was used with confidence down to 10 meters visibility.

A general rule was that an aircraft about to land had the right of way over any incoming airplane. Landing aircraft also made a circuit of the airport to ensure that the aerodrome was clear and, if necessary, to receive landing instructions from the traffic officer. If two aircraft approached at the same time, the one at the lower altitude had priority. If necessary, an aircraft could be instructed not to land; the tower fired a red pyrotechnic signal and flashed the call sign with a visual signaling lamp. At night, the tower flashed a red light as a signal not to land or flashed a green light giving the call sign of the aircraft in Morse code, followed by intermittent flashes. Other regulations prohibited aerobatics within 4,000 meters of the aerodrome and instructed aircraft to turn within 500 meters of the aerodrome. All these rules applied to a height of 6,000 feet (2,000 meters) in the aerodrome vicinity. There is evidence, however, that unauthorized aerobatics—popularly called stunting—was prevalent at Croydon well into the late 1920s. The officer in the tower controlled all the aerodrome lighting, red obstruction lights, amber boundary lights, and a neon beacon with a range of 40 miles, which emitted a series of coded flashes indicating Croydon. A GEC 10-kilowatt landing floodlight and an illuminated wind-direction indicator were also controlled by the tower. Red-and-white or black-and-white signs, of inverted "V" section, were used to denote parts of an aerodrome that were unsuitable for landing or where work was in progress.

From a safety point of view, en route control came to depend almost entirely on wireless. The pilot reported his position at certain definite stages of the flight, particularly when beginning and ending a flight across the Channel. In the tower, a continuous record was kept of the flight progress on a chart, using flags showing nationality and registration marks, from wireless reports and by calculation of the aircraft speed. Cross-Channel traffic not fitted with wireless would circle over the aerodromes of Lympne, St. Inglevert, Ostend, or Calais, both when departing and when arriving. Route traffic services also relayed messages concerning passenger reservations and urgent messages for the operating company. A typical departure message would include the registration of the aircraft, name of pilot, departure time, number of passengers, and weights of baggage, freight, and mail.

In an emergency situation, especially over the Channel, the call "Mayday" would be broadcast when RT was being used. Croydon or Le Bourget could then transmit an SOS message to all shipping. The international air distress signal "Mayday" was invented by F. S. Mockford, officer-in-charge of radio at Croydon in the 1920s, and stemmed from the French *m'aidez* ("help me"). For wireless telegraphy transmission, SOS was used. Visual distress signals included flashing SOS in Morse code or firing red Very lights at short intervals. Less urgent emergencies, for example an aircraft in difficulty but not requiring immediate assistance, were signaled by the word "Pan," transmitted by either radiotelephony or wireless telegraphy (again, still in use today). "Pan" also originated from French—*une panne*—meaning a breakdown. Airliners were first equipped with a medium-band wireless receiving and transmitting set, which functioned after an aerial was reeled out like a fishing line after takeoff and trailed in flight. For example, the routine calls from an Imperial Airways Armstrong Whitworth Argosy operating the prestigious "Silver Wing" service from Croydon to Paris in the late 1920s would be as follows. After takeoff, the Argosy (G-EBLF) called, "Hallo Croydon, Hallo Croydon—L F calling, L F Calling—Leaving Croydon for Paris, Leaving Croydon for Paris—Over." Each detail was repeated to ensure it was heard correctly. Only the last two registration letters were used, or the first and the last two, and there was no phonetic alphabet in use at the time. "Over" indicated that the pilot had switched over his wireless to the receiving position. Croydon then answered, "Hallo L F, Hallo L F—Croydon answering, Croydon answering—Understand leaving Croydon for Paris—OK."

Position reports were given on leaving the English coast and on arriving over the French coast. When in sight of Le Bourget, the Argosy would advise, "Hello Croydon, L F approaching Paris, winding in," indicating that the aerial was being wound in. At a distance of 300 kilometers (200 miles) from Croydon, the Argosy's wireless set was nearing its limit for radiotelephony work, although there were rare occasions when aircraft could communicate to ground stations at distances of over 600 kilometers (400 miles).

On May 15, 1922, a great improvement in en route navigation across the Channel came when a wireless direction-finding watch was introduced at Croydon, Lympne, and Pulham. From a navigational point of view, there was nothing new for aviators to learn about wireless navigation. Instead of a fixed visual point from which to take a bearing, the direction from a wireless station could be derived from a transmission from the aircraft to the station equipped with DF equipment. By adding two conjunctional stations to the controlling station, in the above case Lympne and Pulham to Croydon, the station could use simple geometry to calculate the position of an aircraft. At Croydon, either lines were drawn on a map of the area to "lay-off" the position, or three weighted cords were used to find the intersecting point of the three bearings. This information could then be relayed to the pilot, initially via ground line to the tower and then either by radiotelephony or wireless telegraphy. A DF fix of this type within the London-Continent Airways Area could be given within two minutes and was normally accurate to within two miles. This breakthrough allowed pilots to take off in poor weather, then climb up out of the fog or clouds and set course for their destinations. Since winds aloft could rarely be forecast with accuracy, DF bearings were invaluable to maintaining a correct course. Approaches to destinations obscured by clouds or fog could also be made using

DF. Besides the Croydon-Lympne-Pulham arrangement, DF stations were co-ordinated for Paris to Le Bourget, using Lympne and Valenciennes; Brussels controlled Lympne and Amsterdam or Rotterdam on the London-Brussels route; and Amsterdam was supported by Brussels and Lympne. There were limitations, since the initial Bellini-Tosi DF sets were affected by "night effect," the irregular polarization of radio waves at night, particularly at sunrise and sunset.

The 10 years leading up to World War II in Europe saw air transport not only come of age but stride forward at a phenomenal pace. Over 60,000 miles of organized air routes now crisscrossed Europe, and Croydon handled over 2,000 movements a week at peak summer periods, including 100 airline movements a day. Lufthansa, the European market leader, carried 58,000 passengers in 1930 but recorded close to a stunning 280,000 in 1939. Long-distance flights and sporting events contributed to the public's interest in aviation, and advances in technology brought larger and faster airliners to cater to the rapid growth of air

9.4. The control tower at Paris-Le Bourget opened in November 1937. (John Wegg Collection)

travel. The antiquated biplanes, such as the impressive Handley Page 42, which featured more than its share of built-in head winds, gave way to streamlined airframes such as the Douglas DC-2 and the Bloch 220, which cruised at twice the speed of their predecessors.

With more efficient aircraft came a parallel requirement to speed the flow of air traffic, and comprehensive national air traffic organization became essential. In the cockpit, improved instruments—including the Sperry automatic pilot—and the addition of trained wireless operators to take full advantage of radio assisted the pilot in reaching his destination. De-icing systems blunted the dangers of all-weather flying, and night flying—introduced as early as 1922— became commonplace. By 1934, international law required every commercial airplane capable of carrying 10 passengers to be equipped with radio. Although radiotelephony was still widely used, there was a tendency toward the use of wireless telegraphy, or Morse code, because it had twice the range of medium-wave RT—up to 800 kilometers (500 miles)—was less likely to be misunderstood, and was little affected by atmospherics.

With an increase in night flying in the 1930s, much effort was expended to solve the problem of night effect and develop a direction-finding system that would remain accurate under all conditions. The solution in the United Kingdom was the Adcock-type station, which was first installed at Pulham in the mid-1930s. Homing radio was also introduced, making many calls for positions unnecessary. The Marconi-Robinson homing device was coupled to a standard wireless receiver and used a single loop aerial, fitted to the top of the aircraft fuselage, in conjunction with a trailing aerial run out below the fuselage through a tube. An aircraft flying on course to a ground station did not receive a signal, but when it deviated from the correct course the loop was activated and a signal heard. The direction of the deviation, either right or left, was discerned by switching the trailing aerial into the circuit. With the invention of lightweight homing receivers, almost any aircraft could be so equipped.

Fog was no less a persistent problem in Great Britain and the greater part of continental Europe in the 1930s than it is today; thus a system was needed to prevent midair collisions and to keep airlines moving. At Croydon from November 1933 a "Controlled Zone" was introduced. With a cloud base of less than 1,000 feet (300 meters) and horizontal visibility of less than 1,000 yards, the traffic control officer declared "QBI" conditions, or a bad-weather Controlled Zone open only to radio-equipped aircraft. The letters—part of the basic telecommunications code of three-letter groups—were displayed in an illuminated sign on the control tower. A pilot had to report by radio to the nearest station, stating his position and height and whether he was climbing or descending. Aircraft wanting to land at Croydon were instructed to change frequency to a second channel and were given every assistance for an approach and landing.

In Europe, particularly Germany, a process called "ZZ" was used for a very poor visibility approach. Pilots received a barometric altimeter correction and wireless station sector information. These sectors were selected on the basis of the most favorable air corridor, in consideration of the obstructions and prevailing winds. When the aircraft was overhead the airport, ascertained by ear, the aircraft flew outward for about eight minutes, then turned inbound for an approach. Course corrections were given by radio every minute, and after the aircraft was established on the correct path, the signal to land was given by transmitting the letters "ZZ" in Morse code. Although it fell to the pilot to judge his distance and height from the point of landing, the system worked surprisingly well. Of significant assistance to pilots in poor weather was the introduction of ultrashortwave blind approach and landing systems—such as the Lorenz beam approach pioneered by Lufthansa in Germany. The Lorenz system—which was identifiable on an aircraft by two short rod aerials underneath the fuselage—was first installed at Berlin-Tempelhof and was practical for cloud bases down to 40-50 meters (130-160 feet). The weather or meteorological services were also much improved, with 40 stations operational in the British Isles by 1938. The main airports in the London-Continent Airways Area (Croydon, Paris-Le Bourget, Amsterdam, Brussels, and Cologne) broadcast weather reports in code by wireless telegraphy at 30-minute intervals at fixed times. Anemometers provided local wind information, and upper winds were obtained by using "pilot balloons" filled with hydrogen and observed by means of a specially constructed theodolite.

With radio navigation now the norm, air routes firmly established, and airports taking on a more permanent look, airline advertising could concentrate on comfort over reliability and safety. World War II interrupted the growth of air traffic in Europe, but the development of radar (radio, detection, and ranging), radio, and navigation during the war ensured that the prewar pilot-aid and air traffic control infrastructure would be further improved and consolidated to meet the demands of future air transport generations.

BIBLIOGRAPHY

Armstrong, William. *Pioneer Pilot*. London, 1952.
Burge, C. G., ed. *Complete Book of Aviation*. London, 1935.
Burtt, Philip, ed. *Commercial Air Transport*. London, 1926.

Cluett, Douglas, Joanna Nash, and Bob Learmonth. *Croydon Airport: The Great Days, 1928–1939.* Sutton, Surrey, 1980.

Edwards, Ivo, and F. Tymms. *Commercial Air Transport.* London, 1926.

Finch, Robert. *The World's Airways.* London, 1938.

Golding, Harry, ed. *The Wonder Book of Aircraft.* London, 1927.

Harper, Harry. *The Romance of a Modern Airway.* London, 1930.

Higham, Robin. *Britain's Imperial Air Routes.* Hamden, Conn., 1960.

Hudson, Kenneth. *Air Travel: A Social History.* Bath, UK, 1972.

Instone, Alfred. *Early Birds.* London, 1938.

Olley, Gordon P. *A Million Miles in the Air.* London, 1934.

Sprigg, C. St. John. *British Airways.* London, 1934.

Stroud, John. *Annals of British and Commonwealth Air Transport.* London, 1962.

U.S. Department of Commerce, Joint Committee on the U.S. Department of Commerce and the American Engineering Council. *Civil Aviation: A Report.* New York, 1926.

Wonders of World Aviation. London, 1938.

Virginia P. Dawson

The American Turbojet Industry and British Competition

The Mediating Role of Government Research

The turbojet is a striking example of the commercialization of military technology. Yet the development of military turbojets after World War II and their adaptation for civil aviation in the 1950s have received little historical attention. In contrast to the peacetime development of the radial piston engine by Pratt & Whitney and Wright Aeronautical in the 1930s, the American turbojet industry had wartime roots. World War II brought new companies into the field. Willy-nilly, the aircraft engine industry had to learn to cope with the new reality of government research and testing.

The story of American turbojet development begins with the domination of the turbojet engine field by Great Britain during and shortly after World War II and ends with the commercial success of two American competitors—Pratt & Whitney and General Electric—in the late 1950s. The turbojet engines of these two companies would command the domestic and export fields for the next 30 years.

The contrast between the strong British sally into the turbojet field during World War II and the slide from profitability of the British aircraft engine industry in the late 1950s is striking. To what can we attribute this turnabout? Can we credit the triumph of American-style capitalism over the shortsighted industrial policies of the British Labour Party?[1]

There is no doubt that American engine makers benefited from the policy of mutual technical assistance initiated with the mission of Sir Henry Tizard to the United States in September 1940. The cold war justified continuation of this wartime technical assistance agreement after the war, a fact that worked to the advantage of the United States. American companies reaped a rich harvest of technical expertise through licenses to build the turbojet engines of their British North Atlantic Treaty Organization (NATO) partner. As the technically superior ally, Great Britain had the most to lose in sharing proprietary information with the United States.

Policy is implemented within and between institutions. A social historian of technology, Bruno Latour, has argued—in "Give Me a Laboratory and I Will Raise the World"—that a research laboratory exerts leverage. It has a destabilizing influence on the community it serves. Latour applied his model to the response of the French agricultural and veterinary community to Louis Pasteur's development of the anthrax vaccine.[2] Latour's model can be applied to the role of government research and testing at the end of World War II, particularly as such research relates to the transition from the aircraft piston engine to the turbojet.

My paper will examine the mediating role that a federally funded civilian institution, the National Advisory Committee for Aeronautics (NACA), played in American turbojet development during this period.[3] Of three laboratories under NACA auspices, the Aircraft Engine Research Laboratory (later called the Lewis Flight Propulsion Laboratory), located in Cleveland, Ohio, took a leading role in the testing of turbojet engine prototypes. Because there were no comparable facilities in Great Britain and many British engines were licensed to American manufacturers, the laboratory also tested British engines. It promoted competition and technical innovation among American companies through its testing of full-scale engines. It also acted as a clearinghouse for information on turbojet and turboprop engines, both American and British. Moreover, its basic research on components, especially the axial compressor, assisted both General Electric and Pratt & Whitney in the development of their competing, ultimately enormously profitable, turbojet engines.

In the early euphoria at the end of the war in Europe, few people were aware that American development of the turbojet was late and on a considerably smaller scale than that in Great Britain and Germany. In Great Britain, Armstrong Siddeley, Bristol, De Havilland, Metropolitan-Vickers, Power Jets, Rolls Royce, and Rover all had substantial investment in jet engine prototypes. What impressed an American delegation to Great Britain in early 1944 was the "magnitude of the British effort."[4] The British had as many as 30,000 workers in the general field of jet propulsion. It was clear that British aircraft engine companies believed strongly in the future of the turbojet for both military and commercial aviation.

Reports of the U.S. Army's technical mission to Germany revealed an even stronger emphasis on jet propulsion in that country. A member of the Alsos team, a group of technical experts sent to assess and bring back to the United States examples of Germany's most advanced technology, reported that Germany was "literally sprinkled with high Mach number wind tunnels," which appeared "to have been used extensively for jet work." In the field of jet propulsion, he said bluntly, the United States was "very much behind the Nazis."[5]

The German government had played a key role in supporting aeronautical research "as measured by the number of workers, the number of laboratories, and the modern nature of their equipment, and particularly the construction under way to provide research facilities in advance of those possessed by any other nation."[6] The Alsos team interrogated hundreds of German aeronautical scientists and engineers and confiscated trainloads of documents sent to the United States to instruct the fledgling jet propulsion engineering community. With the German industry shut down after Hitler's defeat, the British were rightly perceived as formidable competitors should the development of turbojet engines become commercially viable.

The American aircraft propulsion community was slow to grasp the potential of a radically new type of propulsion system for aircraft. The origins of the turbojet revolution were European.[7] Air Commodore Frank Whittle in England and Hans von Ohain in Germany independently hit on the turbojet concept, based on long-known principles of jet propulsion. Like Whittle, von Ohain started with the idea that flight required a power plant specially adapted to motion through the air. His enthusiasm stemmed from the insight that an engine that burned continuously was "inherently more powerful, smoother, lighter and more compatible with the aero-vehicle" than the clumsy four-stroke cycle of a piston engine. After experimenting with a ramjet, von Ohain, like Whittle, settled on a design consisting of a compressor plus turbine. He did not discover Whittle's 1930 patent until after the development of his own engine.[8] Von Ohain's engine powered the first flight of a turbojet plane in August 1939. That same year Anslem Franz, Germany's expert on superchargers, designed the first turbojet with an axial-flow compressor.

In contrast to British and German development, American investment in jet propulsion early in the war was tentative and belated. When the British mission visited the United States in September 1940 to inform their American allies of British technical advances in radar and atomic energy, Tizard also dropped some broad hints about British developments in jet propulsion. Vannevar Bush, then chair of both the NACA and the Office of Scientific Research and Development (OSRD), later recalled, "The interesting parts of the subject, namely the explicit way in which the investigation was being carried out, were apparently not known to Tizard, and at least he did not give me any indication that he knew such details."[9] Nevertheless, in response to intelligence reports of European developments, General Hap Arnold asked Bush to set up a government committee to sponsor efforts to develop some form of jet propulsion. Writing that the matter was "of such importance . . . and so definitely require[d] mature and independent judgment of a high order," Bush chose the aerodynamicist William Frederick Durand to chair a Special Committee on Jet Propulsion under the general auspices of the NACA Power Plants Committee.[10]

The Special Committee had a broad mandate to investigate and fund promising jet propulsion schemes. Three respected scientists formed the backbone of the committee: C. Richard Soderberg, a leading authority on turbines, at the Massachusetts Institute of Technology; A. G. Christie, of Johns Hopkins University; and the aerodynamicist Hugh Dryden, of the National Bureau of Standards. Because Bush and other high-ranking government officials believed that the committee should be composed of "personnel other than those who deal with conventional power plants," representation by industry was limited to three companies, all with prior experience in industrial steam turbine design: Allis-Chalmers, Westinghouse, and the General Electric Steam Turbine Division at Schnectady, New York.[11] The minutes and correspondence of the Special Committee do not reveal why Pratt & Whitney, Wright Aeronautical, and the Allison Division of General Motors were deliberately excluded from participation on the committee. It appears that Bush, Arnold, and Admiral John Towers thought the hidebound conservatism of the major piston engine manufacturers would prevent them from contributing constructively to the Special Committee.

By September 1941 the committee was ready to sponsor four jet propulsion projects. Of the four only a project under NACA auspices for a ducted fan had reached test stage at this point. The NACA's project, designed by its premier aerodynamicist, Eastman Jacobs, initially won the support of the committee but ultimately failed, as did a competing design for a ducted fan proposed by Allis-Chalmers.[12] Difficulties with General Electric's design for a turboprop with an axial compressor (TG-100/T31) prompted the company to modify its design into the TG-180/J35 turbojet. Of the committee-sponsored projects, only the Westinghouse 19-B actually reached flight test before the end of the war. Westinghouse designers proudly called it the "Yankee," the first "All-American" jet

10.1. William Frederick Durand (center, right), chair of the NACA Special Committee on Jet Propulsion, and Orville Wright (center, left) tour the Aircraft Engine Research Laboratory during its dedication in May 1943. (Courtesy National Aeronautics and Space Administration–Lewis Research Center)

engine, because unlike the other successful turbojet project based on the Whittle design, it was the product of American engineering know-how.[13]

The role of General Arnold in the choice of General Electric to produce an American version of the British Whittle engine is well-known. It should be emphasized that development of the Whittle engine on American soil took place completely independently of the projects sponsored by Durand's Special Committee.[14] Fearing invasion by the Germans, in April 1941 the British minister of aircraft production, Lord Beaverbrook, released blueprints for the Whittle W2B to the United States and made arrangements for exporting one Whittle engine, the W1X. Arnold chose General Electric's Supercharger Division at West Lynn, Massachusetts, to produce an exact copy of the British engine because of the army's long association with the development of a turbo-supercharger pioneered by Sanford Moss.

10.2. A technician readies the General Electric TG-180 for tests in the altitude wind tunnel at the Cleveland laboratory. (Courtesy National Aeronautics and Space Administration–Lewis Research Center)

So secret was the development of the Whittle engine that only after the project was reclassified from "super-secret" to "secret" early in the summer of 1943 did the army allow the NACA to get involved in testing the General Electric I-A and succeeding models, the I-16 and I-40. The NACA laboratory in Cleveland also tested the Westinghouse 19-B and the General Electric TG-100 and TG-180.

With the war ended in Europe, in May 1945 the Cleveland Flight Propulsion Laboratory was ready to demonstrate the potential benefits of government engine research in the new field of jet propulsion. Representatives from the laboratory were invited to attend the first American conference on aircraft gas turbine engineering, jointly sponsored by General Electric and the U.S. Army Air Forces. Held in Swampscott, Massachusetts, not far from the West Lynn plant, it attracted nearly 200 members of the aeronautical community, including representatives from Great Britain.

Although General Electric engineers and their British colleagues presented most of the 27 papers, Abe Silverstein, chief of the Wind Tunnels and Flight Division at Lewis, had the distinction of describing the NACA's test program. Silverstein's paper was especially useful because of its valuable comparative perspective. The uniqueness of the laboratory's altitude wind tunnel for testing jet engines had enabled the laboratory to provide not only test results of the General Electric I-16 and the I-40, with their centrifugal compressors based on the Whittle design, but also comparable data for other American designs—the General Electric TG-180 and the Westinghouse 19-B, with their more complex axial compressors. Silverstein presented this information in general terms that defined the problems that the engine designer could expect in the design of any turbojet engine. For example, he described "combustion blowout" at low speeds and how the Reynolds number might impair the efficiency of the compressor and turbine at high altitudes.[15] The paper demonstrated the value of government-sponsored testing and revealed the role that the government might play in making test data available to the entire engine industry.

Research by the NACA also promoted innovation in the design of components. For example, in the early postwar period it was uncertain which type of engine compressor would become standard in turbojet design. In the United States there was greater enthusiasm for the axial compressor. Its smaller frontal area made it more compact and better suited aerodynamically for flight than the more rugged, but cumbersome, centrifugal compressor used in the Whittle design. However, the greater aerodynamic complexity of the axial compressor presented enormous scientific and engineering challenges. An axial compressor had to be designed so that air moved smoothly across each of the rows of compressor blades. Compressor failure in the TG-180, for example, was common. NACA research on the eight-stage compressor, research initiated in 1936 for a supercharger application and continued into the late 1940s, laid the basis for the laboratory's compressor expertise.[16]

To Pratt & Whitney and Wright Aeronautical, it appeared that the government had given a head start in the development of a radically new power plant to companies previously outside the aircraft engine field. Would General Electric and Westinghouse become powerful new competitors in the field that Pratt & Whitney and Wright Aeronautical had dominated throughout the 1930s and World War II? In the immediate postwar economy Pratt & Whitney and Wright Aeronautical found themselves in the unenviable position of having enormously expanded facilities for the production of potentially obsolete engines. The very day that President Harry Truman announced victory over Japan, the government canceled more than $414 million in contracts with Pratt & Whitney, and the machinery of its vast production empire fell silent.[17]

10.3. General Dwight Eisenhower visits the laboratory in 1946. (Courtesy National Aeronautics and Space Administration–Lewis Research Center)

As early as 1944, Jerome Hunsaker, the chairman of the NACA, had warned that the Cleveland laboratory appeared to constitute a potential threat to the engine industry. "The idea here is that private enterprise has already developed very superior engines and fuels and does not need government competition in research, invention, and development." Hunsaker reported that industry managers argued that they could make better use of public funds than a government laboratory and wanted government research stopped. Their major complaint was that the NACA was taking the lead in jet propulsion "in collaboration with firms previously outside the aeronautical engine field."[18]

Few had sympathy for the plight of the engine companies. To a report listing industry grievances, OSRD Chairman Bush retorted, "Inasmuch as the Germans have just sprung a clever, new engine on us, which our industry never thought of, their attitude does not strike me forcibly."[19] Recalling with displeasure the resistance of Pratt & Whitney and Wright Aeronautical to developing new engine types before World War II when the two companies were flush with profits, he commented: "The engine people did not do a thing on that subject [jet propulsion] or on any other unusual engine. If we brought new people into the engine field I think we have done a public service."[20] General Oliver Echols shared Bush's reluctance to pander to the engine companies. "Industry," he remarked, "is always looking over its shoulder at its competitors. If their research is one step ahead of their competitors they are satisfied. It has always been apparent they are not interested in the general progress of the art."[21]

Hunsaker worried that without the war to drive American technology, the United States would face competition with the British in civil aviation. The British, he pointed out, anticipated the expansion of their aircraft industry and were proposing to build new facilities. He noted:

> Our competitor is going to be the British. They have had five missions over here recently to study recent additions to American research facilities and to learn everything they can. . . . They are going throughout the United States and they are frank in saying that what we have now is what they propose to build only larger and better. We have a 20-foot-altitude wind tunnel at Cleveland. They will have a 25-foot-altitude tunnel. Their program now calls for the construction of 12 wind tunnels which will constitute a great national research organization for the British empire.[22]

The United States could anticipate not only commercial rivalry with the British in the aircraft engine field but also, more ominously, the potential military threat of the Soviet Union. The superiority of British engines and the perceived danger of British turbojet technology in the hands of the Soviet Union formed a recurring theme in the late 1940s to justify government engine research on an unprecedented scale.

In the early postwar years, the engine companies had no choice but to allow the NACA laboratory in Cleveland to test their engines. The Army Air Forces and the navy insisted that the laboratory evaluate military prototypes. Full-scale testing gave the government an intimate knowledge of the strengths and limitations of a particular engine. Testing played a positive role in preventing the engine companies from growing complacent.

Innovation involved risk. The engine companies were perceived as interested in increasing profits, not in pushing the frontiers of aircraft engine technology. What industry objected to and feared was the sharing of new knowledge through publication, which could undermine the competitive advantage a company might win through its own efforts. Government engine research had a destabilizing effect. By making innovations available to the entire industry through publication, the government forced industry to continue to innovate, in theory pushing competitors to higher technical proficiency. Not only could the government afford to build facilities for testing complete engine systems, but the expertise of NACA engineers went beyond full-scale testing to the study of individual components. They developed theories to predict engine performance and verified these theories in specially designed test apparatus, called "rigs." The NACA tackled specialized areas of research, such as compressors and turbines, combustion and fuels, lubricants and seals, materials, and heat transfer. Through publication and interaction between industry and government engineers, the laboratory encouraged innovation while saving the engine companies some of the costs of development. Government research, even after the adoption of a new policy on proprietary rights, promoted new technology. A designer could not ignore a particular innovation if his company's competitors were likely to incorporate it into their latest engine prototypes.

As long as the NACA had facilities superior to those of the engine companies, it could continue to play a mediating role in engine development by promoting competition among the engine companies through its research and publication of test results. By the same token, the engine companies were determined to build their own facilities, thereby keeping their engine advances proprietary. So important did the construction of facilities for testing appear to Pratt & Whitney, for example, that in 1947 its board of directors authorized $15 million—more than the entire net worth of the company—for a gas turbine laboratory.[23]

By January 1947 the proprietary rights issue had become the subject of debate between the NACA and the Army Air Forces at Wright Field. Colonel H. Z. Bogert, the army liaison officer at the NACA laboratory in Cleveland, connected the issues of proprietary rights with the ability of the United States to compete with the British. An internal NACA memo reported Bogert's conclusion: "The research and development effort of this country must be accelerated to place this country ahead of the British."[24] However, the civilian engineers employed at Wright Field argued that the army did not have the right to violate the proprietary rights of individual companies because the army paid only about 15 percent of the expenses for research and development by companies such as Wright Aeronautical and Pratt & Whitney. But the laboratory's executive engineer, Carlton Kemper, took Bogert's side and argued for a wide distribution of test results. He thought it "was poor policy to spend large sums in operating the Altitude Wind Tunnel and then to make the pertinent information available to only five companies because of the proprietary information in the report."[25]

In a memo written the following month, Kemper described how General Electric, stung when the Army Air Forces awarded the production contracts for the I-40 to the General Motors Allison Division, wanted assurance that the NACA would not release proprietary information to competitors. The company admitted that Allison could produce engines more cheaply because of its government-owned factories. Nevertheless, General Electric was determined that in the future, engineering knowledge would "not be turned over to a competitor at no cost, as was done in this case." The company's decision to stay in the aircraft engine business would mean "real competition" for Wright Aeronautical, Pratt & Whitney, and Allison, particularly since the company had decided to concentrate on development of new designs rather than invest in new production facilities. The company planned to subcontract with other companies for the manufacture of its new engines. Kemper warned that the laboratory's relationship with General Electric was in jeopardy unless a satisfactory solution of the problem of proprietary rights could be found. The company did not object to the release of wind tunnel data as long as the laboratory refrained from discussing how improved efficiencies in the turbine or compressor were obtained. Kemper recommended that the laboratory concentrate on fundamental problems in jet engines, particularly on improvements of specific components. "It is only by having better ideas than industry that we can maintain our outstanding position in the jet-engine field."[26]

To make up for its late start, Pratt & Whitney decided to focus on the development of a turbojet with an advanced design, hoping to leapfrog its competitors. To develop turbojet expertise quickly, it purchased licenses not only for the Westinghouse "Yankee" engine but also for some of the most outstanding British engines. When the company set its sights on the license for the Rolls Royce Nene engine—at that time the best-engineered and most powerful British turbojet—it came into direct conflict with the test program at the NACA laboratory in Cleveland.

Behind the Rolls Royce Nene and the General Electric I-40 lay the genius of Frank Whittle. The Nene, begun in March 1944, eliminated some of the complexity of Whittle's design by allowing the air to flow straight through the compressor and combustor, rather than using the reversed flow of the Whittle engine. Although development of the Nene had begun 10 months after that of the I-40, General Electric "froze" its design at the end of the war, whereas Rolls Royce engineers continued to improve the Nene's performance.[27] The engineering achievement embodied in the Nene was first publicly recognized after the publication of an article in *Flight Magazine* in the spring of 1946. Apparently the British, using the same design as the Americans but in less time and with inferior facilities for testing, had produced a superior engine.[28]

Naturally, the NACA laboratory in Cleveland, with its growing expertise in jet propulsion technology, was eager to test the British engine. With experience in testing all of the American prototypes for the Army Air Forces and the navy, Cleveland engineers were in the ideal position to be able to point out what made British engines superior. Their effort to obtain a Nene for testing coincided with an effort by the navy to test the Nene, perhaps precipitated by the navy's desire to compare the Nene's performance with that of the Westinghouse 19-B and the 24-C, its turbojet with an axial-flow compressor.

In 1946 it was still not clear whether jet engines with axial or centrifugal compressors would emerge as the best production engines. On a visit to the Cleveland laboratory in 1946, Frank Whittle looked with bemused superiority at what he considered the laboratory's misplaced emphasis on axial compressor development. He asserted that the centrifugal compressor would continue to be preferred for its rugged dependability. Some years later, the Italian expert P. F. Martinuzzi (then a consultant for the British) called the abandonment of the centrifugal compressor development by American designers a "pity." He noted, "It appears that the axial compressor types which have replaced the earlier centrifugals are not more reliable [and] are heavier and 'several times' more expensive." Martinuzzi speculated that American emphasis on the axial compressor might reflect "a desire to disclaim British influence."[29] No doubt there was an element of national pride in the enthusiasm for the axial compressor on the part of General Electric and Westinghouse, as well as the NACA. Nevertheless, the greater aerodynamic complexity of the axial design represented a significant engineering challenge.

Toward the end of 1946 the Navy Bureau of Aeronautics obtained two Nene engines and tested them at the navy's engine laboratory near Philadelphia. It was then that the Cleveland laboratory saw its chance. In December, Executive Engineer Kemper recommended that the NACA study the Nene. Such an investigation would be particularly valuable, he wrote in a memo to the NACA Washington office, because the Nene engine was "reported to have higher thrust, lower specific weight, and lower fuel consumption than current American service engines."[30]

So important did the NACA consider this project that it took the unusual step of purchasing a Nene engine directly from the Taylor Turbine Corporation, then the owner of the American license. Meanwhile, at the navy's request, Pratt & Whitney began negotiations in April 1947 to acquire manufacturing and sales rights to the Nene. In December, with the acquisition of the license from Taylor Turbine complete, Pratt & Whitney informed the NACA that it had exclusive rights to the Nene and Derwent series of turbojet engines. The company was, as of that date, actively engaged in their production for the navy. Pratt & Whitney did not object to the testing of the engine but requested that the results be kept confidential because it was now a "proprietary article."[31]

In May 1948 Cleveland engineers completed the preliminary report of the tests of the Nene in the laboratory's new altitude chamber.[32] In the opinion of one engineer I interviewed, the significance of the results from the NACA point of view was their revelation of not only the Nene's strengths but also its limitations. In terms of fuel consumption and weight, the Nene soon would not be able to compete with the engines with axial compressors then under development. This information dispelled any lingering doubts about the strong emphasis on axial compressor development in the United States.[33]

The NACA sent the report to Pratt & Whitney, Rolls Royce, and the military services. At the same time the NACA requested that the report be made available to other American manufacturers that possibly needed "this research information to facilitate fulfillment of military contracts."[34] Anticipating trouble with Pratt & Whitney, NACA Director Hugh L. Dryden, in a meeting of the Power Plants Committee, brought up the general problem of proprietary rights and the distribution of NACA reports. Dryden pointed out that the NACA did not want to undermine the "competitive free enterprise system" but felt that "it was necessary to reconcile the interests of the military services, the engine manufacturer involved, and the engineering profession . . . interested in establishing a general body of knowledge on aircraft engine research."[35]

The general manager of Pratt & Whitney, W. P. Gwinn, strenuously objected to the distribution of the Nene results. "From our point of view the information ceases to be confidential once it is given to competitive firms, either directly or indirectly. While an excellent report, in our judgment, it does not contain research information." The company opposed the disclosure of "certain performance and design characteristics of a foreign engine" to which it had "exclusive American rights."[36]

The case of the Nene involved not merely the question of proprietary rights but also the issue of national security. As a goodwill gesture, the British Labour government had permitted Rolls Royce to sell the license for the Nene to the Soviet Union in 1946. Vladimir Klimov, one of the premier engine designers for the Soviet Union, developed the Nene to permit about 30 percent more air to pass through the engine. This became the VK-1 engine, which powered the Il-28 aircraft, the standard tactical bomber for the Soviet forces after 1950. The fact that the Soviet Union's capable designers had precisely the same technology as the American aircraft industry contributed to the argument against withholding information on the Nene's performance. Dryden pointed out that Pratt & Whitney had never objected to receiving reports summarizing the performance of the engines of its competitors.[37] Since the Nene was superior to any engine produced in the United States, national security made it imperative that American engines surpass the standard the Nene had set. Because of the Nene's challenge to the American jet engine community, it became known as the "Needle engine."[38]

In September, Gwinn responded to the NACA. He made it clear that maintaining Pratt & Whitney's competitive position was paramount. "I cannot get around the two basic facts involved in this situation; that is, that the Nene engine is now a proprietary article belonging to this Division, in severe competition with engines of other American manufacturers and that the publication of the report will furnish information of value concerning it to our competitors."[39]

Dryden brought up the urgent need for a policy statement on the "release of information on specific engines" when the Power Plants Committee met in December.[40] He pointed out, "It would be uneconomical for the NACA Lewis Flight Propulsion Laboratory to construct engines for conducting research in

10.4. The Soviet Il-28, with twin VK-1 turbojet engines, was designed by Vladimir Klimov. VK-1 engines produced a static thrust of 2,700 kilograms (5,955 pounds) for an engine weight of 900 kilograms (2,000 pounds), as compared with a static thrust of 2,270 kilograms (5,000 pounds) for an engine weight of 780 kilograms (1,715 pounds) for the original Nene. (Courtesy G. Novozhilov, General Designer, Ilyushin Design Bureau, Russia)

comparison with obtaining engines built by the engine manufacturers." In general, specific engines were "supplied by the military services for research requested by them. In just one case the NACA purchased the engine." If the NACA was forced to purchase all of its engines with public funds, he warned that proprietary rights would receive no protection at all. With the present system, design improvements made by a particular company would be disclosed to other manufacturers only after a certain time lapse. Although the total number of reports relating to this problem was relatively small, Dryden admitted the need for a policy that would provide a satisfactory definition of proprietary rights.

This issue set in relief the question that most bothered industry: Why did the laboratory feel compelled to engage in work so close to development? Government engineers argued that only with knowledge of state-of-the-art engines could they analyze problems that might affect a whole class of engines. Although the components of the piston engine could be tested in isolation from their function within specific engines, it was necessary to study the jet engine as a complete system. The machine itself was a teacher. Expertise came from running engines. "The reason you have the expertise," one engineer I interviewed remarked, "is that you learn in the facilities. You don't get your expertise by a slide rule. . . . You get your expertise by working with real hardware and real conditions."[41] In a field that was so rapidly changing in the early postwar period, without experience with actual engine prototypes, NACA engineers could not be sure that their work would be relevant to the engine problems needing solutions.

The debate over proprietary rights brought to the surface the basic philosophical issue dividing the government and the engine companies: how to reconcile the invisible hand of the free enterprise system with national security. Could competition be protected if it meant that in the event of a war the United States might have to rely on inferior engines? As one of the military members of the Power Plants Committee stated during the debate over the Nene, "One problem from the Government point of view is how desirable improvements which are known to the Government can be made in engines being purchased by the government."[42]

There was a conflict between the national interest and what would be most profitable for the individual companies. The NACA Power Plants Committee reflected this larger problem in microcosm. The minutes of the meeting in which these issues were discussed reported, "The Power Plants Committee is responsible to the nation as a whole, while the members of the committee from industry are responsible to the stockholders of their companies." Proprietary rights were necessary, but the question was "how much compromise there should be in the best interest of the country."[43]

In general, there were two classes of information that the industry might find objectionable, if released. The first involved negative information that a competitor sometimes used to run down a product. The second type could involve, for example, a superior component like a combustor. With enough information a competitor could engage in "reverse engineering." It was possible to deduce why the combustor was superior and make similar improvements, thereby denying the innovating company the fruits of its investment in development. Pratt & Whitney's representative on the Power Plants Committee, Leonard S. Hobbs, argued, "A man is not improved by turning over to him what a good man did." To which Professor Edward S. Taylor retorted that improved performance "is an excellent stimulus to everyone else to obtain similar improvements." Edward P. Warner, the distinguished editor of *Aviation*, took the government's side of the argument: "Everyone recognizes the desirability of releasing information that stimulates the other man to do as well."[44]

The resolution of the proprietary rights issue gave the upper hand to the engine companies, to an extent compromising the mediating role the laboratory had played up to that point. The NACA won the privilege to distribute its report on the Nene because the engine was purchased before Pratt & Whitney acquired the license, but it had to accept new limitations on the dissemination of technical information. The new policy, hammered out in debates within the Power Plants Committee, the NACA Executive Committee, and the Industry Consulting Committee and approved in June 1949, stated that to preserve a manufacturer's competitive position, technical information on models or components under active development would be withheld unless a specific agreement was reached with the manufacturer. Information on production models could be furnished only after review. In addition, the manufacturer was to receive the list of companies and individuals to whom the NACA intended to send information. Finally, any oral communication released by the NACA before a report was issued was subject to review.

The debate over the Nene revealed an even more troubling question. Why did British engines continue to be superior to their American counterparts, despite the inferiority of British facilities for engine testing? Dryden ruefully suggested that a "lack of money for facilities" had forced the British "to make the best use of their brains." Moreover, through the Gas Collaboration Committee, set up during the war, the British had been able to foster "a much closer collaboration between the engine companies in technical matters." Dryden cited the attitude of Rolls Royce executives on the release of information, attitudes "in refreshing contrast to those of Pratt and Whitney, for example."[45]

As late as 1948, the general lack of coordination and communication among members of the American propulsion community was noted by Martinuzzi. On a trip sponsored by the American Society of Mechanical Engineers, he remarked, "The general trend is tackle the problems independently of past experience and of what competitors are doing."[46]

A series of official British and American missions in the mid-1940s through the early 1950s enhanced American knowledge of British aircraft technology. In June 1947 an American delegation visited major British engine manufacturers, as well as the British government laboratories, the National Gas Turbine Establishment at Whetstone, the National Physical Laboratories at Teddington, and the Royal Aircraft Establishment at Farnborough. The tour ended with visits to American engine companies to educate them concerning the latest British advances.

The NACA representative from Cleveland, Walter T. Olson, noted that the general spirit of collaboration among British manufacturers had enabled them to seek common solutions to problems. However, he added that British development of engines with axial-flow compressors appeared to be behind that of the General Electric TG-180 and the Westinghouse "Yankee" engine (J34/24C). Of particular interest was the Rolls Royce Avon engine, slated for the Canberra Bomber and the De Havilland Comet. The British were counting on the Avon to power the world's first passenger jetliner. The Avon engine was "without question the 'blue chip' project," Olson wrote, because many British aircraft companies with projects in the design stage planned to use the Avon engine.[47] Olson noted that Great Britain lacked altitude chambers to test full-scale engines and facilities to test components, such as compressors, at high speeds.[48] The National Gas Turbine Establishment was the only organization in Great Britain conducting large-scale cascade tests over a wide range of conditions. But Olson revealed, "The cascade results are inaccurate because of boundary layer effects in the cascade test rig itself."[49] Clearly, Olson thought that the NACA's work on compressors based on the Jacobs-Wasielewski eight-stage compressor was superior to what he saw in England.[50]

The Korean War marked a turning point in the development of the turbojet. Before the Korean War, more than half of the aircraft engines produced in the United States were of the piston engine type. By the end of the war, the balance had shifted, primarily because of the reequipment of the navy with jet planes.[51]

The Korean War also signaled the end of British dominance of the turbojet engine field. During the war, Pratt & Whitney was the licensee for the production of the Rolls Royce Tay, or J48, the last clearly superior British engine. When Wright Aeronautical bought the license for the British Armstrong Siddeley Sapphire, a turbojet with an axial compressor, the company found that the thrust of the engine was too low for the aircraft it was intended to power. The failure of Wright's development of the Sapphire contributed to the company's slide into bankruptcy.[52] Similarly, Westinghouse dropped out of the field not long after the British attempted to assist the company with its foundering 24-C engine. On a visit to Cleveland in 1953, the Rolls Royce representative confided that he had been "directed by Lord Hives to follow through on the collaboration between the two companies and see if Rolls Royce could 'make an engine company out of the bloody buggers.'"[53]

Shortly before the end of the war, Pratt & Whitney, years behind Westinghouse and General Electric in acquiring turbojet expertise, came out a winner when it tested the new JT3 (J57), an engine of its own design. The JT3 had better fuel economy than its competitors and more than double their thrust. The innovative design feature of Pratt & Whitney's engine was an axial compressor with a double shaft (also called a dual-rotor or dual-spool), a feature that dramatically increased the efficiency of the compressor. This engine placed the company in the forefront of aircraft propulsion development.[54]

But Pratt & Whitney did not hold the position for long. General Electric responded to Pratt & Whitney's JT3 with the J79. The compressor of the J79 had variable stators to enhance its efficiency.[55] The variable stator design, I should point out, had been discussed in an NACA technical report in 1949 and no doubt influenced the design of the J79 compressor.[56]

By the late 1950s the American turbojet industry had matured and narrowed to two competitors: Pratt & Whitney and General Electric. After two tragic crashes of the Comet in 1954, the De Havilland Company lost the commercial market to the Boeing 707 and the Douglas DC-8, both powered by versions of Pratt & Whitney's JT3. Although the British had set the stage for the development of the commercial transport market, they lost their lead to the United States.

The development of superior NACA facilities for testing engine prototypes contributed to this achievement. This view is supported by Rolls Royce representatives who visited the Cleveland laboratory in 1955. They lamented that their company had been "led up the garden path" by the Labour and Conservative governments, which had promised "to provide full-scale test facilities for the British gas turbine industry since 1945."[57] The politicians failed to deliver the promised full-scale test facilities for the British aircraft industry. Although

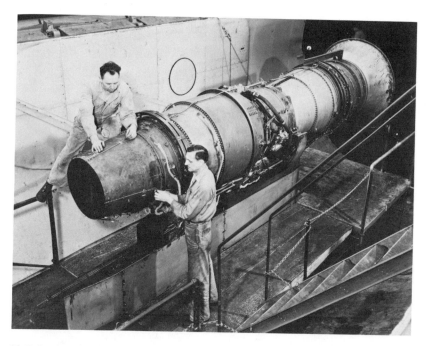

10.5. Pratt & Whitney's J-57 is mounted for testing in the NACA altitude wind tunnel. (Courtesy National Aeronautics and Space Administration–Lewis Research Center)

in 1955 the British made plans to build a large altitude test facility to test full-scale engines at the National Gas Turbine Establishment at Pyestock, with a second at Bedford, these facilities came too late to recoup the British lead.

The cold war justified the continued sharing of British engine technology with the United States—an exchange heavily weighted in favor of the United States. NACA engineers developed an intimate knowledge of British engines, knowledge that they could share with American manufacturers. American engine companies received a financial boost from large defense contracts, necessary because of the dominant role of the United States in the North Atlantic Treaty Organization (NATO).

Gerhard Neumann, who developed the variable stator compressor system now standard in most jet engines, published a poem in his autobiography, *Herman the German*. The poem captures the exuberance of General Electric's design team after they had developed the GOL 1590 (forerunner of the J79, begun in 1951), the engine that enabled General Electric to compete with Pratt & Whitney's JT3.

10.6. A full-scale multistage turbine test apparatus is installed in the Engine Research Building at the NACA Lewis Flight Propulsion Laboratory, 1952. (Courtesy National Aeronautics and Space Administration–Lewis Research Center)

> But in our merriment, let's pause
> To wallow in some self-applause . . .
> All hail the 1590 then
> Designed by most ingenious men.
> Conceived to beat Pratt's dual spool,
> Beat their weight, consume less fuel.
> The edict was, "Go full speed, boys.
> Hang the smoke, and damn the noise!
> With single-spooled high pressure rotor,
> Create a money-making motor!"[58]

The poem expresses the ethos of the engine industry—beat the competition and make a profit. But it characteristically leaves out a third element in the company's success—the role of government research and testing. I say "characteristically" because engine companies are reluctant to admit they receive the benefit of government expertise. Nevertheless, I believe that it is important for historians to try to ferret out this neglected aspect of the history of the turbojet.

This is not to detract from the creativity of the designers of Pratt & Whitney's JT3 or General Electric's J-79. Clearly, the government did not design whole engine systems. But the Cleveland laboratory provided engineering knowledge in the form of testing and research on components. In the early postwar years, before the engine companies and the military developed their own test facilities, research by the Cleveland laboratory helped to push the United States ahead of Great Britain in the turbojet industry. It seems unlikely that the American companies could have won the race to develop commercial turbojet aircraft without the cold war and the fortuitous availability of government contracts and engineering support.

Today, as national debate in the United States focuses on the proper role of the government in support of industry, the case of the development of the turbojet may offer some insight. Precious tax money invested in government facilities for testing in the early postwar period helped establish a new industry.

NOTES

1. See Keith Hayward, *Government and British Civil Aerospace: A Case Study in Post-War Technology Policy* (Manchester, Eng., 1983), chapter 1.

2. Bruno Latour, "Give Me a Laboratory and I Will Raise the World," in Karin D. Knorr-Cetina and Michael Mulkay, eds., *Science Observed* (London, 1983), 141–70.

3. For an institutional history of what is now the NASA Lewis Research Center, see Virginia P. Dawson, *Engines and Innovation: Lewis Laboratory and American Propulsion Technology,* NASA SP-4306 (Washington, D.C., 1991). For a general history of NACA, see Alex Roland, *Model Research: The National Advisory Committee for Aeronautics, 1915–1958,* NASA SP-4103, 2 vols. (Washington, D.C., 1985). Particularly helpful for this study were several documents edited by Roland in volume 2.

4. Minutes of the Executive Committee of the NACA, January-June 1944, Box 9, Record Group 255, National Archives, Suitland, Md.

5. Alsos Mission Report, March 4, 1944, entry 187, Box 137, Intelligence Division Alsos Mission File 1944–45, National Archives, Washington, D.C.

6. Minutes of the Executive Committee of the NACA, January-June 1945, Box 9, Record Group 255, National Archives, Suitland, Md.

7. See Edward W. Constant II, *The Origins of the Turbojet Revolution* (Baltimore, 1980); Robert Schlaifer and S. D. Heron, *The Development of Aircraft Engines; The Development of Aviation Fuels: Two Studies of the Relations between Government and Business* (Cambridge, Mass., 1950); Frank Whittle, "The Early History of the Whittle Jet Propulsion Gas Turbine," *Proceedings of the Institution of Mechanical Engineers* 152 (1945): 419–35; Leslie E. Neville and Nathaniel F. Silsbee, *Jet Propulsion Progress: The Development of Aircraft Gas Turbines* (New York, 1948).

8. Hans von Ohain, "The Evolution and Future of Aeropropulsion Systems," in Walter J. Boyne and Donald S. Lopez, eds., *The Jet Age* (Washington, D.C., 1979), 29.

9. Vannevar Bush to H. H. Arnold, July 2, 1941, 47/208, Papers of H. H. Arnold, Manuscript Division, Library of Congress. On the Tizard mission, see Daniel J. Kevles, *The Physicists* (New York, 1979), 302–3.

10. Bush to William Frederick Durand, March 18, 1941, Records of Committees and Subcommittees, Record Group 255, File 117.15, National Archives, Suitland, Md.

11. John Towers to Bush, March 17, 1941, NACA Committees and Subcommittees, Record Group 255, File 117.15, National Archives, Suitland, Md. Members of the committee were Durand, C. Richard Soderberg, R. C. Allen (Allis-Chalmers), L. W. Chubb (Westinghouse), A. G. Christie, Hugh L. Dryden, Brig. Gen. O. P. Echols, Jerome Hunsaker (ex officio), Capt. S. M. Kraus, U.S.N., George W. Lewis (ex officio), and A. R. Stevenson, Jr. (General Electric). For greater detail on American efforts at developing jet propulsion, see Dawson, *Engines and Innovation,* chapter 3.

12. For an excellent description of NACA's project headed by Jacobs, see James R. Hansen, *Engineer in Charge: A History of the Langley Aeronautical Laboratory, 1917–1958,* NASA SP-4305, (Washington, D.C., 1987), chapter 8. In 1943 the U.S. Navy canceled its support for the Allis-Chalmers design for a ducted fan with double paths of cool and hot air when the company obtained the license to build a British Havilland-Halford jet propulsion unit.

13. For the most comprehensive history of the Westinghouse project, see [W. R. New], "The History of Westinghouse in the War Aviation Gas Turbine Division, Engineering Department," Westinghouse vertical file, National Air and Space Museum, Washington, D.C.

14. See the recent article by Daniel Ford, " 'Gentlemen, I Give You the Whittle Engine': How War Made England Choose between Protecting Its Technology and Defending Its Borders," *Air and Space* (October/November 1992), 88–98.

15. Abe Silverstein, "Investigations of Jet-Propulsion Engines in the NACA Altitude Wind Tunnel," *Aircraft Gas Turbine Engineering Conference* (West Lynn, Mass., 1945), 255–70.

16. See Brian J. Nichelson, "Early Jet Engines and the Transition from Centrifugal to Axial Compressors: A Case Study in Technological Change" (Ph.D. diss., University of Minnesota, 1988); John T. Sinnette, Jr., Oscar Schey, and J. Austin King, "Performance of NACA Eight-Stage Axial-Flow Compressor Designed on the Basis of Airfoil Theory," NACA TR 758, 1943, report first published as NACA Wartime Report E4H18, August 1944; and John T. Sinnette, Jr., and William J. Voss, "Extension of Useful Operation Range of Axial-flow Compressors by Use of Adjustable Stator Blades," NACA TR 915, 1948. NACA data on the use of variable stator compressor blades contributed to the design (begun in 1951) of General Electric's enormously successful J79.

17. Pratt & Whitney Aircraft Division, United Aircraft Corporation, *The Pratt & Whitney Aircraft Story* (West Hartford, Conn., 1950), 152.

18. Jerome Hunsaker, "Notes on Discussion at Meeting of NACA, July 27, 1944," August 8, 1944, document 34 in Roland, *Model Research* 2:688, appendix H.

19. Ibid., 687.

20. Ibid., 688. See also document 35, appendix H: "Notes of Discussions at Meeting of National Advisory Committee for Aeronautics, April 26, 1945," n.d., 690–93.

21. Ibid., 688.

22. Ibid., 689.

23. Robert B. Meyer, Jr., "Classic Turbine Engines," *Casting About* (November 1986). The facility was completed in 1950 and named the Andrew Van Dean Willgoos Gas Turbine Laboratory.

24. Carlton Kemper, "Conference Called by Colonel Bogert at Wright Field, January 23, 1947, Regarding Proprietary Material in NACA Reports for the Army Air Forces," NASA-Lewis Records, 34/317.7, Cleveland, Ohio.

25. Ibid.

26. Carlton Kemper, "Visit to General Electric River Works, Lynn, Massachussetts, with Colonel Bogert to Discuss Their Objections to the Method of Handling Proprietary Material in NACA Reports," memorandum for director of research, February 3, 1947, NASA-Lewis Records, 34/317.76, Cleveland, Ohio.

27. Schlaifer and Heron, *The Development of Aircraft Engines,* 373, 476.

28. See *Flight,* April 18, 1946, and Schlaifer and Heron, *The Development of Aircraft Engines,* 373, 476.

29. P. F. Martinuzzi, "Gas Turbines in the United States," *Flight,* October 7, 1948, 439. John Sanders recalled Frank Whittle's comment in an interview with the author, April 6, 1985. The Whittle visit is described in *Wing Tips,* July 19, 1946, NASA-Lewis Technical Library, Cleveland, Ohio.

30. Carlton Kemper to NACA, "Investigation of Rolls-Royce Nene Jet-Propulsion Engine," December 9, 1946, NASA-Lewis Records, 34/623, Cleveland, Ohio.

31. W. P. Gwinn to NACA, December 3, 1947, RG 255, Power Plants Committee, Box 4, File 112.05, National Archives, Suitland, Md.

32. Zelmar Barson and H. D. Wilsted, "Preliminary Results of Nene II Engine Altitude-Chamber Performance Investigation I-Altitude Performance Using Standard 18.75-Inch-Diameter Jet Nozzle," NACA RM E8E12, May 25, 1948, NASA-Lewis Technical Library, Cleveland, Ohio.

33. Interview with John Sanders, Cleveland, Ohio, April 6, 1986.

34. J. W. Crowley to L. S. Hobbs, May 25, 1948, RG 255, Box 4, File 112.05, National Archives, Suitland, Md.

35. Power Plants Committee Minutes, May 21, 1948, RG 255, File 112.02, Box 9, National Archives, Suitland, Md.

36. W. P. Gwinn to J. W. Crowley, July 9, 1948, ibid.

37. Hugh L. Dryden to W. P. Gwinn, August 2, 1948, ibid.

38. Whitney Aircraft Division, *Pratt & Whitney Aircraft Story,* 168.

39. W. P. Gwinn to Hugh L. Dryden, September 8, 1948, RG 255, Box 9, File 112.02, National Archives, Suitland, Md.

40. Power Plants Committee Minutes, December 10, 1948, ibid.

41. Interview with Bruce Lundin, July 15, 1986.

42. Power Plants Committee Minutes, December 10, 1948, RG 255, 112.02, 11, National Archives, Suitland, Md.

43. Ibid.

44. Ibid., 12.

45. Executive Committee Minutes, September 9, 1948, RG 255, Box 14, File 112.05, National Archives, Suitland, Md.

46. Martinuzzi, "Gas Turbines in the United States," 439–41.

47. Walter T. Olson, "Tour of Aircraft Gas Turbine Industry in England," August 22, 1947, NASA-Lewis Records, 34/621, Cleveland, Ohio.

48. Ibid., 87–88.

49. Ibid., 4.

50. See note 12 for references to this work.

51. Charles D. Bright, *The Jet Makers: The Aerospace Industry from 1945–1972* (Lawrence, Kans., 1978), 15.

52. On Wright's demise, see Robert W. Fansel, *What Ever Happened to Curtiss-Wright?* (Manhattan, Kans., 1991).

53. John H. Collins, Jr., "Visit of Mssrs. L. Dawson of Rolls-Royce and R. P. Kroon, V. V. Schloesser, and M. Norton of Westinghouse Electric Corporation, on June 5, 1953," NASA-Lewis Records, 232/150, Cleveland, Ohio.

54. In 1952 Pratt & Whitney received a Collier Trophy for the JT3, the first award for a power plant in 21 years. See "Presentation of the Elmer A. Sperry Award to Leonard S. Hobbs and Perry W. Pratt," booklet, AIAA Ninth Annual Meeting, Courtesy of United Technology Archives, East Hartford, Conn. The dual-spool concept may originally have been British.

55. The development of General Electric's J79, headed by Gerhard Neumann, began in 1951. The J79 was flight-tested in 1955. See *Seven Decades of Progress: A Heritage of Aircraft Turbine Technology* (Fallbrook, Calif., 1979), 84–91.

56. See Sinnette and Voss, "Extension of Useful Operation Range."

57. Carlton Kemper, "Visit of Personnel from Rolls Royce Ltd. England to Lewis on January 10 and 11, 1955," January 19, 1955, NASA-Lewis Records, 232/150, Cleveland, Ohio.

58. Gerhard Neumann, *Herman the German* (New York, 1984), 219.

 **PART THREE**

Economic and Social Constraints Affecting the Development of Commercial Aviation

Helmuth Trischler

Introduction

The overall subject of this session—economic and social constraints affecting the development of commercial aviation—refers to the prevailing social construction theory. In this context, technology does not follow any kind of inner logic but instead is subjected to political, economic, and social influences. Technology, in short, is a product of human activity.

The various projects to develop civil aircraft for supersonic transport (SST) demonstrate the interdependence among technical, economic, and political influences. The great advantage of the SST is speed. With an increase in the number of passengers and a prosperous world economy in the 1950s and 1960s, the need for the development of a civil supersonic airplane seemed obvious. Market research carried out by R. E. G. Davies proves that the promoters of the European Concorde project expected far too much. They assumed that within a few decades, commercial aviation would include hundreds, even thousands, of supersonic aircraft. Simple arithmetic, however, demonstrates that there was no market for a supersonic airplane during the 1960s. The demand for such an airplane for the North Atlantic market never would have exceeded one dozen, even under the optimistic supposition that 5 percent of all passengers would buy an expensive ticket for the supersonic flight. This calculation shows a maximum of 36 SSTs for the world market. Results of retrospective market research prove the continuing validity of these calculations. There is still no market for a supersonic airplane, a fact that taxpayers in Europe should bear in mind when making any decision about launching an SST or an HST (hypersonic transport) program.

To explain why SST projects have been carried out in Europe, the United States, and the Soviet Union without any economic basis, one should look at other than purely economic factors. An analysis of the American SST program, which was blocked by Congress in 1971, indicates that the program was killed by a coalition of opponents who put forward political, social, and environmental arguments. James R. Hansen's paper stresses this view, taking it further and correcting it. He examines the strategies used by supporters to vindicate the SST project. He also analyzes how SST proponents, especially the prime contractor, Boeing Company, reacted to its cancellation by Congress. Thus, Hansen points to internal, financial, and technological constraints, as well as to the public protest by a broad coalition of opponents.

It would be interesting to take a comparative approach to the SST, concentrating also on the development of the Soviet supersonic jet, the Tupolev Tu-144. Contrasting the completely different political decision-making process in a totalitarian regime to the decision-making processes in European and American projects could lead to new and interesting findings.

In contrast to the glamorous SST, rotary-wing aircraft often seem cast into the shadows. The helicopter is considered predominantly as a military aircraft, bearing little relevance to civil aviation. It is too noisy, too expensive, too slow, and too unreliable. John W. R. Taylor calls into question this popular view. The helicopter is shown as a means of transport with a function separate from, rather than competitive with, fixed-wing aircraft. The helicopter is best qualified to supply remote and inhospitable regions. It is essential for sea and mountain rescue services. These and other examples prove that the helicopter has found its own place in aviation.

■■■■
■■■■
■■■■ John W. R. Taylor

Constraints Impeding the Commercial Use of Helicopters

The average, hardheaded financial director of a major airline would summarize the subject of my paper in a few uncompromising words: helicopters are too costly, too slow, too noisy, and too accident-prone. The director could produce valid statistics to support each allegation, yet the overall scenario portrayed would be utterly misleading.

Our hypothetical director would have found support for these assertions from the earliest days of powered flight. On January 15, 1906, Wilbur Wright, just over two years after he and his brother, Orville, had made the first powered airplane flights, commented in a letter: "Like all novices we began with the helicopter (in childhood), but soon saw that it had no future and dropped it. The helicopter does with great labor only what the balloon does without labor, and is no more fitted than the balloon for rapid horizontal flight. If its engine stops it must fall with deathly violence, for it can neither float like the balloon nor glide like the aeroplane. The helicopter is much easier to design than the aeroplane but it is worthless when done."

Wright was wrong—if you'll pardon the pun—on several counts. The helicopter does *much* more than a balloon and is capable of quite rapid horizontal flight. Thanks to the technique of autorotation, devised by Juan de la Cierva in the 1920s, it does not "fall with deathly violence" if its engine stops, provided the pilot is competent. And it is certainly no easier to design than an airplane. After the first flights of the Wright brothers, 36 years of tireless, and usually profitless, experimentation, by skilled engineers of many nations, were required before Igor Sikorsky's VS-300 lifted off the ground on September 14, 1939, as the progenitor of virtually all modern helicopters.

Not everyone agreed with Wilbur Wright at the time he wrote that letter, addressed to Arnold Fordyce in Paris. Thomas Alva Edison, the American technological genius, made an oft-quoted remark in 1905: "The aeroplane won't amount to a damn thing until they get a machine that will act like a hummingbird. Go straight up, go forward, go backward, come straight down and light like a hummingbird."

With the benefit of nearly a century of hindsight, we know that Edison too was wrong. The airplane has become one of the most brilliant achievements of the 20th century. Also, using Edison's own analogy, if I wanted to send a message by natural means to somebody, I should tie it to the leg of a carrier pigeon, not a hummingbird. As soon as we regard the helicopter as a different kind of vehicle with unique capabilities, rather than as just another airplane, it starts to make sense.

We have not yet arrived at the optimum form of that vehicle. The origins of the helicopter are usually traced back to Leonardo da Vinci's sketch, drawn between 1483 and 1485, of a flying machine that was intended to screw itself up, vertically, into the air by means of a man-powered rotating spiral vane. Leonardo called the vane a *helix,* Greek for "screw." Add *pteron,* Greek for "wing," and we have *helix-pteron,* "helicopter," "screw-wing." Leonardo gave us our generic term, and that's about all.

A man-made helicopter toy was lifting itself into the air day after day, in China, nearly 19 centuries before Leonardo's time. Devised in about 400 B.C., it was described in some detail by Ko Hung, a scientist, in A.D. 320 and found its way to Europe via the silk caravans.

When Leonardo was eight years old, in 1460, an artist in France included one of these mini-helicopters in a religious painting. The toy was no more than a four-blade rotor, a few centimeters in diameter, that could be sent spinning up into the air by pulling a string. Our unknown artist showed it in the hands of the Christ child. What I find particularly interesting is that the painting hangs in the cathedral at Le Mans, France, the site of the first European demonstration of the Wright airplane, at Hunaudières racetrack on August 8, 1908.

Wilbur may never have seen the painting. But at Kiev in Russia at that time, the young Igor Sikorsky had been so fascinated by what he read in the news-

12.1. Igor Sikorsky, father of the modern helicopter. (Courtesy Sikorsky Aircraft)

papers about early flying machines that he determined to build one. In his childhood he had read the science fiction novels of Jules Verne. He found the illustration of Verne's *Clipper of the Clouds* especially inspiring and decided to concentrate on helicopters. In the context of my paper, it is interesting to note that one of his reasons was that he believed helicopters would be safer than airplanes. By 1909 there had been about one fatality for every 2,000 miles of flight achieved by an airplane and a few crashes for every 100 miles.

Sikorsky's first two helicopters, built in 1909–10, were completely safe, since they failed to leave the ground. He realized that the technology of 1910 was too primitive for a practical helicopter. For the next three decades he turned to fixed-wing aircraft, building in the process the first four-engined airplane and the amphibians that put the young Pan American Airways on the map. Then, in 1939, he achieved his lifelong ambition with the VS-300—the first completely successful single-main-rotor helicopter.

Like his four-engined Le Grand airplane of 1913, the VS-300 was constructed on the eve of a world war. Successors to the Le Grand were the Ilia

Mourometz bombers of World War I. Descendants of the VS-300 were evaluated by armies and navies in World War II and made the helicopter an indispensable part of the military inventory during the Korean War of 1950–53.

Anyone who knew Sikorsky—especially those familiar with his deeply inspiring books that reflected his Christian faith—would understand how he delighted in former Supreme Allied Commander General Alfred M. Gruenther's remarks that before Korea, 80 to 90 percent of soldiers who received head or abdominal wounds in combat died; in Korea, quick helicopter evacuation from the battlefields cut this figure to 10 percent.

Sikorsky had always regarded the helicopter's ability to save lives as one of its primary commitments. In a talk to the Wings Club in New York City in November 1964, he told how he had in his possession a brochure published in Paris in 1862—more than 100 years earlier—entitled *L'Aéronef, Appareil de Sauvetage* (The Aircraft, a Device for Saving Lives). He told his listeners, "This brochure gives a reasonable description of the helicopter, and also includes answers to a number of rather naive criticisms which were meant to demonstrate the impossibility of such a machine." He added, "The brochure ends with the following prophetic statement: 'And then I, a modest narrator . . . will have the happiness to see people rescued at sea, and victims of fires and floods saved by this apparatus.' "

"Prophetic" was a well-chosen expression. Sikorsky quoted an article entitled "Tampico's Great Airlift Rescue" from the September 1956 issue of *Reader's Digest,* which described activities after a devastating flood hit the Mexican city:

> The US Navy carrier *Siboney,* with 13 big Sikorsky helicopters, 31 Marine pilots and relief supplies, put out of Norfolk, Virginia. . . . When the final score was totalled it was found that Navy helicopters had snatched 9,262 lives from the flood's maw, 2,445 by hoists. They had saved other thousands by landing Mexican medical aid on 164 missions, and delivering 197 tons of food at points which only they could reach. [Tampico's] Mayor Ravize put in words the common feeling: "Something wonderful happened here. Suddenly there were no Mexicans, no Americans, no border—just human beings rediscovering the brotherhood of man. These few days have been worth a century of diplomacy between our countries."

By the time Sikorsky gave his talk to the Wings Club, more than 100,000 lives had been saved by products of the still-young U.S. helicopter industry, nearly half of them by Sikorsky aircraft.

Sikorsky told how, after floods hit Hamburg in 1962, helicopters saved at least 1,117 people and carried thousands more to safe areas, often in minimal visibility and with wind strengths far beyond all handbook limits. The H-34s and H-21s were deliberately flown against chimneys to knock them down. The wheels of the helicopters were bounced against roofs until they broke through, allowing trapped families to climb out through the hole and into the helicopter. Crewmen jumped from the helicopters onto slippery, sloping roofs to chop holes and liberate families trapped in attics.

Flood, fire, famine, shipwreck, motorway accidents, mountain-climbing crises—all made increasing demands of helicopter operators. Capabilities increased in parallel with aircraft size; turbines replaced piston engines; new avionics and equipment allowed day-night, all-weather missions.

Typical has been the day-to-day routine duty of the British Royal Air Force and Royal Navy search-and-rescue units. The number of people removed alive from a hazard, or transported for urgent medical attention, increased from an average of around 1,000 a year in the 1950s to 1,868 in 1990. Television news shots of a Sea King or Wessex helicopter hovering over a ship on the rocks or engineless or on fire in mountainous seas have become commonplace. Crewmen drop from a cable onto the ship's deck or into the sea in a desperate rescue bid. They are hauled up by the same hoist, often steadying a litter or cradling a victim in their arms. Only helicopters, and a unique breed of men of many nationalities, perform such work as routine.

What begins as a noncombat task for military pilots sometimes develops into a commercial operation later. For example, some British coastal helicopter search-and-rescue services are now being entrusted to private operators, and some of the bases are being closed under the Defence Ministry's cost-cutting program. There is no sign of constraints in such business, but of course the missions are not exactly commercial—unless one counts human lives as being the most precious commodities on earth.

In multibillion-dollar, multinational businesses, like oil and gas exploration and the servicing of offshore rigs, costs are evaluated differently. Time is money, and the financial benefit from ferrying men and equipment between shore and rig in helicopters is easy to show. The work could not be done round the clock, as daily routine, by any other high-speed vehicle. So, typically, helicopters transport 90 percent of personnel working in the oil and gas fields of the North Sea. Constraints are secondary to cost-effectiveness—the stuff of which accountants' dreams are made.

The passengers this time can be counted in millions, not thousands. Bond Helicopters, Bristow Helicopters, and British International Helicopters, the three major operators handling traffic between the British mainland and offshore rigs, carried a peak total of 2,533,890 passengers in 1990, on 349,818 sectors, totaling 132,771 flying hours. Bristow accounted for 53.4 percent of the flight time and had the largest fleet, with 16 Sikorsky S-61Ns carrying up to 24 passengers each, 27 French Super Pumas with seats for 19 to 23 passengers, and 19 smaller helicopters. The combined fleet of the three operators now numbers 135 helicopters.

The scale of this operation is huge by commercial helicopter standards. Aberdeen has the largest heliport of its kind anywhere in the world, handling 30,000 passengers each month. Every weekday around 60 Bristow flights leave Aberdeen to fly to offshore rigs and platforms. Their 95-percent despatch reliability is an industry standard and the envy of many airlines. So much for the alleged constraint of poor reliability.

Worldwide, it is true that the accident rate for helicopters does not match the best airline statistics. Data produced some time ago by Britain's Civil Aviation Authority suggested that the fatal accident rates for jet airliners, turboprop airliners, and large twin-engined helicopters were in the ratio 1.5 to 4 to 10 (1.5 for jets, 4 for turboprops, 10 for large helicopters). Statistics made available recently in Great Britain show that, in almost 30 years of helicopter operations in the British sector of the North Sea oil and gas fields, 9 aircrew and 70 passengers were killed in support flights, with another 8 crew and 4 passengers lost during search-and-rescue and training missions.

The conditions under which North Sea helicopters operate bear little comparison to those experienced as routine by scheduled airline operators. As a start, the "airfields" of the former are tiny platforms, bounded by tall metal structures, high above an often-stormy sea and often approached in appalling weather. In such an environment, the ability of a helicopter to hover and inch its way to a safe touchdown—in the words of Edison, to "go forward, go backward, come straight down and light like a hummingbird"—alone enables it to do the job.

The same is true of so much else that helicopters do daily, as routine, especially in places like Papua New Guinea's jungle highlands. It is often forgotten that airplanes hauled heavy freight into airstrips hacked out of the tropical jungle of New Guinea in the 1920s and 1930s. (According to the BBC, a fleet of four trimotor Junkers G-31 and single-engined W-34 transports lifted more freight into the goldfields of Bulolo in one month, in 1931, than all the airlines of the world had carried in the previous twelve months.)

Today it is not gold but oil that benefits from the greater versatility of helicopters, in Papua New Guinea as much as in offshore oil fields. The pacesetter among the operators is Aerolift International of Singapore. Just as, between the world wars, Guinea Airways realized that the Junkers G-31, with its 7,000-pound payload, was unique in its ability to deliver to the goldfields pieces of steel dredges that weighed up to 3,000 tons when assembled, so Aerolift decided to take advantage of heavy-lift helicopters that Russia's highly skilled engineers were eager to export.

A Mil Mi-26, the world's largest production helicopter, and the first three of four Kamov Ka-32s arrived in Papua New Guinea in mid-1990, with the Kamovs airlifted in a single An-124 freighter. Put to work under oil-exploration contracts in the Kutubu basin, in the highlands, and on such work as power line construction, they have since clocked over 5,000 hours.

Utilization of the Mi-26 was lower than expected for a time, since the oil companies were unable to take full advantage of its 20-ton maximum lift capability; but the Kamovs impressed from day one. Their contra-rotating rotors make them much less sensitive to crosswinds than are other helicopters; the absence of a tail rotor removes the danger of tail rotor strikes in confined spaces and makes the helicopters considerably less noisy—although noise does not matter so much in the heart of a New Guinea jungle as at a city-center heliport.

More significant is that a Ka-32, with a fuselage about the same size as that of a Puma, will lift more than 11,000 pounds, compared with 7,055 pounds for a Boeing Vertol 107 and 5,400 pounds for a Puma under the same conditions. These latter two had been standard equipment before the Kamovs arrived.

Fuel consumption of the Ka-32 is, inevitably, higher, at 1,585 pounds per hour compared with 1,210 pounds per hour for the Vertol and the Puma; but this becomes less important when the customer is in the oil business and is responsible for providing the fuel. More impressive to the pilots has been the Kamovs' cruising speed of 135 knots, which reduces to around 100 knots with a heavy, high-drag external load. The Vertol is restricted to about 100 knots at 7,000 feet *without* a load; the Puma's permitted limit is 80 knots when carrying 4,960 pounds or more.

Aerolift is employing these Russian helicopters in other places as well. In Myanmar (what we used to call Burma), four Ka-32s, supported by a Bell 212, have flown more than 2,500 hours under contract to Amoco. Tasks have included helping in the construction of the largest heli-borne rig in the world, north of Mandalay. In Cambodia, two Mi-26s are distributing aid on behalf of the United Nations Technical Assistance in Cambodia (UNTAC) program, as well as supporting UN forces in the field. As an alternative to their maximum internal payload of 45,000 pounds of freight, they offer an easily removable seating configuration for 76 passengers and can carry more than 100 people in an emergency.

Aerolift achieved in Papua New Guinea what it describes, a little strangely, as the first certification of a Ka-32 "in the West." Such certification is not straightforward. In America, for example, attempts by a logging company to bypass normal U.S. certification procedures, in order to operate an Mi-26 in Alaska, were bitterly opposed by U.S. helicopter manufacturers and rejected by the Federal Aviation Administration. In an editorial in *Helicopter International* magazine, Elfan ap Rees pointed out: "If Russian helicopters are given exemption from US certification, why not British or French or, horror of horrors, ex-US military? Where will be the case for stopping surplus Sikorsky H-3s becoming S-61s, or for Bell Kiowas metamorphosizing into Jet Rangers?"

In a hard commercial world, helicopters must clearly battle against formidable constraints other than "too costly, too slow, too noisy, and too accident-prone." Before becoming overcritical of protectionism, one should study the facts presented at the 68th annual meeting of the U.S. Transportation Research Board in Washington, D.C., in 1989. J. Colin Green, corporate director, Technology Planning, United Technologies Corporation, explained that, excluding what was then the Eastern bloc, there were eight major manufacturers of turbine-engined helicopters in the world, plus another seven significant competitors. He then said: "To make my point clear, we have 15 players in a market whose total demand is for some 100 vehicles a month. . . . Market size is more important than market share. While a fair share of a large market is possibly a living formula, 100 percent of an economically trivial market spells disaster." He estimated that the combined military and commercial helicopter fleets of the United States and Europe then consisted of around 22,150 vehicles, of which 15,400, about 70 percent, were military. Whereas 65 percent of the military helicopters were above 5,000-pound gross weight, 84 percent of the commercial helicopters were below 5,000-pound gross weight.

Clearly, constraints or not, the commercial helicopter business is peanuts in terms of world economics. Without military contracts, few of the 15 manufacturers counted by Colin Green would find the business viable. The long-term consolation for those tough enough to survive the recession and the "peace dividends" is—as stressed repeatedly in this paper—that there is no alternative to rotating wings for some of the economically, and humanely, vital tasks that helicopters perform.

It is not untimely in such a context to refer to an operation that was commercial only in the sense that it deeply affected the lives of a huge number of people. In economic terms, it earned no profits. From those most intimately involved, it demanded courage and self-sacrifice to an extreme degree. And it could happen again, at any one of many places worldwide, without warning and with unpredictable consequences. The story is so remarkable that I trust you will excuse me for telling it in some detail, not in my own words but mainly in those of my good friend and helper Sergei Sikorsky, the son of Igor, based on *his* talk to the Wings Club in New York in 1989.

Chernobyl #4 nuclear reactor exploded shortly after midnight on Saturday, April 26, 1986. The intense heat of the reactor (some 4,000 degrees Fahrenheit) created a plume of radiation, ash, and dust 30,000 feet high. All that day about 300 to 350 plant workers and firemen fought the heat and flames, ignoring the heavy radiation to which they knew they were being exposed. All civilians were evacuated from an area within an 18-mile radius of Chernobyl. Helicopters were called in to help deal with the catastrophe. One of them circled the reactor in order to photograph it and determine the damage. After studying the hastily developed photographs, local nuclear scientists said that the ruined reactor had to be capped or sealed as soon as possible to choke out the fires and to stop radiation from venting out of the rubble and further contaminating the countryside.

Guards Colonel Serebrayakov volunteered to fly directly above the stricken reactor, and through the radioactive smoke plume, to determine the best approach path, altitude, and air speed to start dropping chemicals and special materials to cover the reactor. When he returned, he recommended that the drop helicopters be flown at about 30 mph but not lower than 600 feet above the reactor because of the danger of engine flameout due to the intense heat of the reactor, even at that altitude. On that first Sunday, the 27th, Colonel Serebrayakov and Colonel Yakovlev each flew 22 missions over Chernobyl, dropping burlap bags hastily filled with a mixture of marble chips, lead, and boron. Between them they dropped 60 tons of protective material. On the following day, 93 tons of clay were dropped in sandbags by volunteer crews. More Mi-6 helicopters arrived, and by the fourth day 700 tons had been deposited. By May 8 the total had reached more than 5,000 tons, practically sealing off the reactor.

The work continued through May. Even after the reactor had been covered, and the surrounding land carpeted with liquid synthetic rubber compounds to trap radioactive dust, helicopters were still the only vehicles able to conduct temperature and radiation checks. They did this by hovering 800 feet above the reactor and lowering Geiger counters and other measuring equipment on long cables into the wreckage. A Swedish scientist commented, "Without the heroism of the helicopter crews, who knowingly flew in extreme radiation during the first five days to seal the reactor, it would have been not a Russian tragedy but very probably an international disaster."

One of the pilots, Anatoly Grishchenko, a test pilot from the Gromov Flight Research Institute, died in 1990, despite a half-million-dollar bone marrow transplant in the United States. Others await similar treatment, but no cash is available. Ours has become the first century in history in which the achievements of mankind are limited deliberately, not by what man has the skill and courage to venture but by what dull-minded people permit to be spent. Even life itself no longer takes precedence over financial constraint.

In such circumstances, what chance is there for the commercial helicopter? God willing, Chernobyl was a once-only threat to life on a considerable portion of our planet. Now, as always, any hope of a genuine commercial future for the helicopter must depend on carrying civilian passengers and freight on a massive scale.

In a post–World War II flush of enthusiasm for the newly discovered go-anywhere capability of helicopters, glossy magazines were packed with predictions of a time when everyone would have a family helicopter in the garage. Everyone would fly, just as they now drive cars. But, as homebuilt aircraft and microlight manufacturers learned to their cost, not everyone wants to fly. It is easy to imagine the resulting chaos if everyone did.

This brings us to one highly important constraint that is often overlooked. Although, technically, helicopters are able to go almost anywhere, there are in fact few places where they are allowed to go. In a society that breeds protest in the name of civil liberty, the mere mention of helicopters landing near homes or offices produces a rent-a-crowd swarm of folk with banners proclaiming: "To hell with helicopters."

Also worth bearing in mind is the admission in Bell Helicopter's *Rotorbreeze* newsletter: "In the US helicopter industry, there is not a single financially successful commercial helicopter that is not a direct descendant of military aircraft." If rotating-wing passenger services are unlikely to expand on a vast scale until larger, faster, technologically advanced types are available, where will these types come from now that military expenditure is unpopular?

When I was with the Fairey Aviation Group in the 1950s, we thought we had one answer. The Rotodyne was an elegant twin-turboprop VTOL (vertical take-off and landing) transport, with a conventional high wing and a four-blade torqueless rotor. During takeoff and landing, the turboprops drove compressors that fed air to pressure-jets at the blade-tips. There it was mixed with fuel and burned, to produce high rotor power. After takeoff and transition to forward flight, engine power was switched to normal turboprop mode while the rotor autorotated.

The Rotodyne prototype showed tremendous promise, carrying up to 35 passengers in public demonstrations. In its planned production form, with two 5,250-shaft-horsepower Tyne turboprops, it was intended to seat up to 70 per-

12.2. Rotodyne convertiplane landing at the Westland Heliport, London. (Courtesy Westland Helicopters)

sons, with a nominal range of 250 miles at 201 mph with 57 passengers. It offered true airliner comfort, and even New York Airways planned to order 5, with an option on 15 more. But it *was* noisy.

Development produced suppressors that promised to reduce the noise of the pressure-jets to 95 EPNdB. Fairey claimed that the current noise level was less than that of an underground railway (metro) train approaching a London platform. Fairey's engineers were instructed to aim for 90 decibels. Whether even this would have enabled the further development of the Rotodyne concept—in a time when 400-knot BAe 146 fixed-wing airliners operate at a STOL (short takeoff and landing) strip in the heart of London's dockland—is debatable. Quiet jets like the 146 may be rare and airports in cities even rarer; but the question is irrelevant, since the Rotodyne program was canceled in 1962.

Since then, many helicopter operators have launched passenger services, typically between New York's airports and the city center and between London's Heathrow and Gatwick airports. The more successful operations have been in areas where alternative forms of transportation are slow, often unpleasant, or even hazardous.

British International Helicopters and its predecessor, British Airways Heli-

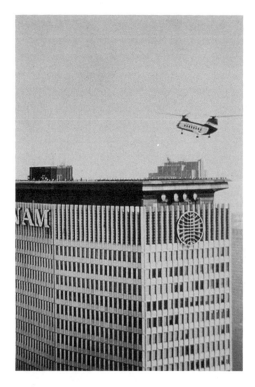

12.3. Airport-to-city-center helicopter landing on the roof of Pan Am's New York headquarters. (Courtesy Pan American Airways)

copters, have carried 2.1 million passengers between Penzance in Cornwall and the Isles of Scilly since taking over from small Rapide biplanes in 1964. The longest-running helicopter service in the world, it operates Sikorsky S-61Ns, which take just 20 minutes for the trip with up to 32 passengers.

S-61s are also the workhorses of services operated by Greenlandair, in regions with some of the most savage weather faced by an airline. The company's 16 helicopters of various types and 8 fixed-wing aircraft fly into 9 airports, 15 heliports, and 37 helistops in a country 1,700 miles long and 600 miles wide. They link isolated fishing villages with the larger towns and carry, each year, roughly three times Greenland's total population.

The S-61 was the first commercial helicopter able to operate down to negative two degrees centigrade at 3,000 feet or below, in any weather, with no risk of engine flameout or icing problems. Bristow operates this aircraft's General Electric engines for 18,000 hours between major overhauls, with 2,000-hour light intermediate overhauls. Generally, therefore, it must be said that today's helicopters do superbly well what they are given to do. Bigger and faster types might do more, although experience with the Mi-26 suggests that some problems increase with size. For example, Mil's chief test pilot has explained that safe autorotative landing after a total engine failure would demand particularly skillful piloting but has been demonstrated successfully.

What, then, does the future hold for the helicopter industry? Optimists suggest that the performance offered by the Rotodyne's modern counterpart, the very different tilt-rotor Bell/Boeing V-22 Osprey convertiplane, might introduce a new era of rotating-wing progress. Much depends at this stage on whether the U.S. military will order it in large numbers, as once planned. The U.S. Marines, in particular, want to be all-STOL by the year 2015. Something like the V-22 would seem to be essential for them.

Minimum changes to the current V-22 configuration would offer a non-pressurized 31-seat CTR-22B (civil tilt-rotor) transport with a range of 600 nautical miles and a cruising speed of 240 knots. With a new pressurized fuselage, a developed CTR-22C would carry 39 passengers at 282 knots, and the tilt-rotor team has projected a 75-passenger CTR-7500 that would cruise at 300 knots. With any of these types, the team figures that 117 pairs of cities in the United States could find work for 1,268 CTRs on city-to-city air links. Europe could absorb 615 aircraft for use on 57 links, Japan 501 aircraft on 26 paired-city links. A Japanese organization advocated the development of a network of 600 heliports in Japan, of which 23 have been opened to date. Another Japanese company, Ishida, is funding in the United States a tilt-wing transport that could use these heliports.

Is this the shape of the future? Increased speed would certainly offset the advantage currently enjoyed by fixed-wing aircraft like the BAe 146, and there is no reason heliports should not be built over already busy and noisy freeways. The helicopters would hardly be noticed by a generation brought up in discotheques.

BIBLIOGRAPHY

Boyne, Walter J., and Donald S. Lopez, eds. *Vertical Flight: The Age of the Helicopter.* Washington, D.C., 1984.

Everett-Heath, John. *Soviet Helicopters.* London, 1988.

Jane's All the World's Aircraft.

Sikorsky, Igor I. *The Story of the Winged-S.* New York, 1967.

Taylor, John W. R. *Helicopters and VTOL Aircraft.* New York, 1960.

■■■■
■■■■
■■■■ James R. Hansen

What Went Wrong?

Some New Insights into the Cancellation of the American SST Program

It was not just one compelling force but rather a myriad of constraints that came together to kill the American supersonic transport (SST) program in 1971. Most observers of the SST debate at the time, and most historians since that time, have focused on the coalition of social and political activists who stimulated intense public concern over the environmental damage the proposed supersonic airliner allegedly would do if ever allowed to thunder across the skies at its designed cruise speed of Mach 2.7. But in fact other, far less public but nonetheless critical constraints, both financial and technological, also played into the termination of the SST program, including factors internal to the private affairs of Boeing Company. These undermining, and as yet mostly unexamined, forces were perhaps as compelling as the noisy activism of the SST public protest movement. In this essay, itself just a slice of a more comprehensive analysis to be done of the SST proponents' private and public reaction to the 1971 SST cancellation, I hope to introduce some of these other, more hidden, constraints, which will then require a much deeper investigation.

On March 24, 1971, the U.S. Senate, in one of the most dramatic votes in its history, refused to authorize another penny for the construction of two supersonic transport prototypes, thereby effectively killing an immensely controversial eight-year-old government program for which more than one billion dollars already had been spent. Like most previous votes on the national SST program (including the one six days earlier in the House of Representatives, which had also gone against further SST funding), the climactic vote in the Senate, which denied $134 million for the go-ahead on the two prototypes, might easily have gone the other way. The defeat came from the slimmest majority possible in the 100-member upper house: 51 senators voted to deny further funding. At the last minute, two uncommitted senators, John Sherman Cooper (R-Kentucky) and Sam Ervin (D-North Carolina), the latter soon to become famous for his role in the Senate Watergate hearings, decided to vote against the SST. From tobacco-growing states, the two men apparently wanted to get back at Warren Magnuson, a pro-SST Democratic senator from the state of Washington (where Boeing Company, the prime contractor for the SST, was located) for supporting some strong anticigarette legislation. As Magnuson himself would reflect in the days following the culminating Senate vote, if he had only been a chain-smoker, or if the supporters of the SST had only been wise enough to cut the proposal down to the cost of just one prototype instead of two, the SST proponents "might have prevailed."[1]

But instead, by the narrowest of margins, the proponents of the SST lost the battle for the funding of the two prototypes, which cost them the war. Various attempts to revive the SST program followed, but after the March 24 Senate vote, the American supersonic airliner was generally believed to be dead—the victim of a mercy killing or of a wanton murder of a precious brainchild, depending on one's opinion about the good sense of building and flying a commercial supersonic airliner. Even if, as some people felt, the opponents of the SST had not quite been able to kill it off, they had at least put the SST concept into a deep and languishing sleep from which it would not recover for a very long time.[2]

For many of those who ardently supported the American SST and who were most actively and passionately involved in its ambitious development, the Senate vote came as a stunning and personal blow. Many of these individuals remember their exact circumstances during the critical week when the SST was killed. For example, Richard D. Fitzsimmons, a staunch SST advocate and head of President Richard Nixon's National Aeronautics and Space Council, sat in Vice President Spiro Agnew's box above the floor of the House of Representatives when the very close House vote of March 18 (a vote of 215 to 204) went against the SST. He had to listen to the yelling and cheering of vocal supporters from The Friends of the Earth, an anti-SST interest group, who were sitting nearby in the public gallery. For Fitzsimmons, the loss was more than disheart-

13.1. Tiny scale model of early SST design. As early as the late 1950s, American aeronautical engineers had their eye on the potential of large supersonic airplanes for both military and commercial applications. Here, in a photo dating from 1961, a research engineer at NASA Langley Research Center in Virginia eyeballs the shape of a tiny wind tunnel model of a supersonic transport configuration. (Courtesy National Aeronautics and Space Administration–Langley)

ening; to this day, some 21 years later, he remembers it as the most upsetting and infuriating moment of his life.[3]

In his mind, Congress was making a huge mistake in canceling the SST program. The program was probably going to be stopped anyway before a commitment to production was made, since it was becoming increasingly clear that the operating economics and the range of the flashy supersonic airliner were just not going to be competitive with those of Boeing's new 747 wide-body.[4] But the SST program—Fitzsimmons thought—should nonetheless be allowed to continue to the point of flying one or possibly two prototype aircraft. In that way, much good research would be accomplished that could be used elsewhere in the industry. Furthermore, as Fitzsimmons and the other SST proponents were to repeat (and mutter to themselves) over and over again in the coming months and years, it was going to cost the U.S. taxpayers more to cancel the SST—and settle all the existing contracts, pay the cancellation fees, and wind down the program—than it would to proceed with building and flying the first airplane.[5]

John T. Swihart, the chief engineer for Boeing's Production SST Airplane Development, remembers *exactly* where he was and what he was doing when he first heard the news of the vote to terminate the SST program. He was on his way through the Dayton, Ohio, airport when he was paged and told over the telephone by a colleague in Seattle the bad news of the March 24 Senate vote. Swihart was headed for Kalamazoo, Michigan, where he and another one of the country's leading champions of the SST—Professor Wilbur C. Nelson of the University of Michigan, head of an organization called FAST ("Fly An American SST")—were scheduled to debate a student activist group, the Michigan Student Environmental Confederation, on the campus of Kalamazoo College.[6]

For several months it had been Swihart's duty as SST project manager to influence public opinion in favor of the SST. Swihart had trained a small army of capable younger people, most of them Boeing employees, to go out and speak in favor of the supersonic transport to any group that would receive them. When paged in the Dayton airport and told of the Senate vote, he first wanted to head right back home to Seattle, but an organizer of the event in Kalamazoo insisted that the debate go on as scheduled. As Swihart remembers, it turned out to be one of his better debates because he could make the arguments in favor of the airplane, but instead of always being on the defensive, he could now take the offensive and tell the audience: "These are the facts, but politics has prevailed."[7]

The decision to cancel the SST was totally incorrect, Swihart told the crowd that evening, because it was a political decision, not the technical or business decision that it should have been. The cancellation was due to antiadministration and antitechnology feelings brought on by the growing unrest (however justifiable) over the increasingly unpopular war in Vietnam. It was, he believed, an opportunistic political reaction sparked by demagogues like William Proxmire, the crusading Democratic senator from Wisconsin, as well as by the hysterical claims of environmentalists and other rabid anti-SST interest groups, who together were doing their utmost to stir up public fears of the social and environmental hazards, most of them farfetched, that the supersonic airliner would inflict if built and allowed to fly on a regular basis. It was hysteria fueled by the press, by liberal instruments like the *Washington Post* and the *New York Times,* and by the three major television networks, some of which, according to Swihart's reliable sources inside the media, had been following an unofficial policy that nothing favorable about the SST was ever to be published and that, instead, scary headlines and stories about the SST were to appear almost daily.[8]

On technical and business grounds, the killing of the SST program made no sense, Swihart told the skeptical Kalamazoo crowd. Boeing already had 15 percent of the first prototype airplane built; the U.S. aircraft industry was five months from the major assembly of what he told his audience would be "the most advanced airplane in the world"; and, again, it was going to cost the country more to cancel the SST program and pay off the contracts than it would to finish the first prototype.[9]

Adding immeasurably to the damage Swihart was predicting was the fact that the United States was surrendering the future of a promising new commercial flight regime—surrendering to the French and the British, and even to the Soviets, what Swihart and most other SST proponents believed to be "the next frontier" and "next logical step" in the evolution of air transportation. In doing so, the nation of the Wright brothers and the DC-3 was turning away from several new flight technologies that would surely be studied and developed in an ongoing national SST program, dramatic new technologies such as fly-by-wire electronic controls, digital stability augmentation systems, high-temperature composite structures, cathode-ray-tube flight deck instruments, and a jet power plant that in tests had already demonstrated 73,000 pounds of thrust.[10]

But politics had killed the chances for all that—or so the SST proponents lamented. The SST was President Nixon's most vulnerable program. The Democrats had made it their number-one target—unofficially, of course—on their antiadministration hit list. This was in spite of the fact that the national SST program had been started by a Democrat, President John F. Kennedy, and advanced by another Democratic regime, led by Lyndon Johnson. So strong was the political opposition to the SST by 1971 that even the most arrogant policymakers in the Republican White House were afraid to support the American SST program very openly. Even Fitzsimmons's National Aeronautics and Space Council, which was headed by Vice President Agnew and composed of the secretaries of the major agencies of the federal government and which had spent many months preparing support papers designed to influence public opinion just before the final congressional votes, stepped to the side at the crucial time before the votes and kept quiet about the SST. In many public ways, the executive office did likewise, figuring (probably wrongly, in retrospect) that the controversial SST program had a better chance of being approved if President Nixon did not publicly challenge the Democrats and the anti-SST coalition.[11]

These were only some of the initial, fragmentary explanations of how and why the national SST program was canceled, as seen in the individual reactions of Richard Fitzsimmons and John Swihart, two of the most ardent and best-informed proponents of the American supersonic airliner. Other explanations can be found in the reactions of pro-SST organizations such as the National Committee for an American SST, based in Washington, D.C., the Committee for an American SST, based in Seattle, and (my personal favorite) the Aerospace Truth Squad, based in Los Angeles. Of course, a great many pro-SST reactions can be found in the numerous editorials and letters to editors that appeared in newspapers around the country, in national magazines, and in the professional trade journals. One letter to the editor, appearing in the leading magazine of the aircraft industry, *Aviation Week and Space Technology,* on April 12,

13.2. Soviet Tu-144 SST. Believing that its engineers had solved the very significant problems plaguing its pioneering—yet patchwork—SST design, the Soviet Union flew the Tu-144 supersonic airliner to the Paris Air Show in 1973. At Le Bourget airport, before some 300,000 spectators, the airplane broke up in the air and was destroyed in a spectacular crash that killed its crew of five, plus eight persons on the ground. (Courtesy National Aeronautics and Space Administration–Langley)

1971, came from John Swihart himself. In it, the angry Boeing engineer did his best to refute a single allegation against the SST: what Swihart called "the out and out lie," knowingly and dishonestly perpetrated by SST critics, that the regular operation of supersonic airliners would cause such a decrease in stratospheric ozone that more and more people would get skin cancer.[12]

But it is dangerous to generalize about the pro-SST reaction from just a few individual cases because not everyone in favor of the SST agreed with Fitzsimmons and Swihart about the demise of the supersonic airliner. Other SST proponents felt that Congress made the *correct* decision in 1971, but for the "wrong reasons." Congress killed the SST for environmental reasons—concerns over the effects of sonic booms, over airport noise, and over ozone depletion—when in fact the decision should have been made, they believed, because the technology for an economically viable SST simply was not yet in hand and building the Boeing design would therefore have been a grave mistake.

A number of aeronautical engineers who had been advocating the develop-

ment of a supersonic airliner were not nearly as confident about Boeing's Model
2707-300 (Dash-300) SST airplane as Boeing engineer John Swihart apparently
was. Several who had been very closely monitoring the technical progress of
the SST program did not agree with Boeing's choices for the airframe design:
neither its original plan for the structurally complicated and heavy variable-
sweep or "swing-wing," which had won the Federal Aviation Administration
(FAA) competition in 1966, nor its change to a fixed delta wing, a design not
terribly unlike the Lockheed configuration that had *lost* the 1966 FAA competition but to which the Boeing engineers had turned so quickly, and in quiet des-
peration, during the spring of 1968.[13]

Some of the most skeptical engineers worked for the National Aeronautics
and Space Administration (NASA). After primary responsibility for the national SST program had been given to the FAA in 1963, NASA had been assigned to evaluate the SST concepts proposed by the aircraft industry and then
to assist the FAA in monitoring the contracts and grants of the resulting national
program. By the late 1960s, some of the NASA consultants clearly recognized

13.3. Lockheed L-2000 SST mockup. In spite of this impressive mockup, the fixed-
wing Lockheed L-2000 SST lost the national SST competition in 1966 to Boeing's
innovative variable-sweep design. (Courtesy National Air and Space Museum)

13.4. "The Airplane That Never Was": a mockup of the Boeing 2707 fixed-wing SST design that was selected in 1969 but canceled in 1971. (Courtesy National Air and Space Museum)

that the tradeoffs necessary just in the propulsion area to meet even minimally acceptable airport noise standards were going to increase the gross takeoff weight of the proposed supersonic airliner to unacceptable levels. A few of the NASA men who spent quite a bit of time at Boeing in 1970 and 1971 remember how Boeing personnel were addressing this nasty synergism involving noise and takeoff weight by frantically designing and redesigning various airframe and engine combinations, with little success.[14]

Thus, when Congress killed the funding for the Boeing prototypes in 1971, many of the strongest SST proponents inside NASA accepted the termination as justified. Program costs were beginning to mount rapidly, and it was becoming obvious to many of NASA's experts that Boeing's prototype could serve only as another research vehicle and not as one that would lead directly to the development of a commercially successful SST. Breakthroughs were needed in too many areas, including aerodynamics, propulsion, sonic boom noise, and "hot" structures. "Another research vehicle was not really needed at this time," according to one NASA researcher, because of the existence of the supersonic SR-71 and the Concorde. What was needed, in the view of most of the NASA

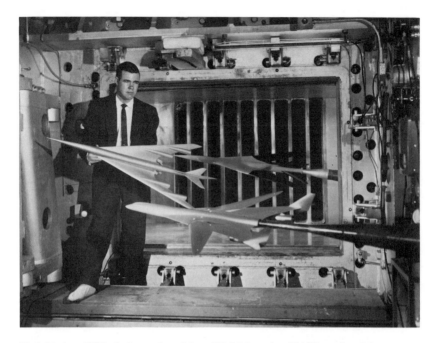

13.5. Various SST wind tunnel models at NASA Langley. NASA explored the performance potential of a wide range of SST configurations, including the three shown in the test section of this Langley wind tunnel during 1963. Notice that two of the three possess variable-sweep wings. (Courtesy National Aeronautics and Space Administration–Langley)

engineers, was a continuation and intensification of a broadly based research program. However, it *was* a mistake, the NASA engineers felt, given the ongoing promise of the SST to revolutionize long-range over-the-ocean transportation, for Congress to curtail the funding of basic SST research efforts.[15]

At NASA's Langley Research Center in Virginia, a group of researchers had grown very enthusiastic about an SST design of their own, known as SCAT-15F ("Supersonic Cruise Air Transport"). This was an innovative, fixed arrow-wing version of an earlier NASA swing-wing SST concept that surfaced during an in-house feasibility study made during the 1964–65 period. For their pet SCAT-15F, the engineers at Langley had churned up a lot of enthusiasm. SCAT-15F incorporated some aerodynamically sophisticated principles of wing design, wing-fuselage integration, engine placement, and favorable lift interference, principles that had been validated in the process of developing computer-aided supersonic design methods in the early and mid-1960s. Both Boeing and Lockheed had considered the SCAT-15F during 1965 and 1966, preparatory to the FAA design competition. Although neither company adopted the configuration as its primary SST concept, both companies incorporated certain features of SCAT-15F into the final contractor designs. In the late 1960s, Boeing was still exploring SCAT-15F as a backup to its delta-winged Dash-300. Wind tunnel tests showed that the SCAT-15F had superior supersonic cruise efficiency and an amazing resistance to an aerodynamic flutter problem that was in fact vexing the Dash-300. As far as many of the SST advocates at NASA Langley were concerned, it would be better to scrap the national SST program as it was and keep working on concepts like the SCAT-15F (for which a group of NASA engineers held a patent) than it would be to go ahead and build a defective airplane like Boeing's Dash-300.[16]

As for the feelings at Boeing itself, to this day there are many questions to answer about how people at the top of the company actually felt about the cancellation of the SST program. We know that publicly, most of them, like John Swihart, sounded terribly disappointed and upset. T. A. Wilson, the Boeing president, called the Senate vote "a blow to all of us at Boeing." The day after the vote, Wilson announced that some 7,000 workers in Seattle would probably have to be laid off as a result of the termination, 4,500 of them coming directly from assignments on the SST program and the remainder from support jobs.[17]

There is no reason to question the authenticity of the anger and the disdain felt by the Boeing rank and file, or by the people of the larger Seattle community, or by most members of Boeing's SST team, about the cancellation of the SST. Their feelings appear to have been genuine, as evidenced in some of the colorfully exaggerated and frivolous ways in which they let their anger out: for example, with their boycott of cheese from the dairy state of Wisconsin—a dig at the SST arch-foe, Senator Proxmire of Wisconsin—which was the idea of a Seattle restaurant chef, and with their printing of bumper stickers that said, "Proxmire Eats Margarine" and "Ban Wisconsin Beer Not The SST!"[18]

Whether we can be so sure about the authenticity of the Boeing corporate management's feelings about the SST cancellation is not so clear. Most of the NASA engineers working with the company on the SST believed at the time, and still believe, that Boeing's leadership was actually relieved when the program was canceled. Already by 1967, many of Boeing's best people had been taken off the SST project and put to work on the wide-body that evolved into the 747. In short, there was a financial conflict between the two airplanes being built by the company, a problem that somehow had to be resolved.[19] By the end of the 1960s, the very survival of Boeing depended on the completion and wide-

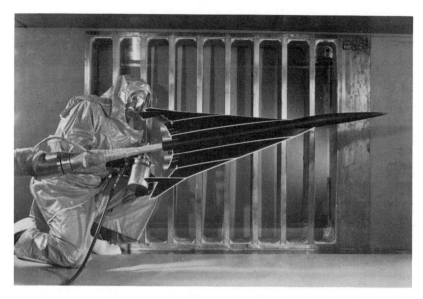

13.6. SCAT wind tunnel model at NASA Langley. A NASA engineer in protective clothing prepares a model of the SCAT-15F for tests in Langley Research Center's Unitary Plan Wind Tunnel in late 1970, less than a year before the cancellation of the American SST program. (Courtesy National Aeronautics and Space Administration– Langley)

spread sale of the 747. The company had to focus its efforts, and more and more of its best people, on the wide-body program, which had major technical problems of its own to solve, and not on the SST.[20]

To be sure, no one in Boeing has ever publicly conceded that the company wanted the SST canceled or that the demise of the SST was a blessing in disguise—or even that the decision could have saved the company (and maybe its customers) from financial disaster. The competition with Lockheed for the right to build the supersonic airliner had been "one of the most dramatic and exhausting" in the history of the company—in the history of *either* company— so why would Boeing have been willing to give up the fruits of winning that battle?[21] The market for SSTs in 1967 dollars, according to Boeing's own estimates (which of course were completely oblivious of the fuel crisis soon to be brought on by the Yom Kippur War in 1973), stood between $25 billion and $50 billion. If the company had been able to go ahead with the supersonic airliner as planned, if the Arab-Israeli conflict had not caused the OPEC countries to force up the price of oil so dramatically, and if the price of jet fuel had stayed at 10 cents per gallon, Boeing might have been able to provide the 300-to-325-passenger, 3,750-nautical-mile-range, 1,800-mph airplane it was hoping for, a vehicle that would have revolutionized the industry once more, just as Boeing's 707 had done when it had been introduced in 1958. No one at Boeing in 1971 knew this would not be the case. Thus, in the company's view at the time—its *official* view, anyway—an SST that could cut the flight time from New York to Paris by half or more was still a very attractive option for both the airline operator and the traveler. There was no reason, at least not in 1971, for Boeing management to feel anything but unhappy about the SST cancellation. This is the conventional line that one hears from SST proponents and opponents alike, demonstrating a mutuality that should lead one to believe that Boeing "went to the mat" and put 100 percent of its weight behind its SST effort right up to the time of the cancellation.[22]

Still, there is enough mystery surrounding Boeing's actions (and lack of actions) related to the SST to warrant some serious historical investigation. Even at the time, informed people criticized Boeing for what appeared to be the company's "apathetic" approach to the SST battle. For instance, in the March 29, 1971, issue of *Aviation Week,* editor Robert Hotz, an outspoken defender of the SST, published an editorial in which he charged that a major reason for the defeat of the SST program was "the defeatist attitude of Boeing." In the SST battle, the aircraft industry had put up no more than a "semblance of a political fight," resulting in "another sad case of too little, too late." Primarily at fault was Boeing's top management, "mandarins in their walled city of Seattle who have apparently learned little from their shattering experience of the past year." According to Hotz, the fate of the SST should serve notice, if any was needed, that the aerospace industry could "no longer survive with such political naivete and aloofness from the fray."[23]

But was Boeing really being so naive and aloof from politics, or did its top managers actually know quite well what they were doing once it dawned on them—possibly sometime in 1969 or 1970, when an economic depression hit the aircraft industry—that they might soon be caught in the predicament of trying to sell two competing airplanes to the same customers: one, the big 747, on which the company was spending its own money; the other, the SST, which the government was backing but which was not quite there yet technologically and whose potential development would undoubtedly affect the market for the new wide-body?

Technologically, by 1971, many members of Boeing's SST team, as well as the NASA engineers who were consulting with them, grasped that there was absolutely no way for the Model 2707-300 SST to make the performance criteria, not on the delta wing, without increasing engine size. But the bigger Boeing made the engine, the worse the aerodynamic flutter problem got. Eventually, the engineers at Boeing and NASA understood that isolated advances in the disciplinary technologies of supersonic flight were meaningless unless they could be integrated into an airplane that met all—not just some—of the mission requirements. This, in the end, proved to be perhaps the major engineering lesson learned from the American SST experience: that although technology integration and design interrelationships are important in the development of any aircraft and for any flight speed, they are absolutely determinative in the development of an SST. Only the very best possible combination of aerodynamic, structural, and propulsion technologies can meet the extreme performance requirements and the stringent environmental constraints placed on a commercial supersonic airliner.[24]

In the case of the Dash-300 SST, that optimal combination simply had not been achieved by 1971, and most of the Boeing and NASA engineers working in the program knew it. If Congress had not canceled the funding of the program, and Boeing had gone ahead and built the prototype, the resulting airplane could easily have failed to meet its design criteria, and Boeing would have lost its investment. On the other hand, if the government canceled the SST program, the company would get most of its money back; the company would not have to be trying to sell an SST and a 747 at the same time; yet the Boeing organization would still have cornered most of the SST field. Given the termination of the national SST program, no one else in U.S. industry was going to set out on the development of an SST very soon. When it was once again time to do so, Boeing would still be in the leadership position. The whole business would turn out just fine, better than if the prototyping stage of the national SST program had been continued. A columnist for the *Seattle Post-Intelligencer* made this point at the time, writing that the cancellation of the SST program would actually benefit Boeing by improving its short-term earnings and its ability to compete in the wide-bodied subsonic jet market. One can only speculate that the source for the columnist's point was a corporate executive at Boeing.[25]

The "high finance" and big business dealings of the international aircraft transport industry have been called a "sporty game." John Newhouse, the author of numerous works on international finance, in fact used the phrase "the sporty game" as the title for his incisive 1982 book on the aircraft transport industry. Newhouse heard the phrase from one of his interviewees in the industry, who told him: "This is a sporty game. Both airframe and engine people will very frequently represent something that turns out to be somewhat beyond their reach in order to get a job."[26]

If the aircraft transport industry does play such "a sporty game," then all sorts of gamesmanship are played besides saying you *can* do something that you *can't*. The game might also include saying you *do want* to do something that you really *don't*. Extending the sports metaphor to the game of golf, where competitive inequalities are overcome by the outside agency of artificial handicaps, to misrepresent your past performance in order to get a higher handicap is called "sandbagging." By extension, this colloquial expression means to misrepresent your competitive status in order to gain an edge on people who are assuming your earnestness and forthrightness. This sports colloquialism, then, leads to my main question: Might Boeing have "sandbagged" its own SST effort, perhaps to protect its interests and its multimillion-dollar commitment to the 747? Had the leaders of the company reached the point by 1971, as one NASA engineer told me, that "they would really rather not have [had] an SST going"? If so, how did that private corporate conclusion affect the public debate and the political lobbying in support of the proposed supersonic airliner? Did it weaken or misdirect it? What directions, if any, did Boeing give to the pro-SST lobby on the eve of the crucial congressional votes of 1971? What sort of test data about the performance of the Dash-300 in comparison with the alternative SST configurations, notably the NASA SCAT-15F, was Boeing furnishing to the FAA in the months and weeks before the votes? What did those numbers show; what did Boeing want them to show; and what did NASA engineers really think about them? If Boeing did not support the prototype phase of the SST program as strongly as it might have, what impact, if any, did that ambivalence have on the crucial congressional votes of 1971? Did Boeing's private feelings about the economic and technological problems of its proposed supersonic airliner themselves constitute a major constraint working to defeat the national SST program? John Swihart, as Boeing's SST project manager, might have been doing everything he could to win support for continuation of the national SST program—after all, that was a project manager's job—but were Boeing's corporate managers doing the same? If they were not, then why not? These are only some of the questions that have not yet been raised by historians of the American SST program. To answer them, scholars somehow will have to get into the company archives at Boeing, as well as into the SST records from NASA, two collections that Mel Horwitch unfortunately did not penetrate for his otherwise superb 1982 book *Clipped Wings,* a history of the American SST conflict.[27] Furthermore, historians must also conduct interviews with key individuals from NASA and Boeing who were directly involved in the national SST program and who may now be willing, some 20 years later, to share their personal recollections.

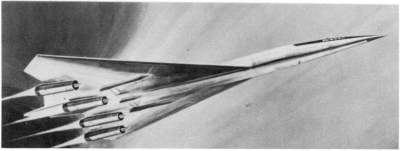

13.7. Artist's conception of the Boeing 747 and 2707 SST. It remains a question for historians to answer: Might the Boeing Company have "sandbagged" its own SST effort (below) to help protect its interests and multimillion-dollar commitment to the 747 wide-body (above)? (Courtesy National Air and Space Museum)

In the wake of their defeat in 1971, most proponents of the supersonic transport program blamed the anti-SST public protest movement for the demise of their pet project. They blamed "environmentalists," "sociologists," "naysayers," "know-nothings," "Luddites," and many other sorts of allegedly misguided and misinformed opponents who, the SST proponents believed, wanted to stamp out technology or at least put technology under very strict social controls.[28] For their part, the opponents of the SST also embraced this interpretation, self-serving as it was, of what went wrong with the SST, as have most historians who have written about the SST debate since that time. It is possible, however, that all of the parties involved have focused too much attention on only one side of the SST debate, that much about our interpretation of "what went wrong" falls short of a complete understanding because we have not delved deeply enough into what went on inside the pro-SST camp, and that the anti-SST public protest movement, apart from constraints working within the pro-SST camp, could not have killed the program.

If this thesis proves even partly correct, our historical understanding of the cancellation of the American SST must undergo some revision—because "too much," as well as "too little," therefore has been made in the past 20 years of the demise of the SST. On the side of "too much" is the conviction that anti-SST activism almost alone was responsible for killing the SST program. Also on the side of "too much" are sweeping generalizations like the one made by the French historian Jean Gimpel, who in the ruminating conclusion to his 1976 book *The Medieval Machine* suggested that the refusal by the U.S. Congress to allocate funds for the supersonic transport in 1971 represented "a complete reversal of the traditional attitude of the United States toward technology" and signaled the start of America's decline as a world civilization.[29] This is "too much." Conversely, on the side of "too little," we do not know enough about the SST history that was internal to NASA, to Boeing, and to the pro-SST camp in general, largely because the conventional wisdom about "what went wrong" has disguised the importance of this side of the story.

There is still much to learn about the death of the American SST program and much to discover from the reactions, public and private, of those placed too conveniently and monolithically inside the pro-SST camp.[30]

NOTES

1. By far the best book on the demise of the U.S. national SST program is Mel Horwitch, *Clipped Wings: The American SST Conflict* (Cambridge, Mass., 1982). The chapter entitled "Final Confrontation" (309–27) provides a detailed narrative and analysis of the decisive congressional votes against the SST in 1971.

2. A scholarly history of what has happened in the field of supersonics in the United States since the demise of the SST program has not been written. The best account so far, which concentrates on NASA's continued research and development activities, is *Supersonic Cruise Technology* (Washington, D.C., 1985), by F. Edward McLean, a retired NASA engineer. Although highly technical, this book offers some important insights into the history of the SST and other U.S. supersonic airplane programs. In preparing my paper, I also benefited from reading an unpublished paper (dated November 1982) entitled "The Supersonic Airliner Fiasco, 1956–1976," by the distinguished American aviation historian Richard K. Smith.

3. Letter from Richard D. Fitzsimmons, Newport Beach, Calif., to the author, January 8, 1992. Fitzsimmons's letter was in response to an extended questionnaire that I had sent to him and to 15 other individuals who had played prominent roles in the ad-

vocacy of the national SST program in the 1960s and 1970s. My questionnaire asked the following eleven questions:

1. What do you think now, 20 years later, about the decision by Congress to terminate the SST program? What is your understanding of *why* the program was killed? Was the decision correct or mistaken? On what grounds do you personally make that judgment?

2. How would you evaluate the performance to date of the Anglo-French Concorde? Is it a successful aircraft? On what basis do you make that judgment?

3. How would the world of aviation be any different if the United States had built an SST 20 years earlier?

4. What sort of first-generation SST would we have built in the 1970s if the national SST program had not been canceled in 1971?

5. Do you remember your personal reaction when hearing the news that Congress had terminated the SST program? In what circumstances did you hear about it (where were you, who told you, etc.). How would you describe your reaction?

6. Did you remain heavily involved in SST-related studies after the 1971 congressional decision?

7. How active have you been since 1971 in advocating the renewal of a national SST program? What are the chances for such a renewal taking place by the end of the century?

8. How would you describe your present feelings about the potential of an American SST? Does it make sense technologically? Explain your answer in some detail. If it makes sense technologically, does it make sense economically? Will it ever?

9. Is it inevitable that the United States will build an SST? How and why will it happen? What possible developments in global population, politics, or economics might affect the American policy on an SST?

10. If NASA or the aerospace industry once again begins to advocate a national SST program, who or what will be its major opponents? What arguments will the opponents be making? What can pro-SST people do to counter those arguments?

11. What will happen to the American aircraft industry if we do not move rather quickly to build an American SST?

The goal of my questionnaire was to begin building a qualitative data base from which to understand the point of view or mentality of those who have been—and still are—SST proponents. Everyone to whom I sent this questionnaire responded, a reflection of their continued enthusiasm for, or interest in, the subject of an SST. In response to my questionnaire, Fitzsimmons was kind enough to send back a handwritten letter of eleven legal-sized pages. For the purposes of this paper, only a small fraction of the responses from Fitzsimmons and the others proved relevant. The rest of the collected information will be instrumental in helping me to formulate a more comprehensive analysis of the SST proponents' private and public reaction to the 1971 SST cancellation.

4. On the development of the Boeing 747, see Laurence S. Kuter, *The Great Gamble, the Boeing 747: The Boeing Pan-Am Project to Develop, Produce, and Introduce the 747* (Tuscaloosa, Ala., 1973), and Douglass J. Ingells, *747: The Story of the Boeing Super Jet* (Falbrook, Calif., 1970). In John Newhouse's *The Sporty Game* (New York, 1982), a penetrating study of the modern American aircraft manufacturing business, chapter 6, "Bigger is Better," offers some important insights into the genesis of the Boeing 747.

5. This was a common argument, expressed by the SST proponents even before the Senate vote. It is, of course, impossible to say just how expensive the SST program would have become if the funding for the prototypes had been approved. Given the cost of conducting the flight experiments, the program could easily have turned out to be more expensive than the proponents suggested.

6. John T. Swihart, typewritten response to SST questionnaire, Bellevue, Wash., December 11, 1991.

7. Swihart, questionnaire, answer to question 5.

8. By 1971 many people had grown disenchanted with the "magic" of the airplane as a result of the continuing bombing in Vietnam. Moreover, two years had passed since the first lunar landing (*Apollo 11*) in July 1969, and the enthusiasm for the aerospace enterprise as a whole was waning. In the following years, media skepticism increased due in part to the dramatic problems plaguing commercial aviation, specifically the performance of the Douglas DC-10. One of these airliners crashed near Paris in March 1974, killing 346 people, and another DC-10, flying for American Airlines, crashed in Chicago in May 1979, killing 273. The Chicago crash, the worst in the nation's history, shook American confidence not only in the DC-10 but in commercial airliners in general. On the problems of the DC-10, see Newhouse, *The Sporty Game*, 88–94.

9. Swihart, questionnaire, answer to question 1.

10. What NASA and the American aerospace industry have, and have not, done to research and develop these technologies since the cancellation of the American SST program in 1971 is covered in some detail by McLean, *Supersonic Cruise Technology*. Of course, over the past 20 years the aerospace trade journals have published countless articles about the development of these technologies. On the development of new technologies for the Concorde SST, see Kenneth Owen, *Concorde: New Shape in the Sky* (London, 1982).

11. In the wake of the defeat of the SST, the Nixon administration did express some sharp disappointment, and it continued to do so for some time after the Senate vote. In December 1971, for example, President Nixon had a chance to inspect the Concorde supersonic airliner (which had not yet made its first visit to the United States) in the Azores during a meeting with Prime Minister Marcello Caetano of Portugal and French President Georges Pompidou. "When I arrived at the airport on the 'Spirit of 76,' a Boeing 707 airliner," said Nixon at a dinner for the heads of state that evening, "I saw parked in front of me a Concorde which had carried the President of France. Our am-

bassador to France, Mr. Watson, pointed out that he had come from France at a speed three times as fast as we had come from the United States. I do not speak in envy; I wish only we had made the plane ourselves." Nixon then went on to declare that "one day" the United States would build its own SST, expressing dismay that Congress had terminated the program. On the Nixon administration's ambivalent attitudes and policies concerning the SST, see Horwitch, *Clipped Wings*, 260–61, 269–71, and 305–7. See also Fitzsimmons's response to my questionnaire, 1–3.

12. Letter to the editor, "Cancer Charge Refuted," from John T. Swihart, Chief Engineer, Production SST Airplane Development, Boeing Company, Seattle, in *Aviation Week and Space Technology,* April 12, 1971, 60. For a news summary of the activities of the various pro-SST lobby groups on the eve of the key congressional votes in 1971, see "Campaign for SST Funding Accelerating," *Aviation Week and Space Technology,* March 1, 1971, 45. Horwitch, *Clipped Wings,* also covers the diverse activities of the various pro-SST groups.

13. Horwitch's analysis of the FAA design competition and of Boeing's move from the swing-wing B-2707-200 (which won the competition) to the fixed delta B-2707-300 (which was very similar to Lockheed's losing design) leaves many questions unanswered, especially regarding what was really going on inside Boeing, NASA, and the FAA concerning the definition of the SST requirements. A complete study of this important event in the history of modern American aviation—the scrapping of variable geometry for the wing form of the proposed American SST—still needs to be written. For Horwitch's limited analysis, see *Clipped Wings,* 182–85.

In *Supersonic Cruise Technology,* McLean (a NASA engineer who worked in the areas of supersonic airplane design and sonic boom and who was a technical adviser in the FAA's ongoing SST evaluations) states that the 1966 decision to go with the B-2707-200 "was less than a clear-cut decision." Moreover, McLean charges that the government's favorable review of Boeing's B-2707-300 proposal in 1968, a review that was performed by the U.S. Supersonic Transport Integrated Configuration Validation Group of which McLean was a part, somehow happened to be done very superficially. "This validation, unlike the previous rigorous FAA evaluations, represented little more than an audit of Boeing substantiating information" (48). Readers might want to reread this note after finishing the entire text of my paper.

One of the respondents to my SST questionnaire, William S. Aiken, Jr., a retired NASA official (now living in Bowie, Md.) who had been deeply involved in NASA activity in support of the FAA's SST program, principally in the noise and sonic boom areas, recommended McLean's book to me. In doing so, Aiken mentioned that McLean had had trouble getting the book published by NASA because of its SST advocacy as well as some of its controversial statements. According to Aiken, who remained continuously involved in support of NASA's supersonic research and development programs into the early 1980s, "It was not an easy job to get it published by NASA just before I retired in 1985." Aiken letter to the author, November 29, 1991, 3.

14. For detailed insights into NASA's role as a consultant for Boeing and the FAA on the SST, see my extended interviews with NASA Langley engineers: Cornelius Driver, Hampton, Va., July 21, 1989; A. Warner Robbins, Hampton, Va., July 19, 1988; and Mark R. Nichols, Hampton, Va., July 6, 1988. Transcriptions of all three interviews will be available in the Historical Archives at NASA Langley Research Center in Hampton, Va., on completion of my SST history project.

For an exhaustive analysis of the FAA's leadership role in the national SST program, see Horwitch, *Clipped Wings,* which was written primarily from FAA sources. In essence, Horwitch builds his story around the FAA's institutional and political inability to do the job for which it was chosen.

15. Mark R. Nichols, typewritten response to SST questionnaire Hampton, Va., February 18, 1992, answer to question 1. As chief of NASA Langley's High-Speed Aircraft Research Division (the former Full-Scale Research Division), Nichols was intimately involved for many years in NASA's supersonic airplane research programs. Not all of my interviewees agreed with Nichols's view that the United States did not need another supersonic research vehicle at the time. For example, NASA's Richard H. Petersen, a leading SST proponent who worked at NASA Ames Research Center in the 1960s and went on to become NASA Langley's center director (1985–91) and associate administrator of the Office of Aeronautics and Space Technology at NASA headquarters (1991–92), counters that the United States did very much need the proposed SST airplane. Neither the SR-71 nor the Concorde would contribute much to solving the particular problems at which the American SST program had been looking. If the United States had flown an SST prototype in the 1970s or 1980s, the country's scientists and engineers could have addressed the environmental concerns "in a reasonable fashion" rather than through "an outpouring of environmental and antitechnology emotion influencing the political process." See Petersen's typewritten response to my SST questionnaire, February 27, 1992, answer to question 1.

If a prototype had been built and flown as Petersen and others had wanted, however, the pressure for going on to a production aircraft probably would have become irresistible. (Dr. George B. Kistiakowsky, the eminent Harvard chemist and former science adviser to President Dwight Eisenhower, made exactly this point in a letter to anti-SST Congressman Henry Reuss [D-Wisconsin] in March 1971; see Horwitch, *Clipped Wings,* 320.) And if there was no production of even a marginally successful SST, the whole effort, given the national mood during the Watergate period, would probably have been noisily denounced as a boondoggle.

16. On SCAT-15F and NASA's other SCAT configurations of the 1960s, see McLean, *Supersonic Cruise Technology,* 42–46 and 50–52. See also my interviews with the following NASA Langley engineers: Mark R. Nichols, Hampton, Va., July 6, 1988; A. Warner Robbins, Hampton, Va., July 19, 1988; Laurence K. Loftin, Jr., Newport News, Va., August 5, 1989; Thomas A. Toll, Hampton, Va., August 29, 1988; and Cornelius Driver, Hampton, Va., July 21, 1989.

17. "Alternative SST Funding Considered," *Aviation Week and Space Technology,*

March 22, 1971, 16; "SST Termination Process Begins," *Aviation Week and Space Technology,* March 29, 1971, 14–15.

18. "Campaign for SST Funding Accelerating," *Aviation Week and Space Technology,* March 1, 1971, 45–46. On Proxmire's critical role in the anti-SST fight, see Horwitch, *Clipped Wings,* 178–79, 217–21, 282–83, and 304–8.

19. "Were it not for the SST," one airline official stated in 1971, "we could see our way clear to buy the larger jets [i.e., the 747] right now" (quoted in Horwitch, *Clipped Wings,* 160). As Horwitch explains, the airlines were concerned that they might be "stuck with a new fleet of subsonic aircraft just as the public was turning to the SST." In this sense, there was indeed a financial conflict for Boeing in building and trying to sell both airplanes. Conversely, "Pan American, the airline most heavily involved with purchasing 747s, was the last of ten American-flag air carriers to participate actively in the SST competition" (ibid.). Initially, Pan Am had planned to send its intercontinental first-class passengers on SSTs, whose total passenger capacity would be 100-percent first-class cabin, and to use the 747s just for its economy-class travelers. By 1971, however, that plan had all but faded away, and Pan Am was expressing serious reservations over the financial wisdom of ever flying both of Boeing's airplanes.

20. An intriguing opinion on this matter was that of John Stack, a former NASA engineer and accomplished aerodynamicist, who in 1962 left NASA to become director of engineering for the Republic Aviation Corporation, which just happened to be Boeing's only major subcontractor for the SST. Stack believed that Boeing at some point in the late 1960s had found a way to use some of its government SST money to help fund the development of the 747. If anyone from the outside was in the position to know about what probably amounted to a creative redefinition of spending categories, *if one in fact took place,* it might have been John Stack. Stack died in 1972, and I report this belief of his secondhand. But it was told to me firsthand by Laurence K. Loftin, Jr., Stack's successor as director of aeronautics at NASA Langley (where Stack worked for over 34 years); and Loftin was ideally positioned during the time period in question to know both about Boeing and about Stack. Thus I believe that the *possibility* that Boeing used SST funds for 747 work merits attention. Laurence K. Loftin, Jr., interview with author, Newport News, Va., July 10, 1992.

21. Newhouse, *The Sporty Game,* 139–41.

22. Swihart, questionnaire, 3.

23. Robert Hotz, editorial, "Toward a Technological Appalachia," *Aviation Week and Space Technology,* March 29, 1971, 9.

24. McLean, *Supersonic Cruise Technology,* 68–70.

25. Quoted in Horwitch, *Clipped Wings,* 309.

26. Newhouse, *The Sporty Game,* 54.

27. See Walter A. McDougall's review of Horwitch's book in *Technology and Culture* 25 (April 1984): 367–69. Interestingly for my thesis, McDougall implies that Horwitch has not looked closely enough inside the corporate history, leaving his readers to wonder "how to explain the curious reticence of the aerospace firms and airlines them-

selves" in heartily promoting the cause of the SST. As McDougall suggests, "A deeper dip into the microeconomics of the industry might have broadened our understanding of the saga of the SST" (369). Such "a deeper dip" should start, as my essay proposes, with a careful study of what was going on inside the minds of the corporate leadership at Boeing.

28. For the various SST proponents' public reaction to the death of the SST program, see Horwitch, *Clipped Wings*, 323–27. See also the numerous editorials and columns that appeared in the major aerospace trade journals and in the newspapers following the culminating SST votes.

29. See the epilogue to Jean Gimpel, *The Medieval Machine: The Industrial Revolution of the Middle Ages* (New York, 1976), 249.

30. To complete the story, I should note the activities of Richard Fitzsimmons and John Swihart after the SST cancellation in 1971. The day after the Senate vote, Fitzsimmons—having heard that Boeing's executive chairman, William Allen, was threatening to reassign all his SST people by the following Monday and to drive a bulldozer into the Boeing plant, clearing out all the drawings, hardware, and reports on the SST—called an emergency meeting of the National Aeronautics and Space Council. In this meeting Fitzsimmons and colleagues found a way to save a few of the ongoing research contracts. Despite this frantic effort, however, most of the major programs designed to obtain some of the biggest technological gains—including the program for the development of the new material, titanium—were lost for good. Within a year Fitzsimmons left the Nixon administration and took a job as director of supersonic transports with McDonnell Douglas, a company that wanted to get back in the SST business and that was thereafter able to support a rather significant level of supersonic activities through the rest of the 1970s as part of a NASA effort known as the Advanced Supersonic Technology (AST) program (later redesignated the Supersonic Cruise Research—or SCAR—program). At McDonnell Douglas, Fitzsimmons assembled a carefully selected team of 125 engineers, scientists, and manufacturing experts and ran the company's supersonic program from 1972 to 1980, when the NASA contract funding assistance ran out and the company chose to cut back on its in-house funding. As for John Swihart, not long after the demise of the SST in 1971, Boeing reassigned him to direct commercial airplane sales in the Far East, and in fact he lived in Japan nearly full-time for a number of years. With his Japanese counterparts, he talked regularly about his SST work, on which he even lectured at their national aeronautics laboratory. When he returned to the United States, Swihart continued to be active in research and development activities and ran product development for the Boeing 767 and for future airplanes. In 1983 he started once more to promote the idea that SST technology had progressed to the point where, with a small but significant effort, the United States could build an airplane that would compare on a seat-mile-cost basis to the Boeing 747-400. Swihart is currently the president of the American Institute of Aeronautics and Astronautics (AIAA).

R. E. G. Davies

SST Market Limitations

A Simple Matter of Arithmetic

The world of aviation is still fascinated by the prospects of supersonic speeds, whether in military applications (although these are far fewer than popularly imagined) or in the search for a successor to the aging Concorde, a technological masterpiece that has now been in service for 16 years. Supersonic aircraft have been proposed by Boeing, McDonnell Douglas, Aerospatiale, and British Aerospace, among others. The problems of further improvement over the Concorde, however, are not to be dismissed lightly.

TECHNICAL FACTORS

In assessing the commercial market for any aircraft for supersonic travel (SST) or hypersonic travel (HST), one cannot ignore certain problems still remaining to be solved by engineers and scientists. The problems must be mentioned to put into perspective the degree of optimism with which an assessment of the market may be judged. Listed below are the most important barriers to further progress.

The Sonic Boom

Overland supersonic flight can be ruled out.

Noise

Anyone within half a mile of a Concorde taking off can *feel* the noise, as well as hear it. Future supersonic or hypersonic aircraft cannot be any louder.

Heat

Passengers will have to be protected against high temperatures caused by fuselage skin friction during flight. For hypersonic aircraft, how long will it take for the aircraft to cool down after landing?

Fuel

In today's airline world, fuel is a vital item of cost. The Concorde burns a ton of fuel for every seat it carries across the Atlantic. Unless a revolutionary engine is developed that will be more economical in fuel consumption than today's jets and that cannot be of benefit to subsonic airliners, then supersonic or hypersonic airliners will always be more expensive to operate.

Ozone Depletion

Severe adverse effects are feared as a consequence of sustained and frequent supersonic flights at altitudes around 60,000 feet (20,000 meters).

Materials

Substitution of aluminum by titanium will not alone be the answer. I understand that research is under way with metallurgical marvels such as submicron dispersoids and dendritic fibers within titanium-aluminide structures. Such a level of scientific expertise suggests that the alchemists' dream of converting base metal into gold would present no problem today.

The Competition

Technological improvements may be a prospect for supersonic airliners, but subsonic aircraft will also improve. Twin-engined transocean service (unheard of about 10 years ago) is already accepted as normal. Highly economical 600-seat airliners may be next.

The Costs

I have never spoken to anyone involved in SST (or HST) projects, be they in manufacturing, government agencies, or consultancy, who questions a development cost of $10 billion, or even higher, in research and development alone, before production begins. This figure, plus the cost of tooling, buildings, and other production items, is put into perspective, based on previous experience, in illustration 14.1.

Selling Price

Such figures are further augmented by marketing, administration, and overhead costs (see illustration 14.2).

Operational Problems

When President Ronald Reagan stole some headlines in 1986 by speculating about the prospects of an *Orient Express* of the air, which would fly people from New York to Tokyo in three or four hours, he did not mention when they would have to leave New York or when they would arrive in Tokyo. Perhaps he did not think about it, but the facts must be faced (see illustration 14.3).

The times at which a New York–Tokyo supersonic airliner can either take off

AIRLINER COSTS
($ billions)

Speed	Type	Development (Research, Prototypes)	Pre-Production (Buildings, Tooling, Design, Manufacturing Systems)
Subsonic	Boeing 777	3	2
Mach 2	Concorde	4	1
Mach 3	SST	10	5
Mach 6	HST	20	10

14.1. Airliner costs.

PRICE
OF
SUPERSONIC AIRLINER

Cost Item ($ billion)	Aircraft Number			
	300	150	100	50
Development	10	10	10	10
Pre-Production	5	5	5	5
Production	40	20	15	10
Overheads, Marketing	20	10	3	2
Total	75	45	33	27
Price per aircraft ($ million)	250	300	330	540

14.2. Price of supersonic airliner.

NEW YORK – TOKYO
TIME SLOT CHOICES

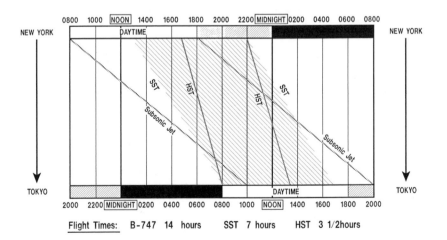

Flight Times: B-747 14 hours   SST 7 hours   HST 3 1/2hours

14.3. New York–Tokyo time slot choices.

or land during daylight hours are very restricted. Even during the short period shown, consideration must also be given to the "jet lag" problem, in addition to simply the inconvenience of a late-night arrival. Currently, an American businessman cannot do better than to arrive in downtown Tokyo at about 10 A.M. (or 10 P.M. New York time) after staying awake for about 16 hours, at which time he is likely to have to face his Japanese counterpart, who is bright and alert at the beginning of the workday. The same considerations must be taken into account in the reverse direction, traveling from Tokyo to New York (see illustration 14.4).

Anyone in the airline business involved in scheduling will immediately recognize the problems of turning aircraft around for operations in both directions at commercially acceptable times. Low utilization across the Pacific is inevitable, even though the Concorde can make a transatlantic round-trip (at almost $8,000 per ticket) in a day.

Preliminary Market Estimates

Based on the inescapable challenges touched on above, and whatever performance improvements might be envisaged, the prospects of producing an airliner that could operate at lower seat-mile costs are negligible.

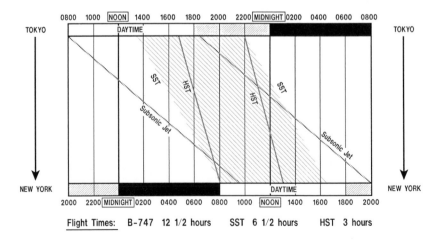

14.4. Tokyo–New York time slot choices.

Any market calculation must, therefore, be based on the first-class air travel market. Another basic assumption must avoid generalizations that imply that air traffic would be attracted to selected hypersonic airport hubs. A Swiss banker is not going to make a subsonic connecting flight to London, Paris, or Frankfurt to fly supersonically to New York when he can take a comfortable 747 direct from Zurich. The same applies to the *Orient Express*. Transpacific travelers from Hong Kong, Singapore, or Bangkok will not connect to Tokyo, for the same privilege, when they can fly nonstop to the United States.

Supersonic or hypersonic airliners will thus have to depend on individual city-pair traffic. This basic truth has been proved by the Concorde experience. Air France routes to Rio de Janeiro, Caracas, and Mexico City were soon dropped because of load factors that were totally unacceptable; and British Airways' expectations of lucrative traffic from the oil-rich Middle East, served via Bahrain, were quickly forgotten. Concorde routes today, after 16 years of operation, can be counted on the fingers of one hand.

One of the problems has been that the engineers, designers, and public relations people rarely asked the economists or the market researchers for information, much less opinions. And if they did and received unpalatable answers, these answers were either suppressed or ignored. The ignorance about the patterns and structure of air travel was appalling. Some of the promotional literature about the Concorde suggested that its market was justified by an assumption that 25 percent of the world's air passengers flew first-class. This was wildly inaccurate. The correct figure is about 5 percent.

At that time, the Concorde was "the only game in town," and let us give credit to this magnificent machine, which I have already described as a technological masterpiece. British Airways and Air France operate it, and so also, for a short time, did Singapore Airlines. The Concorde is a thing of beauty and joy forever.

But what of the Concorde market? There is no need to make highly complicated calculations or to invoke complex econometric studies with dozens of independent and/or dependent variables to explain this situation. But the following assumptions are inescapable:

1. Because of the sonic boom, the market is limited to transocean routes.
2. The North Atlantic accounts for one-third of this market.
3. Of the total traffic volume, only 5 percent is first-class, and this is fragmented between hundreds of individual city pairs.
4. The average load factor is 70 percent.

Twenty-five years ago, I used to make simple calculations on the back of an envelope to demonstrate the cold facts of the case. The market potential could

Concorde Market (1980s) Mach 2

North Atlantic Passengers (one way) : 20 million/year
    of whom 5% first class : 1 million "
    of whom 40% on top city pairs : 400,000 "
    Plus 50% for upgrading : 600,000 "

Annual Productivity of Concorde (100 seats)
    One round trip per day : 200 seats
    × 70% load factor : 140 passengers
    × 365 days per year : 50,000 "

North Atlantic Concorde Market
    600,000 ÷ 50,000 = 12
World Concorde Market : Maximum 12 × 3 = **36**

14.5. Concorde market (1980s) Mach 2.

U.S. SST Market (1990s) Mach 3

North Atlantic Passengers (one way) : 30 million/year
    of whom 5% first class : 1.5 million
    of whom 40% on top city pairs : 600,000
    Plus 50% for upgrading : 900,000

Annual Productivity of U.S. SST (150 seats)
    One round trip per day : 300 seats
    × 70% load factor : 210 passengers
    × 365 days per year : 76,000 "

North Atlantic U.S. SST Market
    900,000 ÷ 76,000 = 12
World U.S. SST Market : Maximum 12 × 3 = **36**

14.6. U.S. SST market (1990s) Mach 3.

<u>Hypersonic Market (2005)</u> <u>Mach 5</u>

North Atlantic Passengers (one way) : 50 million/year
  of whom 5% first class : 2·5 million "
  of whom 40% on top city pairs : 1 million "
  Plus 50% for upgrading : 1·5 million "

Annual Productivity of HST (250 seats)
  One round trip per day : 500 seats
  × 70% load-factor : 350 passengers
  × 365 days per year : 127,750 "

North Atlantic HST Market
      1,500,000 ÷ 127,750 = 12
<u>World HST Market:</u> Maximum 12 × 3 = **36**

14.7. Hypersonic market (2005) Mach 5.

<u>World SST/HST Market 1980-2010</u>

Decade	1980s	1990s	2000s
North Atlantic Passengers (millions)	20	30	50
N.Atlantic SST/HST Passengers (thousands)	600	900	1,500
Annual SST/HST Passengers per aircraft (thousands)	50 (Concorde)	76 (U.S. SST)	128 (H.S.T.)
Aircraft required for N. Atlantic	12	12	12
World Market	**36**	**36**	**36**

14.8. World SST/HST market, 1980–2010.

be expressed as shown in illustration 14.5. The same applies to the faster and bigger SST of the currently proposed next generation and even to a hypersonic marvel of the next century (see illustrations 14.6 and 14.7).

Interestingly, one of the revelations is that the productivity of the new projects increases in parallel with world traffic growth (see illustration 14.8). This growth is optimistically forecast to be substantial, even though world air traffic as a whole has stagnated during the past three years. Travelers today seem to have run out of spending money—known as discretionary income in economists' parlance—because belts are tightening everywhere, and the traveling public is endlessly seeking lower fares, not higher speed.

A FEW WORDS OF WARNING

I am constantly bewildered at the way in which scientists, engineers, and mathematicians, accustomed to precise calculations based on irrefutable data meticulously compiled, assembled, and analyzed, can suddenly throw away these praiseworthy standards when the subject of supersonic or hypersonic aircraft is introduced. Nobody ever discusses the costs. Nobody ever wants to think about the market.

Above all, do not listen to the often repeated argument that the jet age succeeded because the traveling public would always pay for speed. The 707s and the DC-8s, and even the first-generation Comets, succeeded because they were more economical to operate than their piston-engined predecessors, the Constellations and the DC-7s. The anticipated high cost of the fuel-greedy engines was offset by the low cost of the kerosene, by the absence of engine vibration on the airframe, and above all by the amazing reliability of the jet engines, leading to an unprecedented decrease in the maintenance costs. No piston-engined airliner of the old generation could match the seat-mile costs of the big jets. The introduction of economy-class fares coincided with the introduction of the jet age in 1958. Lower fares, not speed, were the attraction.

CONCLUSIONS

Beware of those who constantly quote past predictions that turned out to be mistaken. The examples are always carefully selected. Little is said of those who predicted, for example, that the biplane would be superseded, that the airship would never be commercially successful, that landplanes would usurp flying boats for transocean travel, or that helicopters would not be tolerated for city-center commercial operation. There were many who challenged contemporary convictions that were fashionable at the time. And they were right.

Let the air transport industry, therefore, come to terms with reality. It would not accept the prospect of widespread jet travel until the Comet proved that it could be done. Concorde operations were regarded skeptically—and rightly so—by airline managements that had to answer to their accountants and their shareholders. Equally, to improve standards for future generations of air travelers, the airline world must closely examine all claims for supersonic feasibility and ask to see those claims demonstrated before indulging in dreams of fantasy and, as a result, burdening the taxpayer.

Beware too those SST protagonists who blithely start their advocacy with, "Assuming a market of 250 (or 350, or 500) . . ." The market cannot be assumed; it must be calculated. The limitations are formidable, largely because the costs of achieving parity with subsonic economics will be extortionate. There are other directions in which the billions of dollars of research and development money can be better spent.

Contributors

ROGER BÉTEILLE is executive vice president and general manager of Airbus Industrie. An engineer and test pilot, he was head of the Flight Test Department at Sud-Est Aviation during the testing and certification of the Caravelle jet airliner. He joined Airbus Industrie as senior vice president following its creation in 1970.

HANS-JOACHIM BRAUN is professor of modern social, economic, and technological history at the Universität der Bundeswehr, Hamburg. He is the author of books on technology transfer, technological development, the German economy in the 20th century, and British economic policy in the 19th century.

EMMANUEL CHADEAU is professor of economic history and fellow of the Institut Universitaire de France at Université Charles de Gaulle–Lille. His works include *Historie de l'Industrie Aéronautique, de Blériot à Dassault, 1910–1950* (1987), *Latécoère* (1990), *Saint-Exupéry* (1994), and *Le Pari Technologique, Naissance d'Ariane, 1970–1973* (1994).

R. E. G. DAVIES, who had a lengthy career in aviation economic research in Great Britain and the United States, is curator of air transport at the National

Air and Space Museum, Smithsonian Institution. His books include *A History of the World's Airlines* (1964), *Airlines of the United States* (1987), and *Airlines of Latin America* (1984).

VIRGINIA P. DAWSON is a consultant for the Winthrop Group, Inc., a firm specializing in the preparation of corporate histories. She is the author of *Nature's Enigma* (1987) and *Engines and Innovation: Lewis Laboratory and American Propulsion Technology* (1991), a volume in the history series of the National Aeronautics and Space Administration.

HANS DEGEN, who was trained as an architect and environmental planner, is the elected head of city planning in Winterthur, Switzerland. He has done historical research in the field of Swiss aviation and is working on biographies of pioneer aviators.

DEBORAH G. DOUGLAS is a doctoral candidate at the University of Pennsylvania and a research collaborator with the Aeronautics Department at the National Air and Space Museum, Smithsonian Institution. Her publications include *U.S. Women in Aviation: 1940–1985* (1990).

JAMES R. HANSEN is chairman of the Department of History at Auburn University. He also has served for the past 13 years as a historian for the National Aeronautics and Space Administration. His three books include *Engineer in Charge: A History of the Langley Aeronautical Laboratory, 1917–1958* (1987).

ROBIN HIGHAM, a pilot in the Royal Air Force from 1943 to 1947, is professor of history at Kansas State University. He is the author of numerous books and articles, including *Britain's Imperial Air Routes, 1918–1939* (1960), *Air Power: A Concise History* (1988), and a still-sequestered official history of the British Overseas Airways Corporation.

WILLIAM M. LEARY, a former flight operations officer for KLM Royal Dutch Airlines at Gander, Newfoundland, is professor of history at the University of Georgia. He is the author of histories of the China National Aviation Corporation, Civil Air Transport, and the U.S. Air Mail Service, 1918–27.

W. DAVID LEWIS is Distinguished University Professor at Auburn University. He is the coauthor, with Wesley Phillips Newton, of *Delta: The History of an Airline* (1979) and the coauthor, with William F. Trimble, of *The Airway to Everywhere: A History of All American Aviation, 1937–1953* (1988).

HOLGER STEINLE is deputy director and head of the Air and Space Department of the Museum of Transportation and Technology in Berlin, Germany. He is the coauthor, with Michael Hundertmark, of *Phoenix aus der Asche: Die Deutsche Luftfahrt Sammlung Berlin* (1985).

JOHN W. R. TAYLOR, an engineer by profession and a member of the design staff of Hawker Aircraft from 1941 to 1947, served as editor-in-chief of *Jane's All the World's Aircraft* from 1959 to 1989. The author of numerous books on aerospace topics, he is editor emeritus of *Jane's*.

HELMUTH TRISCHLER is director of research at the Deutsches Museum, Munich, and seminar lecturer for modern history and the history of technology at the University of Munich. His books include *Luft- und Raumfahrtforschung in Deutschland, 1900–1970: Politische Geschichte einer Wissenschaft* (1992).

JOHN WEGG, who had a 17-year career in commercial air transport, is the author of a history of Finnair and books on the aircraft of General Dynamics and the Caravelle. He is editor-in-chief of *Airways* magazine.